JUST A LITTLE
Love & Joy

From tragedy to triumph, this is the story of one
of America's greatest Paralympians

Curtis Lovejoy

T&J PUBLISHERS

A SMALL INDEPENDENT PUBLISHER WITH A BIG VOICE

Printed in the United States of America by
T&J Publishers (Atlanta, GA.)
www.TandJPublishers.com

Cover design by Timothy Flemming, Jr. (T&J Publishers)
Book format and layout by Timothy Flemming, Jr. (T&J Publishers)
Photography by Christopher Evans (Clearly Focused Media Works) and Drea Nicole (Drea Nicole Photography)

ISBN: 978-0-9997806-8-8

To contact author, go to:
www.TheCurtisLovejoy.com
love1982002@yahoo.com
Facebook: Curtis Lovejoy
Twitter: @curtis_lovejoy9
Youtube: CLovejoy988

DEDICATIONS

First, I would like to thank my Lord and Savior, Jesus the Christ. Without Him, I would be nothing. Thank you Lord for planting a willing spirit in me to serve you at an early age. You shaped me, molded me, and are using me for your glory. Now I realize why you put all of the people in my path that you placed. Now, it's time to show the world your love and joy!

I would also like to dedicate this book to my mom who's now in heaven, Mrs. Sallie L. Lovejoy. She is who I drew my strength from. She would always remind me to take whatever I was going through to the Lord in prayer.

Also, to my late father, Mr. James R. Lovejoy, you were the disciplinarian in the family who taught me to always set goals for myself and achieve them. Both you and mom shielded my siblings and me from drama in this mean old world until we were able to deal with it on our own.

To my late grandmother, Mrs Earleane Atkinson, who lived to be 112 years old, you reminded me not to worry and would always tell me whenever I encountered trouble, "This too share pass. Put it all in God's hands."

Also, to my grandmother Mrs. Bessie H. Lovejoy, who lived to be 92 years old, you always had a switch for me and my siblings with our names written on it!

To all eleven of my siblings—with only three of us remaining—thank you so much for sacrificing your lives and time so that I would be the chosen one. You all believed in me, and I never took your faith and confidence in me for granted.

To my play-mother, Mrs. Helen Ponder, you were always there adding your two cents to make sure that I didn't get beside myself. Even now, you continue to encourage me. Thank you.

To Rev. Timothy Flemming, Sr., thank you for continuing to remind me of God's goodness and ability to take even a bad situation and turn it into a blessing. You've been so inspirational in my life I can't put into words my gratitude towards you and the entire Mount Carmel Baptist Church family. You all helped to mold and shape me into the faith walker I am today. All of you are my 2nd family.

To my 3rd family, Team USA, I love and appreciate all of you. What you see is what you get!

To the late Pernell Cooper (USA weightlifter) and Joe Mueller (USA Fencer), thank you for all of your support and encouragement. You always reminded me that I had something great on the inside of me that set me apart from the rest of the world. You'd always tell me that I would be the champ one day!

Finally, to my wife, Mamie Lovejoy, you are the greatest prize in my life - my real gold medal! Others view me as a true champion, but they have no idea who really made me a champion before I ever became one. You allow me to be me. You've treated me like a king. You didn't listen to others; you listened to God's voice instead. Even when I couldn't see my way, you kept me on the right track. You saw what was ahead of me. Without you and my entire village there wouldn't be a Curtis Lovejoy! Yes, with all that's within me, I truly love you, Mamie.

TABLE OF CONTENTS

FOREWORD

Curtis' journey to become one of the most decorated athletes started 30 years ago at southeast Atlanta Natatorium. It was there that we first met and he, a very energetic swimmer, expressed an interest in swimming competitively.

Immediately, I discovered Curtis was not your average swimmer. His physical potential was somewhat unbelievable. He could swim nonstop for hours. And then there was something else… a certain quality that I've never been able to describe. As I was coaching him I would find myself in awe at how he was able to move with such ease and precision.

Curtis was always focused. In the beginning of his competitive swimming career he was constantly preparing to reach the next level. But it was the challenges outside of the swimming pool that dared to stop him.

There were times I would remember Curtis telling me how he wasn't treated the best at swimming meets. Or how the airline had not provided the proper accommodations for a wheelchair. I remember being struck with how imperative it is that he start preparing for obstacles he would face outside of the pool.

As an athlete you have to train mentally to prepare your body to perform at each event. I set out for Curtis to take that same approach and apply it to everything in life. He already had the talent and discipline – he had to become faithfully determined to succeed.

We picked up this routine where during practice we would discuss life and how it related to swimming. Sometimes we would share our good and bad moments in life. This was never a pity party. But learning the extent of what he faced – further showed me Curtis is an immensely strong person.

It is with faith, integrity, preparation and a burning desire to be the best that Curtis was able to become the most accomplished and decorated male athlete in Paralympic history for U. S. A.

Leading up to the 2000 Olympics, Curtis wanted to participate in Fencing and Swimming. He would come to practice each day telling me he could do it. But he was constantly being told that it had never been done before. With a spirit of "why the hell not" Curtis challenged these beliefs that it could not be done. It is because he had this courage and unwavering belief in himself he was able to prove the naysayers wrong and become the first athlete to win Gold medals in two non-related sports.

We were both disappointed when Curtis did not make the 2016 Paralympic Olympics Team. After not hearing from him for a while I became concerned. But my worry was unnecessary ... Curtis came to me ready to get back in the water and train to make the National Team. Once he accomplished that goal he said, "We have to get ready for the 2020 Olympics in Japan." That's the spirit of an incomparable Champion.

It is without a doubt that Curtis is one of the greatest athletes of our time. But what is most admirable about him is his deep spiritual belief that anything is possible.

—Tommy L. Jackson
Head Coach, City of Atlanta Dolphins Swim Team

INTRODUCTION

"**E**VERYTHING IS GOING TO BE ALRIGHT!!! JUST hang in there!! An ambulance is on the way!!" a man shouted. I was in and out, semiconscious, hearing screams and cries all around me and the high-pitched sounds of sirens as they grew louder and louder; and yet, everything seemed dream-like; everything seemed surreal like Dorothy trapped in her little wooden house while it was being spun around by the powerful winds of a mystical and majestic tornado. Briefly, I felt like I was trapped between two worlds: this world and the afterlife. I couldn't tell which one I was actually in, or if I was simply between the two while transitioning from one to the other. Glimpses of my loved-ones' faces kept flashing before my eyes alongside the flashes of halted cars, broken glass and twisted metal, grass, concrete, guardrails, and a utility pole. Everything was spinning—all of those sights blending into one another until becoming one big hazy, foggy scene. Suddenly, everything began to fade to black.

"Open your eyes, sir!!! Don't leave me!!! Talk to me!!" the man shouted in my ear after sensing that I was losing consciousness; his impassioned pleas, like a lasso, pulled me back into consciousness and into a world that would forever be different to me—one where I would have to get used to living without things I once took for granted, one where I would have to adjust to new environments and activities, one filled with a level of pain I had never experienced before but also to a glory I had never before tasted. That fateful day in November of 1986, my world was turned upside down.

My life changed in the blink of an eye. I can testify that nothing in life is certain—not our next breaths, our next steps; not tomorrow, next week; not our plans, not the realization of our goals and dreams. There is only one thing that is certain: when we place our lives in the hands of God, all things will work together for our good in the end.

The car accident that occurred on November 11, 1986, actually saved my life because it took me in a direction I would not have gone if it was left up to me. Behind my tragedy, I discovered an ability I didn't know I possessed and a strength I didn't know I had. Also, in subsequent years, I ended up doing and accomplishing things I never dreamed I could do and accomplish. A tragedy blessed me to travel around the world multiple times representing the USA and catapulting my name and causing it to be immersed in the bright lights of international fame and etched in the annals of history. A tragedy blessed me to be privileged with audiences with great people including United States Presidents who invited me to the White House on several occasions and also with other world leaders. A tragedy blessed me to come face to face with some of the celebrities I used to watch on the big screen in movie theaters as a child growing up, and I have been blessed with the privilege of coaching many of them through their own tragedies. My accident has given me the honor of having my picture placed in school textbooks across America and on postage stamps. In the end, I can say that which was meant for evil turned out to work for my good.

I didn't learn how to swim until I reached my 30s. Until then, swimming pools terrified me. You couldn't get me near a swimming pool. Whenever I was close to a swimming pool, the only thing that would run through my mind was the thought of drowning—I would recall incidents where several of my peers drowned. I had surrendered to the fear of swimming and it followed me well into my adulthood and dominated my life continually. Now, I am experiencing the loss of the use of my legs. Before this, I'd run from the water; actually, I'd run from a lot of things. My strength, in many cases, actually was my weakness, and my mobility paralyzed my progress. I was my own hindrance in life. Ironically, having the use of my legs had handicapped me in many ways because I misused them. I ran from my own blessings. I even ran from love. But after losing the use of my legs,

I had no other choice but to stop running and face the things I didn't want to face.

Whenever I slide into the pool and begin gliding through the water it's like my natural habitat. It's like I'm a fish enjoying the smooth therapeutic and lucid hands of the water massaging me like a masseuse pressing away the cares of the world. The water takes my mind to a place of serenity. During these times, I begin to think about the things that brought me to this point in my life. I begin to think about how I went from doing the norm to doing the impossible and how I made it through the darkest season of my life.

What held my sanity intact when I felt like I was about to lose my mind? What sustained me mentally and physically when I no longer possessed the strength to stand on my own? What put my life back together after it was broken into a million pieces? *What?*

What kept me going? It was my faith. It produced a joy in my heart, and an incredible love for my family and friends. But most of all, it was the supernatural presence and power of God that kept me going. Like in the poem *Footprints*, there were times when God had to simply pick me up and carry me forward.

Regardless of what you go through in life, understand that you can make it with the help of God and the right attitude. You *will* make it. These kinds of situations come to show you what's on the inside of you waiting to be unleashed. Never give up because you have a purpose and a greatness on the inside of you that the world needs to witness.

CHAPTER 1:
JOE THE COCOMO

I CAME INTO THIS WORLD ON MAY 13, 1957, AT 7:55.25 pm at Grady Memorial Hospital in Atlanta, Georgia after seven long hours of labor. I was born to James Robert and Sallie Lena Render Lovejoy. I was the youngest out of thirteen children. As was customary in their day, my mother and father married when they were only teenagers. Once married, my parents had no reservations about starting a family, so they began producing children right away. Out of all of their children, only seven lived to reach maturity. My mother had two sets of twins that died while babies from what is known as Crib Death (or Sudden Infant Death Syndrome). She had one son who was killed by a drunk driver, and another child who, to this day, still remains a mystery to me. Among her living children were four boys and three girls.

19

My mother was more than ready for me to hurry up and come into this world. As a baby, I was an extremely active—constantly kicking and moving around inside of her womb. And came, I did very responsive, attentive, happy, bubbly, outgoing, and charming: the traits that epitomizes my last name (Lovejoy). I admit using these traits to my advantage since I was the youngest. Cute and charming, nearly everyone in the family showered me with affection and attention except one sibling: my brother, Willie Lewis (WiLewis); he was next to the oldest child. My siblings were James Robert, Jr., Willie, Rose Lee, Sallie, Carl, Diane, and then me, Curtis, who also donned the nickname "Joe the Cocomo". I received this nickname from my uncle Harrison Randolph. Despite being blind, having lost his sight at a young age, my uncle managed a grocery store where I would take the liberty of eating all of the broken cookies at the bottom of the jars therein.

I enjoyed being spoiled by my parents. I was nursed by my mother until I was 3 years old and slept in the bed with my parents until the age of 8 years old. Being the youngest and the baby in the family certainly carried a few perks.

Our family wasn't rich, but strangely, therein lay a hidden blessing. We had to bond as a family. At times, it seemed like we were a little too close. My siblings and I slept four to a bed and we became acquainted with one another's stinky feet. We'd occasionally tussle over the covers on the bed. Quickly a sense of hierarchy began to resonate with me because I saw myself in the pecking order. When mother and father weren't around to shield and protect me from this *order* and grant me special privileges, being the baby, I had to face the reality of being at the bottom of the food chain. Living in the house with eight siblings can drive you insane. Just trying to make it to the dinner table to get a drumstick was death-defying. If you were the last to get to the dinner table you would only get the neck, which had no meat at all, only bones. At the top was James, who carried the responsibility of being the role model. He carried this role with pride. He went on to be the first in our family to earn an MBA (Masters in Business Administration). He was my father's pride and joy. While in college, my father made sure that James' tuition and school expenses were treated as top priority. Next was Willie who donned the nickname "Sweet Doctor Love". He was given this nickname because whenever he would drink that Crown Royal, his personality would change. Actually, alcohol would bring out the zestfulness in him along with other less appealing attributes. Aside from that, WiLewis spent the majority of his time honing in on me like a hawk trying to pinpoint my flaws just to prove to mom and dad that I wasn't the perfect little angel. He always tried to get me in trouble out of jealousy of the attention I was being showered with. WiLewis was the cause of the many whoopings I received growing up. He enjoyed calling me "a little spoiled brat," and he would occasionally say things like, "Y'all let him get away with murder. He's going to grow up and be a little sweet punk. He looks like a girl!" My mother would simply admonish him for his harsh rants. My brother Carl was the quiet one. He had the patience of Job. He never raised his voice at anyone and he never physically fought back when being attacked or bullied. Carl simply wanted peace. He was non-confrontational. He'd cry when there were arguments and fights in the family. Carl loved God and his family, but his problem was that he would spend too much time in the bathroom—sometimes, up to two hours—and you'd never want to use the bathroom behind him. Now, my sister Diane was the complete opposite of Carl. She was the warrior in the family. She would take up for me and Carl. She was also known as the black sheep of the family. Rose was a little more conniving. She would always scheme and connive to get her way, especially when it came to daddy. She would always agree with daddy to temper his mean streak and have her way. There was just one thing standing in her way, momma. Momma could see right through her, and she would always put her in her place. Rose was a party animal, but she was a bit too pessimistic at times, which was a nuisance. Sallie took more after mom. She loved being active in sports and she loved to cook. Both Rose and Sallie would chastise me whenever mom and dad weren't around.

As a family, we stuck together and enjoyed doing things together. We were rich with love and support, and we all knew each other. None of us discounted and overlooked the blessing we had in two parents. My mother was a nurturer. She would cook, clean, starch and iron our clothes each day, and she made sure that she was there for each one of us with care. She was a good listening who showed us love and affection. She was such a source of strength for the family, making us all believe that we could accomplish anything we wanted to in life. She certainly made me feel like I could conquer the world. I stayed by her side everywhere she went, and by her hands was laid a foundation of prayer and faith in my life. She prayed all of the time and about everything. She was what we call a prayer warrior. Her prayers covered us all. Her faith under-girded us all. It didn't matter what we wanted to do in life, where we wanted to go, or what happened to us in life; we had a strong foundation to stand on, one that provided the moral clarity we needed in order to make the right decisions for ourselves in life when our parents were not around.

My father instilled in us an understanding of the importance of hard work. He was a hard-working man. He had a janitorial business and he also worked on the side as a cook at The Jiffy Teddy Bear Grille on Stewart Avenue (since renamed Metropolitan Avenue). He was also the disciplinarian in the household. He had zero-tolerance when it came to disobedience and would keep an inventory of all of the things we did wrong as children. Whenever we filled up the tolerance meter, he would give us a good old fashion whooping while calling out everything we had done wrong. The longer the list, the longer the whooping. It was wise to keep a short list. But even after chastising us, dad would come right behind that and love on us just so that we'd know he wasn't angry with us—he just preferred to not see us walk down a dark path towards destruction due to not receiving correction. And yes, it worked. We all turned out just fine. We turned out to be healthy, responsible, morally upright adults. It is because of our father that the drive to succeed was instilled in us starting at an early age. From him, we learned to never be lazy, don't make excuses for our failures in life, and to never just sit down and do nothing. We were either going to work or go to school. No one would be sitting still.

Our family lived for the weekends. Fridays for us was snack day: fried catfish, coleslaw, French fries, Kool-aid, hot dogs, and peanut butter cookies (my favorite). Every Friday, as a family, we'd all go down to the Atlanta Municipal Auditorium or the Sports Arena for the main event of the professional wrestling matches. My favorite superstars were Dusty Rodes, The Assassin, and Abdullah the Butcher. In one incident, mom got into a fight with a lady who was sitting behind us. The lady spilled her drink on my mom's hair, which she would get fixed every two weeks. Mom immediately jumped-up and turned and looked at the lady who remained unapologetic and unremorseful. At that moment mom asked, "Oh, so you not going to say nothing?!" The lady just sat there, solemn-faced. Mom then turned around as if letting the incident go; but then, she did a 360-degree turn and knocked the hell out of that lady and began pulling her by her hair. She pulled the lady all the way down to her row. Meanwhile, daddy was just making his way back from the restroom. Diane, Sallie, and Rose jumped up to watch mom's back just in case somebody wanted to intervene and stop mom from beating the lady senseless. I was glad that my dad wasn't caught up in the middle of the brawl...being that he was known to pull out a pair of brass-knuckles and a switchblade. Back at home, my siblings and I loved to wrestle around. WiLewis loved to demonstrate on me different wrestling moves he'd seen. He'd lock a Sleeper Hold or Full Nelson on me in a heartbeat. Once, after locking me in a hold, he rendered me unconscious. My parents were very upset with him and placed him on punishment for a month. Diane loved to drop kick everyone and you would never see it coming because she was so skinny and quick. Sallie, however, thought she was Bruce Lee. She'd go around judo chopping everyone like a Ninja. It was our routine each Friday after watching wrestling to stop by Krystal and get forty hamburgers, eight sides of French fries, two whole delicious chocolate pies with whipped cream on top, two Coca-Colas, and five milkshakes—the best nightcap before hitting the sack and turning out the lights for bed. Sometimes my siblings would keep up a little raucous when it was time for us to be asleep. I would often wonder why daddy wouldn't barge out of his room and storm into our rooms and break up the raucous. It later dawned on me why daddy was so preoccupied: he and momma were busy *taking care of business.*

After mom and dad had finished doing their thing with the door shut, I'd sneak into their bedroom and slide into the bed between them. I knew they were pretending to be asleep. *Pretending.*

After long and wild weekends, Sunday mornings would come. The sunlight oftentimes dashed through the windows of the house as if washing away the residue of yesterday and ushering in a fresh new day. Every Sunday we would get up and go to church as a family. Afterwards, we'd come back home and eat Sunday dinner. My mom made dinner every Sunday. That was one of our greatest bonding times as a family. At the dinner table on Sundays, dad would give us an overview of where we stood as a family and what the future held for each of us. It was at the dinner table on Sundays that our father would speak destiny over our lives and empower us to be and to do great things in life. And every Sunday evening, just when the sun began to set, dad would load us all up into his baby blue, four-door 1965 Chevrolet and drive us to the Atlanta airport so that we could watch the planes landing and taking off. His hope for us was that each of us would see ourselves soaring as high as we could in life. He wanted our eyes to be transfixed on that which transcended our current reality. He wanted us to...dream.

Chapter 2

MILLION DOLLAR SMILE

THE FIRST SIX YEARS OF MY LIFE WENT BY LIKE a whirlwind. Time just flew by. My body was growing just as rapidly as my curiosity about the world around me. It was during these quick years that I learned a number of lessons and was scolded for a number of infractions: "Joe, don't come in my room!!" "Don't touch the stove!!" "Stay out of adult conversations!" "You're not old enough to do that!" "Why are you staring at me?! It's impolite to stare!" "It's impolite to point! Stop that!" I, perhaps, had more questions than infractions lined up: "Why do I have to wear underwear?" "Can I have some of that what you're drinking?" "Why do people keep saying I'm so cute?" "Momma, what are those things over there staring at me?" "Momma, why do girls have *that* and boys don't?" "Momma..." At times, mom would say, "Boy, you ask too many questions. Why are you so quiet in church, but can't keep your mouth closed at home?"

The alarm clock would go off early in the morning signaling that it was time to for school. I'd rise, wipe the sleep out of my eyes; wait for my turn to get into the bathroom, which was usually taken over by one of my sisters who had to do much more than me in the mornings just to get ready. All of us had pretty white teeth. We were even questioned by others who wanted to know how we kept our teeth so white. Once, when my dad was asked that question, he simply replied, "Ajax." Every day we were dressed to impress when going to school. Mom would lay our clothes out each night before bed, and she made sure that regardless of whatever we were wearing we were always matching, always neat. We may not have had a million dollars, but we dressed and carried ourselves like we had millions in the bank. We were taught to never hold our heads down.

My sisters Rose and Sallie would take turns walking me to school every morning. Whenever we were late they would take an alternate route through the alley. I'd always tell mom when they did this, which would usually land them in trouble at home. They began calling me a tattletale and would often take turns pulling and jerking my arms on the sly just to get back at me.

Everyone in the family realized that I had a gift for manipulation, and they didn't bother capitalizing on it for their own personal uses. When my siblings wanted to get something out of our parents, they'd use me to get it. In one case, my siblings wanted to go to the big fair back-to-back. They knew that if they had asked daddy to take them back-to-back, he would have said no; so they put me up to the task. I used my charm and convinced daddy to give in to our demands. It was as simple as taking candy from a baby. But it wasn't just my siblings that used me to get what they wanted; my parents even got in on the action.

Grandma Earlene Atkinson lived in Greenville, Georgia, which was about an hour and ten minutes drive from Atlanta. Our family would go down there to visit her during her church's homecoming services where the table was spread afterwards. Grandma cooked the best cornbread, collard greens, oxtails, candied yams, sweet potato pies, and the sweetest iced tea in the world. Everyone in her community, from the youngest to the oldest, loved her cooking. One person even traveled 1400 miles just to taste her food. Grandma was wiser than a fox and full of wisdom. She'd often tell me, "Joe, you can't turn a jackass into a racehorse!" She grew her food on the farm and cooked every day. She held the respect of everyone around her. She'd spend her time feeding the hungry, clothing the naked, picking cotton; she owned her home and worked part-time as a nurse. She never was sick, and she had this old saying: "You will understand it better by and by." She outlived her husband, Mr. Atkinson. While Mr. Atkinson was alive, he and daddy didn't talk much. Mr. Atkinson was always kind to one side of his family, but mean and cold towards us. Daddy would make it a point to arrive at grandma's house one hour before homecoming service was over, before Mr. Atkinson made his way back home. Daddy then gave everyone instructions on what to do: Rose and Sallie were the lookouts, Carl and Diane were to be playing out front, WiLewis was to be working on the car with the hood up, and I was to be with mom and dad around the back of the house where the smokehouse was—that was where Mr. Atkinson stored all of his meat. I was the only one small enough to climb through the window of the smokehouse. Inside it was pretty dark but I followed daddy's instructions. He told me to grab four hams and four hog legs. My heart was racing a hundred miles per second. I was only 3½ feet tall weighed 55lbs when wet; therefore, I wasn't tall enough to pull the hams off the nails they were hanging on. But all I could hear was mom and dad saying, "You can do this, Joe!!! Just take your time and be patient!!" I replied,

"But it's stuck!" Daddy simply responded,

"Keep pulling!!"

"But it's stuck!"

"You can do it! Do you want to eat some of your mom's baked ham?!"

"Yes, sir!!"

"Then you better pull that hog off of that nail!!"

It was extremely difficult pulling those hogs off of those hooks. And the whole time while struggling to get those hogs down, I could hear daddy hollering, "What's taking you so long?!" I could also hear mom telling dad, "We need to hurry up! It's about time for Mother to be coming home!" The distance between the church and the house was about the same as that of a football field.

Rose and Sallie screamed, "Daddy, church service is over!" After hearing that I yelled, "I'm coming out!!" But dad hollered back, "No, not until you get the four hogs first!"

"But we don't have enough time!" I hollered.

"GET THE FOUR HOGS, JOE!!!" he retorted. By now, I've urinated on myself. It was about 90 degrees in that smokehouse and I was running out of time. I suddenly mustered up enough strength to pull not one, not two, not three, but four hogs off of the hooks. Each hog was bigger than I was. I couldn't see my way around that smokehouse, so I began tossing the hogs out of the window. I tossed the first one out. I then heard dad say, "Damn! You hit me on the head with one!"

"Come on, Joe!!" dad yelled.

"Okay, I got another one!"

"Throw it out!" dad yelled. By this time I could hear Sallie, Rose, Diane, and Carl yelling, "Mr. Atkinson and Grandmomma are on their way!!"

"Hurry-up, Joe!" dad urged. I rushed and got the second one out, then the third one; and while I was getting ready to toss out the fourth hog, I heard dad holler, "Come on out, Joe!!!"

"But I got one more!!" I responded.

"Come on out!! Just leave it!!" So I stepped up on the stove and dad grabbed both of my arms and pulled me out of the smokehouse. I ripped my shirt on the way out. I was soaking wet with sweat. By this time my mom had gone to the front to meet her mother; WiLewis was blocking the driveway with his car, pretending to work on it. Mr. Atkinson, being distracted by it, stopped to assist him with the battery cable. Meanwhile, the other siblings had hidden the meat on the side of the house. Daddy walked around to the other side of the house to meet them. I could hear Grandmomma saying, "Where is Joe?" Dad replied, "Oh, he's in the backyard playing." Neither grandma nor grandpa (Mr. Atkinson) suspected a thing.

THAT WAS A CLOSE CALL!!! Mom and dad were just standing around with big smiles on their faces trying to conceal what they had just done; or better yet, what they'd just made me do on their behalf. Perhaps, they felt justified in stealing those hogs due to grandpa's apparent, yet, unexplained animosity towards dad mainly. He did take kindly to mom, just not to the rest of mom's immediate family (dad and the rest of us) for whatever reason. He was a hard man to understand. But, in either case, Mr. Atkinson, before we left, escorted us all to the smokehouse where he supplied us with one big ham and one small ham. Daddy cut his eyes at mom and smiled.

While on our way back to Atlanta all of my siblings were asleep. I was still wide awake. At that moment daddy told me that he was sorry that he made me take Mr. Atkinson's meat without his consent. He then asserted, "Mr. Atkinson will never miss it anyway. Joe, you did well. Now, this doesn't mean that you can take what you want from others. You did this for the family." Mom had a look on her face that said *we'll pay for this sin*, but daddy began singing, "Mr. Big Stuff, who do you think you are?" no doubt in reference to Mr. Atkinson, who he thought of as arrogant and very suspicious of him. They never got along. Daddy kept his distance from him. All mom ever wanted was peace between the two of them.

I had been used by my siblings too on my parents, and by my parents on my grandparents. My smile was a tool for manipulation, and so was my small size. However, my size would eventually change...but not my smile. I'd continue to use it along with my charm in the upcoming days. At times, my smile and my charm would serve me well. However, there were also times when they didn't serve me well.

JUST A LITTLE LOVE & JOY

CHAPTER 3:
A JOB CALLED "MOM"

DAD WORKED HARD TO PROVIDE A HOME FOR US. But watching my mother revealed to me that keeping a home intact is equally, if not more arduous a task. Family has given me an identity, and I don't believe it was a coincidence that I was born into the family I was. Home has provided for me a foundation in life which allows me to make healthy decisions for myself. All that I am today I can attribute to home. But all that home was I can attribute to my mother. She was the rock and foundation of our family.

My mother made me believe I could conquer the world; she made all of us believe we could conquer the world...including daddy. There's a popular saying: "Behind every good man is a good woman." Well, the Bible says that a woman has the ability to either build a house or tear it down with her hands in Proverbs 14:1. It also says in Proverbs 24:3, "A house is built by wisdom and becomes strong through good sense" (New Living Translation). I truly believe that my strong home, my strong sense of family, and my family's strong bond, manners, morals, cleanliness, respectability, and sense of excellence is evidence of this biblical truth. My mother was a woman filled with wisdom who exercised a lot of good sense in all her ways. She possessed the sense, the foresight, and understanding to recognize and take on the toughest and highest job in the world: being a mother. She had the sense to know that being a mother was an opportunity to contribute to shaping the minds of future leaders. All world-changers and world-shapers had mothers who made them who they were: Alexander the Great, Woodrow Wilson, Ralph Waldo Emerson, Dr. Benjamin Carson, and more. In many cases, men who didn't even have fathers went on to be world-shakers simply through the power of their mothers' influence. Thank God my mother knew that being a mother was a job and not a hobby, that it wasn't a sign of weakness as some people think today. Motherhood is tough, but it's also the most rewarding job.

Years ago, there was a summit where eight scholars were asked the question: Who is the toughest and strongest person in the world? These eight scholars (each of them a Caucasian) unanimously agreed that it was the Black woman. They noted how Black women had endured slavery and sexual exploitation at the hands of their masters. Yes, the slave master would touch their bodies, but not their souls. There was something unique about the Black woman, something that enabled her to bounce back with more power after the worst abuses. Those scholars concluded that they'd never seen anyone endure so much and still remain so strong. Their statements were printed in the *New York Times*.

❦

As a child, I used to stare at my mother. I was mesmerized by how beautiful she was. It wasn't hard for me to see why daddy was so crazy about her, and why he had a bit of a jealous streak regarding her. Standing, she stood at about five feet, two inches; had a medium size frame, wore size seven shoes, and a size 15 dress. She had pretty, shiny, long bouncy black hair that stayed in place when she walked. She had beautiful brown eyes, cocoa butter soft skin, an unbelievable smile that showed her sparkling white teeth, and a soft tone voice that completed her attributes. Her presence was one of class and sophistication. She was everything that a man could want. But her job was never-ending as she worked seven days a week without much of a break. Seeing about her children and her husband and taking care of our needs before her own was a full-time job. Mom never really got a full eight hours of sleep. But what truly amazed me about her was that she never complained about doing what she was doing. Amazingly, she saw motherhood as an honor and a privilege, not a curse and a burden; she saw being a wife as a blessing, not a setback. These were biblical values that have long since been abandoned by the vast majority in our society today. Weak families are perhaps the number one cause of the breakdown in our society today, which leads to an abundance of crime and immorality.

Some of my fondest memories are of those times when my mom demonstrated her endless love towards my siblings and me such as the times when one of us was ill. She would stay up all night long giving medicine, fixing hot tea, and praying over that child. Many nights mom would rock her ill child to sleep.

My mother knew secrets to healing and wellness that many are unfamiliar with today. One Friday after school, Diane got stung by a bee on her arm. She started hollering like she lost her mind. Mom brought Diane into the kitchen and examined her arm, taking notice of the swelling and redness; she then got some cigarette tobacco oil and began rubbing that area back and forth. Suddenly, after five minutes, Diane started feeling better. She then fell asleep in mom's arms.

During the cold November of 1965, you couldn't get me to go outside to play. It was too cold. I'd stay close to the fireplace. One particular night everyone was taking turns taking baths when we ran out of hot water. Sallie decided to boil two pots of water without mom's permission. While trying to carry the pots to the bathroom, she accidentally spilled some of the water on her foot. She began screaming in intense agony and pain, prompting mom to run to the bathroom. The next door neighbor even came over to the house, being nosy and wondering what was going on. Mom had Rose holding

Sallie's arm. "Sallie," mom said, "if you want me to help you, you must tone it down so I can chalk the fire out with the witch-hazel. If you rub it, a blister will come. Trust me! Mom knows what's best." It doesn't make sense to add heat to an already hot surface, but that's exactly what mom did. Sallie finally felt a little comfort. Mom then elevated her right leg and added her special touch by gently stroking Sallie to sleep. The next morning, Sallie woke up with no sign of a blister.

It was the summer of 1966. School was out. I was enjoying a game of marbles outside with my siblings Diane and Carl; we also liked to play hopscotch and jump-rope. My brother WiLewis, however, was into much more dangerous and death-defying stuff. For example, he would try to use garbage bags as capes to jump from high platforms like buildings or the side of the house. Apparently, he thought he was Superman. Mother kept telling him that Superman was make-believe, but WiLewis still did risky things. One day, he and a couple of his friends were playing with dry ice, putting it in their mouths and blowing out ice circles like they were smoking cigarettes. Dry ice will burn your tongue if you keep it in your mouth for too long. Desiring to fit in with my brother and his friends, I asked if I could do what they were doing. WiLewis's response was, "No! You just a baby!" Despite WiLewis's objection, I insisted that he allow me to participate in the game he and his friends were playing, which he eventually did. I just wanted to be accepted by them. So I took a piece of dry ice and put it in my mouth, but I accidentally swallowed it. Immediately, I began to lose my hearing in my right ear, and it felt like my mouth and my insides were on fire. I started running home crying out for my mother who heard my cries from a distance and bolted out of the house and met me halfway. My next door neighbor also heard my cries and screams and rushed out to assist us. They drove us to Grady Hospital. All the way to the hospital, my mom held me in her arms and reassuring me that everything was going to be alright. Her voice was so soothing and comforting; it was like hearing the voice of an angel in my ear wiping away the fear and worry that raged in my soul. Upon arrival at the hospital my mother rushed me to the emergency room and nurses took us to the back and mom explained to them everything that happened. Afterward, they escorted her to the waiting room while they pumped my stomach. The procedure took around forty-five minutes.

☽

Mother was a survivor. She and her sisters were adept at making the best out of what little they had. Mother was the oldest of three sisters: Mae Render-Jenkins was the middle girl and Aunt Hattie Render-Birts was the baby girl. They'd do everything together. They joked, laughed, and shopped together; from head-to-toe that dressed the same, from their outfits to their socks, shoes, and hats (in different colors). Whether going to church, gossiping together, dancing together, playing together, or holding conference call, they remained close. As sisters, they had an unbreakable bond. Mother was the product of close family ties. She understood the importance of family; this concept was drilled into her at an early age. She learned that when facing great difficulty there is a type of medicine that can cure any heartbreak, worry, and stress. She often shared with me her secret to survival: "Laughter" she said, "is good medicine." I noticed she and her sisters loved to laugh. They got together and laughed, laughed, laughed. This secret was undoubtedly one thing that helped me in my later years, during the dark times of my life, during times when darkness would encompass me and nearly send me into a state of delirium and insanity.

Mother was also a big proponent of education despite the fact that she didn't have much education herself. She wouldn't let me nor my siblings play outside until we first finished our homework. She pushed us although she only had a ninth grade education. I became inquisitive of my mother's level of education when doing my homework. I began asking her for help in certain areas only to discover that she needed help herself in those areas. I quickly found myself educating her as I became more educated. When I questioned her about her lack of completing her high school education, she explained to me that she had to drop out of high school because her parents made her help them on the farm and even go pick cotton at times. Times were tough then. In my mother's young years she and her family had no other choice but to work if they were to survive. School was not much of an option for them. My mother got married at the age of fifteen. She came up in an era where hard, back-breaking work and labor was about all they could expect. Hard work and bearing children were the two most important things life offered her; but even still, mother saw the value of capitalizing on new opportunities not afforded to her generation. Mother didn't have a lot of book-sense, but she had more sense than most professors and academics when it came to living life. She was quick to share with us wisdom for living. But when it came to our homework, James would help us out mostly; and when James wasn't around, mom would always say, "God always got a ram in the bush" (referring to her brother, uncle Randolph).

There was one incident, however, that highlighted the necessity of having a decent education, one that revealed how not being well educated affected my mother. My father worked hard. He'd bring home between $125 to $150 in a two-day work period. Both he and mom would discuss how the money should be used: how much should be spent on food, bills, the mortgage, taken out for life insurance, spent on family outings; and lastly, how much should be deposited into the bank each week. Several months had passed and, one day, daddy came in and confronted mom about what he considered to be a blatant misuse of the family's funds. He noticed that our bank account was not reflecting the amount of money that should have been in it; there was a severe shortage. He and mom began arguing over the money. He asked her where all of the money went and accused her of spending too much on nonessentials. Mom stood her ground and adamantly argued that she had not misused the money. The two had a big fight, one that left mom in tears. My sisters went to console her; and as they did, Sallie noticed one of the deposit slips on the table. Curious, she picked it up and then asked mom how much money she had been depositing with each trip to the bank. Mom responded that she had been depositing $100 during each transaction, but Sallie noticed that the deposit slip read $1.00 during each transaction that was deposited. Mom either forgot or just didn't know to add the extra two zeros on the deposit slip, a mistake that the bank teller was picking up on and capitalizing on. Sallie gathered up all of the receipts and gave them to daddy, who went to the bank along with mom and confronted that teller. They spoke to a bank manager who then discovered that the bank teller had been accepting those $100 deposits but allowing mom to get away with mistakenly depositing only a dollar into the bank. The teller knew that mom wasn't conscious or aware of what was going on and had been secretly pocketing the other $99 dollars out of the $100 mom was depositing. When it was all settled the bank teller got fired and arrested and the bank refunded mom and dad a total of $792 (which had been stolen from us for eight months). Afterward, dad apologized to mom for the whole thing and the two made up . . . real good.

I believe that the main reason mom and dad got that whole issue resolved is because mom was a woman of prayer. Even though she didn't realize the bank teller was tricking her out of her money, God knew. As He said in His Word, He will not allow His children to stay in the dark—He vindicates His children. This is why mom would always tell us that no matter what anyone says or does to us, we should "just do right" by others and trust God to take care of us. This lesson would stick with me also in my later years, further helping me to let go of much hurt and pain and allowing me to discover freedom from fear and bitterness through forgiveness. I would certainly need the life lessons taught by my mother. Without them, I would have certainly gone under.

When I think about life today, I wonder what if mom would have been too busy to be a mother. Would I have gained such a strong foundation in my life to help me handle the coming storms? No. I learned much in school, I accomplished much in life, I soared higher than I could have ever dreamed, but none of this would have been possible if mom had not been on her job laying a foundation in my life.

CHAPTER 4:
BULLETS AND FIRE

I MET HER IN BIOLOGY CLASS AT PARKS JUNIOR HIGH
School. Biology was one of my favorite subjects, but
my eyes were on another extraordinary specimen:
a girl named Karen. She provided even more motiva-
tion for me to show up to class. She smelled so good,
was clean with sparkling white teeth, and was very well
dressed in her fitted blue jeans that contoured perfectly
around her curves. Her hair had a bounce to it like my
mom's, her fingernails were clean and rounded, and her
breasts and her lips were as soft as she was petite.

Karen developed a sudden interest in me one day
during class after the teacher asked me to elaborate on
dissecting a frog. I could see the infatuation beginning to
form in her face as I was talking. Her eyes and lips began
to form a pouty expression. I knew what she wanted,

and I was bold enough to give it to her. So, after class was over, I introduced myself to her and told her that she had some lent on her face (which she didn't, but it was my way of flirting and setting her up for my next move). In a sudden move, I leaned in and kissed her right smack on the mouth. She didn't put up a fight or try to reject me either; instead, she embraced me more. That kiss lasted for at least four minutes. "Why are you so bold like that?" Karen asked afterward.

"Well, I guess it's in my genes," I responded. We exchanged telephone numbers. After I got home later on that day from football practice I went straight to my room. I didn't even want to eat. I was mesmerized, entranced, still thinking about that incredible kiss. I had to hide in the closet just to call Karen since mom certainly wouldn't have approved of me dating at such a young age; also, dad had a very strict policy in the house when it came to using the phone. Mom and dad's hope for me at the time was that I'd focus more on books than girls. But as with every teenager, biology had kicked-in; puberty had arrived and it wasn't going anywhere. Now an adolescent, nature was taking its course. I was exploring my world further and doing what was natural and experiencing what was inevitable. It was inevitable that I was going to soon fall in love with a girl. So I'd sneak, call, dream, daydream, and kiss Karen's soft lips whenever the opportunity became available. When Karen and I were on the phone, we would talk about the basic stuff such as our home-life, our parents' strictness, etc.

"Well, Curtis, are you ready for me and can I kiss

you tomorrow in school when I see you?"

"Of course, you can. But why are you rushing me off the phone?"

"I don't have much time on the phone because I have strict parents as well."

"Momma!!!" yelled Rose, eavesdropping on my conversation. "Joe is in the closet on the phone!!!"

"Karen, I got to go. I will see you at school."

"Man, I can't do this anymore!" I exclaimed. I was sick of working with my dad. He worked me like a Hebrew slave. I got paid between $5 to $10 for seventeen hours or more of long, hard work. That just wasn't going to cut it for me. I needed some money. I was tired of dad only giving me a quarter a day for school. Dad claimed that he kept a record of everything we ate and drank and that he'd deduct my percentage from my paycheck. That was cheap. Just plain cheap. I vented to momma, "That's why no one wants to work for dad! He is so cheap! I quit!"

In school, I was working on another task: Karen. I couldn't stop dreaming about her soft lips and that sexy body. This was my first brush with teenage love. At school, we would meet up. That was my time to serenade her with affection, sweet words, and to inch ever so close to the fire of sexual passion. "Hi, Karen. It's good to see you."

"The feeling is mutual."

"Did you dream about me last night?"

"Yes."

"Tell me one thing that ran across your mind."

"Can I show you instead?"

"Yeah, girl. I can't wait to taste your juicy lips."

"I like the way you maneuver your tongue. Have you participated in a kissing contest?"

"No, but I witness my parents doing it all the time. My mom always says that dad is an expert in the kissing department. Now, what did you dream about?"

"Do you really want to know?"

"Yes! Well, I'll tell you what I dreamed about last night first. I dreamed of us being in a park together on a mild, cool day with the sun shining. You were sitting on my lap while I ran my fingers through your hair and held you so close that I could hear each beat of your rushing heart. I let my mind float all around all of the wonderful things that I want to share and do with only you!"

"Curtis, this is my first relationship!"

"Oh, call me Joe. My entire family calls me Joe the Cocomo.

"Is that your middle name?"

"No. That's another story that I'll share with you later."

"Joe, do you really want to be with me?"

"Yes, I do."

"Can you put up with my mood swings? My parents don't like me talking to boys. I've lots of homework to do after school. I'm going out for the cheerleader team and there won't be any time for us."

"Karen, I can deal with all of that and more. With togetherness and communication, we'll get through all of that. You're not going to get away from me that easy. You need to review my sign. I'm a Taurus."

⁂

I found another job. It didn't pay very much, but it beat working for my dad. My eighth-grade football coach, Mr. Goss, asked me and another boy named Sylvester if we would like to work with him for 2 hours after school every Tuesday and Thursday, assisting him. His requirement was simply that I maintain a 3.0 GPA. I was happy about it, but I explained to Coach Goss that I still needed to get my parents' approval first. "You will be working with me in the gym, Joe. Tell you what: I'll call your parents and explain everything to them myself."

"Thanks, Coach." Looking at Sylvester, I said, "This will be great for me because I can use some *real* extra funds. What about you?"

"Right on, Joe!" Sylvester responded.

Mom and dad talked everything over and came to an agreement to let me work for Coach Goss and his assistant, Coach Lavender. Now, I needed to tell Karen about my new job, which I did. She responded, "That's great, Joe!"

"Yeah. Now I'll have some spending money to buy you some sweet things with."

"Joe," Karen solemnly interjected, "since we've been dating for the past three months, I was wondering if you've ever been sexually involved?"

"No. You're my first, and you'll probably be the only one. What do you feel when we're together?"

"I know that my heart starts beating super fast when you kiss and hold me tight, my right breast also becomes very sensitive, and I get a little moist downstairs. What do you feel?"

"Well, my heart does beat, but not super fast. Some mornings, I do wake-up with a splitting headache, wishing that you were near me. I know nothing about sex, only what my dad shared with me. I've seen my dad on top of my mother 'doing the do!' I know when he finishes he just rolls over and goes to sleep. Once, it seemed like mom was upset with him. Maybe she wanted some more but dad must have come too quickly. My mother told me that every woman got two holes: one for intercourse and the other for the exiting of her stool. Karen, when that time comes we'll know what to do. A condom is a safe way."

"Okay, baby. I'll leave it in your hands."

It was April Fool's Day in 1971, but the gunshots were no prank. That day, Sylvester and I were refereeing a basketball game for the 19 years old and under league. There was one player who took exception to a call we had made during the game. That player's name was Jeff. He was upset over a foul call and began pushing Sylvester's buttons. Sylvester then issued another citation to Jeff, citing him for unsportsmanlike conduct. Jeff's team was losing by one point. Jeff issued a threat to Sylvester and I, saying, "If we lose this game, both of ya'll is mine." We certainly didn't take the threat as seriously as we should have since Jeff wasn't pranking us or joking with us. He was dead serious, and we'd find out just how serious after the game was over and his team had lost.

After the game was over I stayed behind in the gym playing basketball; Joe, on the other hand, went and hung out in the lobby. While Sylvester was sitting in a chair, he was approached by Jeff who had a very serious look on his face. Sylvester, agitated by Jeff's confrontation, shouted, "Man, I don't want to hear that noise!" Jeff, without speaking a word, simply stepped back and reached his hand into his coat pocket, and pulling out a 22 caliber handgun he shot Sylvester in the chest right above the heart. People began running everywhere, trying to get out of that gymnasium, but Jeff wasn't done yet. He came into the gym looking for me to finish me off too. When I saw him I immediately took off running, zig-zagging along the way so that he wouldn't be able to get a clear shot at me. Jeff was chasing behind me; he was right on my tail. When we got to the hallway, Jeff took off in the opposite direction, but I kept running. After a while, I stopped running, turned around and went back to the gymnasium. Entering the lobby, I immediately noticed blood all over the floor, and there were drops of blood leading upstairs to the principle's office. It was there that I discovered Sylvester lying on a couch, bleeding profusely. Someone was there with him, applying pressure to the wound while waiting for the ambulance to arrive. Sylvester's shirt was drenched in his own blood. It was a terrifying sight to behold.

The principal began to question me about what

had happened. I was still somewhat in a state of shock. I answered his questions the best I could before the ambulance arrived. Shortly afterward, the Atlanta police arrived and began questioning me and others about what had taken place. After giving my statement to the police, they let me go; and that night, I ran home in about seven minutes what normally took me around twenty minutes. When I got there, mom realized that something was terribly wrong with me. My clothes were drenched in sweat and I was breathing heavily. She could see trauma and shock on my face. She began to question me, asking if I was alright. I explained to her everything that had just taken place. She asked me why Coach Goss or Coach Lavender didn't drive me home. I explained that Coach Goss wasn't present and that Coach Lavender, although on duty, was nowhere to be found. Mom began comforting me, then she gave me a hot bath before sending me to bed. "Get some sleep, Joe. I'll go with you to school in the morning. I love you, son," she said.

"I love you too, mom."

The next day came. The sun rose as if nothing had transpired the night before. The clouds were back to work. It was time to go to school. Time moved forward, but my mind was still stuck in yesterday. The thing that relieved my anxiety and fears was the good report about Sylvester's condition: he was doing just fine. The bullet narrowly missed his heart. Sylvester's mom had already pressed charges against Jeff. Coach Goss was back in his office that morning. He confronted Coach Lavender about his sudden disappearance during the incident the night before. The two began to exchange words in a heated argument, after which Coach Goss landed a right-cross on Coach Lavender's face, causing it to swell-up. Following their altercation it was discovered that Coach Lavender had been silently and secretly suffering from a serious illness for some time: he suffered from amnesia, a condition that made him unfit to serve in the position he was in. At that point mom made me resign from working with Coaches Goss and Lavender. I just had to find another job, but that wasn't an issue for me. I was just glad to be alive. I was glad to feel my mom's arms again. I was excited about seeing Karen's face, feeling her warm embrace and her soft lips. I was even glad to hear my dad's voice. I had forgotten all about how cheap he was. His company seemed priceless to me now.

JUST A LITTLE LOVE & JOY

CHAPTER 5

BECOMING A TEAM PLAYER

"DAMMIT, LOVEJOY!!! WHAT THE HELL WERE you thinking?!!!" hollered Coach Goss, irate over the fact that I had just cost our team a shot at the state football playoffs. It was the fourth quarter and we (Parks Junior High) had 19 points on the scoreboard; the opposing team, Kennedy Junior High, had 24 points on the scoreboard. We only had time for one more play, one that would either send us to the playoffs or send us home. We had the ball on our 2nd yard line with only a few seconds left on the clock when Coach Goss called for a time-out so that he could give us the final play. "Floyd, let's go with 32-quickie right. Tell Lovejoy to power through the hole with everything he got. Okay?!"

"Got it, Coach!" Floyd replied. Floyd approached

the huddle with the play. The crowd was extremely loud, excited and anxious due to the suspense of the moment. Floyd looked at me and said, "Lovejoy, 32 Quickies . . . on 2!!"

"Hold-up! Did he say right or left?" I asked myself. "I think he said left." We were now at the line, getting ready to execute our play. "Ready! Set! Blue 22! Blue 22! Hut! Hut!" I ran left and Floyd went right, which was not the original plan. Unfortunately, Floyd got sacked and we lost the game.

"Damn, Lovejoy!! You were supposed to go right, not left!!" yelled Floyd.

"Man, I thought you said . . . Man, I'm sorry," I said with a look of shame on my face. That walk back to the locker room was one of the longest walks I had ever taken before—it perhaps felt like the Green Mile. I could feel the resentment of my teammates. I could feel their contemptuous eyes burning the back of my head. My teammates were all looking pissed off at me. "These guys are going to kick my ass," I thought to myself.

Coach approached me. "Lovejoy, what were you thinking?! The damn hole was wide open! You don't have anything to say?!"

"Um... Um..."

"You can't hear, boy?!"

"No, Coach!" I responded.

"Oh, so your ass being smart?!"

"No, Coach! I'm serious! I'm deaf in my left ear! When Floyd was calling the play in the huddle, I was reading his lips. I only heard bits and pieces. Just when he said which way to go, one of the players moved and blocked my view with his helmet. I was sure that I partially heard 'left'! But I know and everybody in the stadium knew that the hole that was open was right. I'm so sorry. It's a hard pill to swallow right now." After explaining this, I noticed the look on the coach and the players' faces; it transformed from a look of contempt to a look of compassion.

"I'll inform the school counselor to assist in getting a hearing test scheduled for you ASAP!" Coach Goss said.

"Thanks, Coach."

"No matter whether we lose or win, you're still our brother and we love you," the coach explained. His words further imprinted on me the significance of family over all else. My coach and fellow teammates were like a family. Even though we lost the game and perhaps one of the greatest opportunities of our high school sports career, we understood that the teammates were more important than a trophy.

I loved football and basketball. Basketball was probably my favorite sport though. I may have been shorter than most of my teammates, but my quickness and point guard skills definitely made up for my lack of height. Hearing my name called by the cheerleaders also gave me a rush; it would bring out the best in me and make me work just that much harder on the court. Our basketball team finished the season with twelve victories and four losses. During the athlete's banquet, I received the Most Valuable Player (MVP) and Assists Awards. I was certainly optimistic about the next season.

❧

I was learning the value of being a team player on and off the basketball court and the football field. By now, I'd begun working on another job at Church's Fried Chicken. I was only 14 years old when I started working there. I'd practice in the mirror how to talk and act older than I was just so that I could make an impression. My parents weren't too excited about me getting that job, but they recognized the strength of my spirit. I was very independent. I wanted to have my own money.

I managed to secure the position at Church's illegally to be truthful. I changed my birthday on the application to reflect that I was 16 years old rather than 14 years old. The manager didn't bother to check and verify my information and my parents weren't too happy that I lied. While there, I worked my way up the ladder while there, demonstrating an exemplary attitude, dedication, and hard work. I performed any and all tasks I was assigned without complaining and murmuring; I did them with excellence. The boss was impressed with my work habit, personality, and especially my smile. After about six months in, I got promoted to the management team as a crew chief leader. I was responsible for opening up the store at least one day out of the week, which was Saturdays. My boss, Peggy, excused me from work to attend school activities such as football practice and games. I was averaging 24 to 30 hours a week making $8.75 an hour. Having this kind of responsibility exposed me to the adult world before I fully reached maturity. My ego began to blow up due to this. My eyes were becoming more and more open because of this newfound responsibility and because of the girls. I was beginning to think I was grown, but my ego was starting to place me on my dad's bad side.

I had finally finished Parks Middle School and I was now ready for high school. It was a family tradition that all of us (my siblings and I) attend and graduate from Price High school. I knew what my dad's expectations were, but I decided instead to go and enroll myself in Sylvan Hill High School, which was 95% Caucasian. I did this without my parents' consent. Dad was furious, but mom, on the other hand, saw the bigger picture. She was actually quite understanding of my decision, perhaps sensing that the world was changing and that it would only be beneficial for me to be exposed to different cultures and peoples. She knew what challenges lay ahead of me on the road of life. She also understood what it took to increase my chances of succeeding. Dad's mindset was to pull me out of Sylvan Hill High School and pull me off of my job indefinitely and inflict even more punishment on me, but mom was able to talk him out of it. She stepped in on my behalf and persuaded him to change his mind. But the whole situation reminded me of who was still in charge.

Thankfully, I was allowed to not only attend the high school of my choice, but to continue working at Church's Fried Chicken (CFC). The experience of working built my confidence even more. Earning a promotion made me think I was capable of doing anything. Hard work provided me with a sense of worth that I couldn't have gotten even from the basketball court and the football field. High school sports were good, but they don't carry the same gravity as a job where money, bills, livelihoods, and serious responsibilities are at stake...and not to mention that the impact of getting fired, unlike being cut from a high school basketball or football team, will follow you where ever you go and hinder you up the road should you attempt to find another job. Being a team player in the corporate world is another level of responsibility. At CFC, my teammates didn't just have egos to feed; some of them had mouths to feed; and if this team lost, there was more at risk than just a few egos. We all had to step up. We had to de-bone and cut chicken every day in a 32 degree cooler. We had to process chicken and cook it in a deep fryer at 365 degrees. We had to change hot filters during cooking. We had to do all of this knowing that we risked losing a limb due to a serious accident. The CFC that I worked at was on Stewart Avenue. It was like a small box with just enough space for the staff. There were no drive-through windows, only two walk-up windows. We had a manager and a cook on duty. When it was time for the staff to leave the building at the end of the day, we had to climb out the front sliding window for safety and security reasons. We found that it was also very beneficial for us to feed police officers for free whenever they would show up. Whenever we treated them good they wouldn't mind escorting us out at night after we closed. That was a fair exchange.

"I think we got a winner here" our store manager, Peggy, told the CFC area supervisor while discussing me. That certainly boosted my self-esteem. She told the area supervisor that I was "a quick learner who could adapt to changes," and that I had "a contagious smile." My chest was now sticking all the way out. I realized that I was on to something. I continued to specialize in customer service, making myself known, and gaining a reputation in the community when it came to Church's Fried Chicken on Stewart Avenue. Loved-ones, family members, and schoolmates would regularly stop by for food, and I would usually give them a little something extra. I would get to know my customers while serving them. Some of them would even show up in the store and ask for me by name to take their orders. I'll never forget waiting on one elderly gray-haired man. He approached the window and I greeted him with a warm smile. "How are you doing today, sir? Can I get something for you?" The man just stood there staring me down. Since he didn't respond right then, I figured he needed more time to think about his order, so I gave him a courtesy drink.

"Okay. I'm ready to order. Give me eight pieces, white [meat]."

"There's a five-minute wait on the fresh white meat. Would you care to wait?"

"Yes," the man responded. Then the man stated these words to me: "If you keep that smile on your face always, it will take you around the world." I thanked him for the kind words.

"The chicken is up!" yelled the cook.

"Okay, sir. Let me get your chicken," I said to the man. I then turned and went to get his order, but when I returned to the window he was gone; it was as if he had vanished into thin air. I never saw that man again after that. When I got home I shared that encounter with my mom, and she said, "You just witnessed an angel sent by God! Angels only do specific things for GOD—no more; no less."

CHAPTER 6
THEY COME IN PAIRS

MANY OF MY CUSTOMERS WERE REGULARS; THEY knew me by name and I knew them by their faces. One customer was unforgettable. It was extremely difficult for me not to stare at certain of her *assets*. She would come to the store once every two weeks to order food. I remembered her order by heart: a two-piece breast meal. I would never get the chance to wait on her whenever she came. I would notice her come, and notice her even more as she walked away from the window. But one particular day, she showed up and approached my window to place her order. It was a good day. I tried to maintain eye contact with her, but couldn't help glancing down while she talked to me. She had perfectly rounded breasts; they were big and full. "Curtis, why are you staring at my breasts?" she asked.

"I'm not," I responded defensively. "And I'm sorry that you think so. . . . *How did you know my name?*"

"It's on your name-tag," the girl mentioned. I felt so stupid at that moment. I got trapped in the cross-hairs of embarrassment, but I realized there was no need to continue with the act, so I decided to come honest and clean.

"Yeah, I was looking at your breast. Please forgive me. Can you tell me your name?"

"Angie. You know, lots of guys do that to me. It's a big turn-off to me."

"I'm sorry. I didn't mean to do it."

"It's okay. You were able to bail yourself out of this one. Just be yourself. I'll see you next time."

"See you next time," I responded, watching her as she walked off. My heart nearly sunk into my chest as she walked away. She was the total package. She looked just as good from behind as she did from the front. She reminded me of Pamela Grier. She had a bodacious body with a clean, business appearance and professional mannerisms. *I can't wait to see you next time*, I thought to myself. *That's when I'm going to make my move.*

My mind was just stuck in those few moments, thinking about that sexy Angie. I found myself at the cash register zoned out in a daydream. "Hello. Excuse me!" a customer interrupted. "Are you going to take my order or sit here daydreaming about *her?*"

"Oh, I'm so sorry, ma'am. What can I get you?" I responded to the customer.

CHAPTER 6: THEY COME IN PAIRS

The night was long and interesting. I had Angie on my mind. Oh, how I basked in my fantasies of holding her in my arms, feeling on those full breasts and that round bottom. My sleep had been stolen from me by the sweet thief of burning lust.

The following day came and the sunlight washed away the residue of sleep from my mind. Time to get out of the bed and get ready for school. Brush my teeth. Wash my face. Put on my clean, freshly pressed clothes. Eat my breakfast. Off to school. Sit in class and listen to the teachers describe the mechanics of the English language, the intricacies of science, the elements of world history, and more. But my mind was still pondering one subject: Angie. I was studying the curves of Angie, the bodacious body of Angie, the classiness of Angie, and the sexiness of Angie.

At work, I was prepared to take on the influx of customers that would be gracing the windows to order chicken, fries, biscuits, and soft drinks. I figured that it would be another two weeks before I got a glimpse of the girl who had been depriving me of sleep. My hunger and thirst for the sight of her and the sound of her voice were immense, but I had to pull it together and get to work. And I did just that by quickly rekindling my zeal and excitement for customer service at CFC.

Customers were gracing the two windows. One order after another was being made and filled. The exchange of cash and juicy fried chicken was flowing in and out of the front windows like water. It was business as usual. And then the telephone rang. "Hello, thank you for calling Church's Fried Chicken. How may I help you?"

"Is this Curtis?"

"Yes, this is me. May I help you?"

"This is Angie." Oh, how my soul felt a sense of jubilation and excitement. It wouldn't be another two weeks of longing. The one who stole my sleep was on the phone with me. She called the store to speak to me!

"Oh, what's up?" I said trying to play it cool.

"I know you're surprised that I called you."

"Yes, and no," I replied.

"Well, I have to admit that you've been on my mind ever since I left your store. You fascinated me with your beautiful smile and your dimples. I've never seen a man flirt with his eyes without having a change of facial expression."

"Thank you."

"Now, don't think I'm a freak. But were you breastfed by your mother?"

"Yes. Was it written all over my face?"

"No, but I could sense that you were. So, you love breasts?"

"Yes, indeed. I was actually breastfed by my mom until I was 3 years old. I would fall asleep with her nipple in my mouth. I'm not ashamed about being a baby boy who loves his mother."

"I bet you want to touch my grapefruits, huh?"

"Yes! I do!"

"In due time, Curtis. In due time. Just slow your

role. Are you free this Saturday around twelve noon for lunch?"

"Yes. I can meet you at the Underground Atlanta. I don't have my drivers license yet, though."

"Well, why don't I pick you up."

"Okay. I'll be looking out for you. Will you be driving that Mustang?"

"Yes."

"What type of work do you do?"

"I'm a bank teller at Trust Company Bank."

Angie was four years older than me. I was only 16 years old then, but I acted very maturely for my age. She didn't know my age. My parents didn't know that I was already hooking up with girls and young ladies and was beginning to date. They were still very strict with me when it came to dating, requiring that I wait until I reached my eighteenth birthday before jumping into that world. But I was growing up and experiencing the natural transition that comes with time. My eyes were open already, and my mind curious about the female anatomy more than ever. Sex and sexuality were on my mind as was to be expected with a young man growing up. And due to my parents' strict restrictions in this area, I felt the need to sneak.

I didn't want Angie to see me getting picked up by my parents. I didn't want my parents or siblings to see me getting picked up by Angie. I was very discreet. Angie and I would hang out. While hanging out, I would do most of the talking. She enjoyed my company. She loved the fact that I showed an interest in more than just her breasts; I showed an interest in her. I asked her about everything concerning her: her goals, desires, dreams, etc. I wanted to know what made her tick, and what made her happy.

One day, while hanging out in the park, I noticed that Angie was deeply disturbed by something. I asked her what was on her mind. At that moment she began to open up to me about a dream and an insecurity that she had. "I don't like my job," she told me.

"Listen," I responded, "I love my job. The only way I'm going to get ahead is that I must work hard and smart. If you're not happy, then you need to follow your heart. What does your heart say?"

"I want to be a model. I love to dress for every season," Angie replied.

"Then what's stopping you?" I asked.

"I have too much breast," she replied. I was taken aback for a moment. That which I loved was what she dreaded. Perhaps, that explains why she would become quickly agitated by men who only tended to focus on her breasts when looking at her.

"I think that you need to learn to use what you got and make the best out of it. If you don't like the size of your breasts, then reduce them to a smaller size. I know that it takes money. Just save up for the surgery." After taking the time to listen to and encourage her, Angie thanked me for being such a listening hear and being so positive about everything. She then pulled me closer and gave me a big hug; the softness of her breast pressing against my body was sublime. While holding her, I placed a gentle kiss on her cheek, and then her forehead, and then her eye, and then her nose.

"I don't want to kiss your lips because your heart rate will rise," I said.

"That's what I need," she responded.

"Don't blame me if something happens."

"Believe me. I'm a big girl."

"Okay."

"I've never been kissed like that," she breathed. "Can I have another one?"

"Sure," I replied. Gently, I began kissing all over her face and neck while slowly working my way down to her breasts. She stopped me at first, but the look in her eyes suggested that she wasn't necessarily reluctant to take it further.

"Let's continue this when we get to the car," she said. She then got up, took my hand, and led me back to the car where things got even hotter . . . and steamier.

JUST A LITTLE LOVE & JOY

CHAPTER 7
BALLS AND BRASS BALLS

I CERTAINLY HAD MY SHARE OF GETTING INVOLVED with females who secretly had boyfriends they didn't tell me about only to discover the truth the hard way. I'd grown tired of the games. Quite frankly, I didn't have time to do much of anything. My schedule was filled up with school, sports, and work. Having a serious relationship was something I wasn't really prepared to have at this time.

Over the past six months, I had been busy mailing letters to different colleges and universities, looking to gain a basketball scholarship. It seemed like my efforts had paid off as I received word that several college scouts would be attending my games. When I told my basketball coach Mr. Clark about the recruiting scouts, he just laughed. I didn't quite see the humor. "You are too short to play for any college," he told me. I didn't let his insults get to me. I let them go in one ear and out of the other and I continued to keep my hopes up. As far as working with Coach Clark was concerned, I was glad it was my last year of high school. After graduation, I'd no longer have to look at his ugly face and hear his irritating voice.

Two days after I shared the news with Coach Clark about the college scouts, I received a call from one of those scouts informing me that they were going to be at my upcoming game. I was super excited at the prospect this being my big break, my big opportunity, my ticket to a better life, to college, and more. All I need-ed to do was play an excellent game by demonstrating my point guard skills, which I had done throughout my high school life. I started as a point guard on our basket-ball team. I led our team to many victories on the court; however, when the time came for me to perform on the court in front of the college scout, Coach Clark decided to sabotage my goal by doing the unbelievable: he de-cided not to start me. I sat on the bench throughout the entire game. I just sat on that bench with tears streaming down my face, asking God, "Why me, Lord? Why me?" Chants began to ring throughout the gymnasium from the audience, saying, "Put Lovejoy in! Put Lovejoy in!" But this didn't deter the stubborn, strong-willed coach who was determined to ruin my chances at getting into college on a basketball scholarship.

After the game was over, I angrily got up and took off my jersey and then threw it on the floor of the coach's office. I was sick of dealing with a cruel, evil-hearted man whose only joy was seeing me miserable it appeared to me. At that time, if you were to ask me to describe Coach Clark to you, I'd describe him as having horns, a tail, wearing a red cape, and carrying a pitchfork.

After quitting the team by returning my jersey, I left the building and headed home. It was cold and rainy that night, but the pain that I felt inside far outweighed the fear of getting sick from the weather outside. I began walking home in the dark, feeling like a zombie lacking a soul. Suddenly, a car pulled up beside me; it was my dad. "Get in, Joe!" he yelled. I got in the car. "What's wrong, Joe?" he asked.

"Coach Clark blew my chances for a scholarship. Dad, that asshole thought I was kidding when I told him a college scout was coming tonight to see me play. He just laughed and said that 'I'm too short to play college basketball.' He don't know my heart! He don't know my desires! He can have it all! I quit!!!"

"Joe," my dad cut in calmly, "you don't just throw in the towel like that. If you give up this time, you'll do it again. You're not a quitter; you're a winner! Go back tomorrow and apologize for quitting and then ask to be reinstated to the team. Let him put you off the team. Just remember this: whatever you make your life, we support and love you." Those words from my dad not only consoled me; they laid a foundation inside of me, which to now is one of the guiding principles in my life: Never quit! And never assume that another person has power over your destiny because they don't!

"Okay. Yes, sir," I responded. "Love you too dad."

The next day, when I arrived at school, there was a note on my locker stating that Coach Clark wanted to see me in his office. I remembered my dad's words and the revelation they had given me about being in control of my own destiny, which is what I needed at the moment due to the fact that I wanted to punch him in the face and curse him out, both of which would negatively affect my future in one way or another. I went to Coach Clark's office and closed the door behind me. Coach Clark then looked at me and said, "Last night, I found your jersey in my office on the floor. At first, I thought you were just upset, but apparently you quit? So, I need you to turn in all of your school jerseys and tennis shoes immediately." That wasn't exactly how I hoped things would go, but I had to make the decision that was best for my future at the moment; so I responded,

"Coach Clark, let me explain. Yes, I was very upset with your decision last night." Coach Clark then cut me off and said,

"Curtis, I feel that you should have informed me ahead of time, not right before tip-off. Coaching staff always talk about the athlete holding a great deal of respect and carrying himself or herself in a professional manner. I desire the same respect from you, Lovejoy!"

"Still, I told you that some scouts would be at the game last night to observe me playing, but you decided to bench me with no explanation! Why, Coach?!"

"Boy, I don't take orders from you! You are just children!" the coach fired back. At that moment, I stood up out of my chair and replied,

"No! I'm a mature growing young man who respects all ages! And if I ask you a question, you should reply back in a professional manner!"

"Oh, by you rising out of your seat I'm supposed to fear you or something?" the coach asked.

"Oh, it don't work like that because I do have a father who can stand tall for me! I refuse to meet you at your own game! I'll inform Coach Daniel of the matter because he is the H.N.I.C. (the Head Nigga' In Charge)! You're just an assistant coach!"

"You're off my team!!!" Coach Clark yelled.

"You'll never put me off this team unless I resign from this team in writing!!" I replied.

"Get out of here you spoiled crybaby!!!" the coach responded.

"As long as breath is in my body, you'll never be able to put me in the category of a loser!!" I said before turning to his office.

"Let the doorknob hit you where the good LORD split you!" yelled the coach. Baaammm!!!!!! I slammed the door behind with force while leaving out of that office. I gained a sense of strength from my courage to let the coach know that not even he could force me to quit and give up on what I wanted to do in life. I felt a sense of control over my destiny returning to me. The coach couldn't get to me and make me quit my dreams and goals. I was not a quitter, and I wasn't about to allow anyone to stand in my way. I was a fighter. Like my dad, I wasn't the one to lie down for anyone.

Later, I had a meeting with the head coach, Mr.

Daniel. "Lovejoy," he began, "I had a talk with Coach Clark. He felt intimidated by your words. He underestimated you. That side of you, he had never seen before. I know that he tried to sell you a wolf ticket, but you didn't bite it. I've seen those who did, and it was an ugly picture. So, here's what's going to happen: you will remain on the team, finish out your term, and follow his game-plan. Can you live that?"

"No. Not in my heart. But I'll act according to his agenda," I replied. "Does this mean that I'll sit on the bench for the remainder of the season?" I asked.

"Perhaps," said Coach Daniel.

"Okay," I responded calmly. "My mom always told me there is more than one way to skin a cat. He (Coach Clark) doesn't know who he's messing with," I assured Coach Daniel before leaving his presence. Several games had passed and I found myself just sitting on the bench. Finally, the last game of the season was ready. It was a showdown between our team, Sylvan High School, and Central Macon High School who was ranked #1. They had a powerhouse named Rick who was a wing guard standing 6'2" and averaging 10 assists, 7 dunks, and 80 points per game. He was the player no one wanted to check. Coach Clark decided that this would be his prime opportunity to embarrass me in front of my family and friends and college scouts, so he assigned me to Rick. But I didn't care about how intimidating Rick was; I was hungry like a caged animal just waiting for my opportunity to shine. *Okay, Lovejoy, let's do this. It's our time to shine*, I thought to myself. *Rick may be quick, but*

CHAPTER 7: BALLS AND BRASS BALLS

I'm quicker.

The tip-off came and Rick got the ball. The opposing team set up a pick on me, which allowed Rick to score in the beginning. While guarding Rick, he began to talk junk, saying, "Boy, you can't play me. You're too short. I'm going to dunk all over you."

"You must have the ball to do that," I responded.

Throughout the game, I endured a barrage of elbows, shoves, and more fouls that went unnoticed by the referee. I was sore and aching, but determined to win and make an impression. Half-time came. I remember looking up into the audience and seeing my family. I could read my mom's lips asking, "Are you alright?" I grabbed my head and signaled back that my head was pounding and aching. She gave me an aspirin. Finally, half-time was over and it was time to get back into the game. Coach Clark was loving the humiliation I was enduring. He even winked at me before the start of the second half. I got back on the court, ready for more. In the third quarter, the humiliation began with a 360-degree slam dunk by Rick with me hanging onto his shorts. The entire room went crazy. I realized that I couldn't let him get on a roll. I had to do something to stop him. Rick had the ball again. His teammates set up a double-pick on me this time, but I managed to get around them and positioned myself in front of Rick as he went for another slam dunk. I jumped with him, attempting to block him. While in the air, my life flashed before my eyes. It was like standing in front of a runaway train. Rick's body slammed into mine, sending me to the floor with a hard thump. The back of my head hit the floor hard. The referee then hit him with a "charging" violation. Upset, Rick started running off at the mouth. I got back up and got right back on him, sticking to him closely, not giving him any space to maneuver. He delivered an elbow to my face, for which the referee called "foul". Next, he went for a crossover dribble move that I didn't fall for it, and we ended up bumping heads. As a result thereof, Rick earned his third foul of the night.

We were nearing the end of the third quarter and Central Macon had 48 points; we had 32 points. I went for the ball after it got loose from one player's hands. As I dived for the ball, I tripped on another player. I ended up sliding about 30 feet on the floor and needed help to get up. I was too hurt to continue playing, so I had to be escorted to the bench. There's one thing was noticeable after I go benched: before Rick only had only scored 8 points, but after I got benched Rick scored an additional 30 points in the game. They won the game 78 to 42. Everyone saw and recognized my courage and tenacity, and valued me as perhaps the real MVP (Most Valuable Player) in that game. I was the little guy, the underdog who prevented the number one scorer on Central Macon High School's basketball team from putting the ball through the hoop. It was me, little ole' me who tamed the beast and basically shut him down. Oh, and by the way, I scored 21 of the 48 points our team made. Afterward, I received one of the highest compliments from Rick's Coach. He told me, "You got lots of heart and a relentless will! I wish I had you on my team!"

CHAPTER 7: BALLS AND BRASS BALLS

"Thanks, Coach Jackson!" I replied.

It was well into the first few weeks of my sophomore year in high school and I was on my way to Biology class. When I walked through the door, I greeted the teacher, Mrs. Smith. "Hi, Mrs. Smith. How are you doing?"

"Just fine, Mr. Lovejoy. I hope that you're ready to talk about the human anatomy. I want everyone to go over the body's composition today."

"Oh, I'm ready. I'll go."

"Okay, Mr. Lovejoy."

"I want to talk about the female anatomy because their make-up is mind-boggling to me. I'm overwhelmed by how a pregnant mother can carry a baby in her stomach surrounded by all that H^2O and it survives. When she feels pain and the baby is kicking, that's a sign of life. All the vitamins and nutrients are stored in her breasts. Why is it so hard for a baby to break away from that format? What makes her five senses become stronger? What are hot flashes? Is a mother's love for her children the same as that of a man's love? I know that she carries the baby for nine months, but all of that closeness must measure up to something that can be greater than love. My dad says you can give without loving, but you can't love without giving. Women are emotional creates and man is somewhat strong and curious all of the time. He's the provider and she is a helpmate. Can we say that women are the receivers and men are the givers?"

"Wait, Mr. Lovejoy," Mrs. Smith chimed in, "you

are way ahead of everybody, and most of the students you lost right after you asked the first question. Let me try to answer some of your questions. You can take a seat now."

I went back to my seat and sat down next to a beautiful girl named Pamela, whose curiosity was piqued due to my little dissertation on the female anatomy that I had just given. She was impressed by it. "Hi, my name is Pamela. You can call me Pam," she said, introducing herself after I sat down. "Why you so fascinated with women and ask so many questions?" Pam asked.

"Because I've seen and witnessed so many things that my mother went through. I wanted to know how she was able to go through all of that."

"You too bold."

"Well, that's your opinion," I replied. I then asked her, "Can I ask you a question: Why are your thighs so big and muscular? Do you run track?"

"No. I just love to exercise and keep my body in shape," she replied.

"The average girl that attend school here, their thighs aren't that defined. Your thighs are bigger than mine and I play three different sports!"

"Curtis, they're not the same size."

"I have a tape measurer. So, let me see." At that moment, I pulled out a tape measure and began measuring Pamela's thighs and comparing them to mine.

"Curtis, thighs run in my family," she interjected. After a moment, she realized what I had just done. "You are a smooth talker. I can't believe that I let you do that,"

80

Pamela remarked.

"Just admit it, you're comfortable with me," I said. "Since we're classmates and we both have something in common . . ."

"And what is that?"

"We dig each other, and you'll never know what's next," I responded. Pamela didn't deny anything that I said to her. I knew I was in the door and had her right where I wanted her. It was now time for me to move in for the kill.

Over the next few days during lunch, I would invite myself to sit at the table with her. One day, I approached her during lunch and asked, "Can I sit here with you?"

"Sure, if you can handle the heat," she responded flirtatiously. Then she said, "Listen, Curtis, I think you're very hot, but I'm currently seeing someone." These words didn't deter me. I responded,

"What I want to know is this: Are you dating or coping? You can be with several guys because...I'm currently seeing two girls right now—one of them is too childish for me and the other one has too much drama in her life. So I feel like you're just checking out the stock at Sylvan, and that makes two of us."

"Curtis, I supposed to have lunch with Larry."

"Larry? Who is that? I don't see him here."

"Well," she said nervously, "you need to look slightly to your left." I didn't want to panic and look that way, so I kept my cool and kept looking in Pam's direction instead. Larry then approached us from the side and asked Pamela,

"What's going on here? You want to explain?"

At that moment I cut-in and said, "We're having lunch here. You got a problem with that?" Larry then gave me a look like he was ready to kick my butt all over that cafeteria, and he certainly could have; he was, after-all, the #1 halfback in the nation. His neck size was 18½ inches in circumference, not to mention his arm size. But I couldn't show any signs of weakness. I stood my ground, ready for whatever was about to go down. But Larry just looked at Pamela and said,

"I'll see you later."

After that, Larry walked away, and I looked at Pamela and asked, "Is that who you're seeing? He talks like he owns you." I added, "I know I probably should have kept my mouth closed because I know about Larry's temper. But tell me now if you really want that. If you can look me in my eyes and tell me you want him and that you don't want me, I'll walk away, and you won't have to worry about me in your face ever again. So what is it going to be?"

"I've only known you for three days, but this is the 3rd week of the school year and things have moved so fast between us. I can't get you out of my mind. You're so entreating and a daredevil. That's what excites me about you. Yes, I want to see you, but just give me some time to end this with Larry."

"Okay. You have one week to make that happen," I told her.

"Why are you looking at me like that?" Pam

asked.

"Pam, the quicker you end it, the better you'll feel and the more you can focus on us," I said.

The next day at school my cousin Bob Lovejoy pulled me aside in the hallway and said, "Listen, cuz, this is your 1ˢᵗ year over here at Sylvan. You need to leave Larry's girl alone. Is something wrong with your eyes? Do you see how big he (Larry) is? I told you before school started to stay on the 'DL' (Down Low). Instead of you checking out a low profile girl, you messing with the star football player's girl. Joe, I know that girl is fine as wine, but let that go, man. She's not worth an ass-whooping."

"Bob, I like her, man," I responded. "She's going to dump Larry in one week."

"And you believe that?" Bob asked.

"She reminds me so much of Coffey (Pam Grier); she got the total package man—everything in the right spot. Don't worry, Bob. All is going to be fine. I'll stay out of Larry's view."

"I'm so glad that you didn't go to Price High School," Bob stated.

"Why?"

"Because their mindsets are totally different over there," he said shaking his head.

JUST A LITTLE LOVE & JOY

CHAPTER 8

THE WRONG PLACE AT THE WRONG TIME

I WAS BEING ACCUSED OF CHARGES I KNEW WERE FALSE. I didn't do what I was being accused of doing! I didn't break into the school and try to steal anything, but the police officer questioning me didn't want to hear that. He insisted that I and a few of my peers were trying to commit a crime that day, and he was more than excited about taking us down to the Atlanta Precinct. This would be a greatly inconvenient time to get caught up in such a situation: I'm approaching my senior year, and I've just been promoted to manager at my Church's Fried Chicken store. I'm not trying to throw away everything that I've worked so hard for. I wouldn't be so dumb.

It all started on a Friday. On Fridays, a couple of my friends and I would hang around after school and play basketball. This particular Friday, Coach Daniels, our basketball coach, informed us that the school was being monitored by detectives. He also informed us that the gym would be closed on the weekends from now on. Apparently, there had been an incident that raised alarm around the campus, prompting concerns and meriting police surveillance.

That Friday, me and a few of my friends chose to stay behind and play basketball for two hours. After we finished, we went to the locker room to shower. On our way to the locker room, we noticed a couple of boys trying to break into the school's equipment room. The boys took off running once they noticed we spotted them. We really didn't think anything of it.

After showering, we all left for the evening. We got on the metro bus to go home. Before leaving, we all agreed that we would return to the school gymnasium the next day around noon to play some more basketball. This routine was something we had done plenty of times before. The plan was to shoot some hoops and then go to a house party later that evening. Unfortunately, things didn't go as planned.

The next day, we showed back up at the school. Usually, on Saturdays, there would be a door left cracked open to the gymnasium, but this time we couldn't find a cracked or unlocked door anywhere around the building. We went from door to door, but they were all locked; however, there was one more door left for us to try, and we did. This door was in the middle of the campus. I went to check the door to see if it was unlocked. I pulled on it a little, but it was locked. So, after that, I proceeded to walk away when, all of a sudden, someone swung the door open from the inside. It was the Atlanta police. Once the police officer opened the door, my friends immediately took off running. The officer told me to come here. His facial expression was less than inviting—it was stern and very solemn. For a moment, I stood there, debating whether or not I should run like my friends. I decided to run.

I took off running, figuring that I could outrun the officers. I was panicky and scared, and not thinking straight. The other guys were ahead of me, yelling my name: "Love!!!!" We could hear the sirens behind us. We had circled the building when my hat flew off my head and landed in one of the windows of the school. This thought suddenly entered my mind: *Hold-up. Why are we running? We didn't do anything wrong. We were just trying to play hoops and have some fun. We don't have to act guilty of anything.* That was the moment I stopped running. I just stood there on the corner catching my breath when all of a sudden a police car slammed on the brakes by the corner and an officer jumped out of the car aggressively and yelled, "Get down on the ground!!!"

"No way! I didn't do anything!!" I yelled back.

"I said get down on the ground, now!!!" the officer yelled again. Seeing that I was reluctant to follow his instructions, the officer stormed towards me, detained me, slammed me hard against his car with his forearm pressed against my neck preventing me from moving; then he handcuffed me and told me to spread my legs.

"Man, why you handling me like this?! I didn't do anything!" I said.

"You and your buddies broke into the school!" he claimed.

"No, we didn't!"

"Then why did you all start running?!"

"Cause we were scared and we panicked, sir!" I replied. The officer opened his car door, pressed my head down, and shoved me into the back seat.

My friend, Dennis, believed he got away from the cops, only to bump into an off-duty police officer while running. That officer ended up arresting him and placing him in the back of a squad car. My other friend, Alex, was caught by another officer while he was trying to jump a fence. The other guys got away.

The officers drove me, Alex, and Dennis back to the school in handcuffs. To me, everything seemed unreal like a bad dream. I didn't expect my day to end with me in handcuffs while sitting in the back of a police car, quite possibly facing serious criminal charges that could drastically affect my future. Tears were now flowing from my eyes. Dennis and Alex had the same look on their faces.

One of the officers walked up to the three of us and said, "Listen, boys. I want to help you all. Just tell the truth: you all broke into the school, didn't you?" I was crying so bad snot was dripping out of my nose.

"No, sir! We didn't do that!" I answered. "On yesterday, we saw some boys trying to get into the equipment room, but they ran away when they saw us. That is the truth, so help me God!"

The officer retrieved the cap that blew off of my head and presented it to me saying, "That's the window you came in, and then you opened the door and let your friends in, didn't you?"

"No, sir! That hat blew off of my head while I was running!" I replied. After being interrogated by the police officer, we were sent to meet with the school detective. He searched our pockets. I had on me a hundred dollars and some condoms.

"So, you boys were in the school jacking off?" the detective asked.

"Hell no!" I responded. One of the officers then told the school detective that I admitted to breaking into the school by climbing through one of the windows and then letting my friends in. After hearing him tell the detective this, I yelled, "You liar!! I didn't say that! Don't be lying on me!!"

The officers took me, Dennis, and Alex down to the Atlanta Precinct police station for more questioning and to book us on charges of trespassing, and breaking and entering. An officer explained to us the charges and then stated that we would be transported to a juvenile facility shortly. I then told that officer, "We were at the wrong place at the wrong time. I can't live with myself knowing that I didn't do this. And to witness my parents come down here for something we didn't do and for us to have a criminal record now, that doesn't sit well with me. Please, do me this favor: Take your gun out, put it to my head, and then pull the trigger...because I can't live with myself knowing that I didn't do the things that you are planting on me. I'm not going to let you embarrass my parents and me."

The officer gave me a look as if he couldn't believe what he had just heard come out of my mouth. He then paused for a moment, and then looked at me and said to the three of us, "I'm going to drop all of the charges. If I were to find out that you were lying to me, it won't be a pretty sight. Trouble is easy to find. You hear me?"

"Yes, sir! Thank you, sir!" I responded. "Thank you, Jesus!" I declared.

"Now, when you all get to the juvenile detention facility, they will notify your parents to come and pick you all up. They'll release you then." I was so relieved by those words.

The officer then called our parents and informed them of all that happened. When they notified my parents, my mom told them she would be there in under five minutes. My dad was not so anxious to see me come home though. "You ought to let him stay in there to learn a lesson," he told mom.

"Curtis is a good kid. He never looks for trouble," mom replied. "I'm sure that he has a good explanation for what happened. Let's go!"

I was so happy that Dennis and Alex didn't say anything because they were both 19 years old and I was a minor. I feared that the officers might have been a lot less compassionate and sympathetic towards them. I was given a second chance, and I knew it.

CHAPTER 9
THE UNPARDONABLE SIN

GRADUATION-DAY CAME FOR ME. I WAS JUST GLAD to be able to walk across that stage and receive a high school diploma. My family celebrated this accomplishment with me. I survived high school! I made it to the end without being murdered by the boyfriends of the girls I stole. I survived through all of the drama. But the end of one journey only marked the beginning of another one in the Lovejoy family. Like in most, if not all African American families this is the time it was expected of us to march straight out of the doors of a high school building and straight through the doors of a college or university. And that's what I did. *So, Morris Brown College, here I come!*

I began my freshman year at Morris Brown College in 1975. One of the first things I tried out for was the basketball team. Immediately, I knew I was in for a challenge. At the tryout, Coach Hardinet standing at seven feet one inch didn't take too kindly to short individuals who tried out for the team. Day one of the tryouts, he made his intentions clear, "All of you short people need to leave because there is no way in hell that you are going to make it here. So leave!"

I was unshaken by Coach Hardinet's words. I had an unshakable confidence in my ability to play the game of basketball. I didn't allow him to intimidate me at all. I stayed and worked hard over the next five days, proving myself to the coach on the court. Coach Hardinet even issued an open challenge to any of the short players who wanted on the team, stating that if they could steal the ball from him while on the court and prevent him from scoring, he'd allow them on the team. I not only stole the ball, but I stole the ball from him twice and scored twice on him. Sadly, however, when the coach posted the roster on the board showing who made the team, my name wasn't on it.

After reading that list and finding my name wasn't on it, I felt trapped like in the Twilight Zone. I couldn't believe it! Despite proving myself to the coach, he still cut me. Well, I still wanted to play the game, so I decided to play intermediate basketball. I took out all of my frustrations on the opposing teams. We went undefeated at 6-0. Coach Hardinet took notice of my talent on the court. He was watching.

It was my seventh game, and I showed out. I acted like I was losing my mind on the court in a good way.

CHAPTER 9: THE UNPARDONABLE SIN

I scored 11 points in just under two minutes. After the game, Coach Hardinet approached me. I could see it in his eyes, he was having second thoughts about me and was beginning to regret the decision he made to cut me from the team. He came to me and confessed that he was having second thoughts about me and asked me to show up to the next team practice. But my response to him was, "You can kiss me where the sun doesn't shine." I truly meant that. I left his presence feeling so good. Oh, and, by the way, our team finished the season undefeated.

Although I was in college, I was more focused on my career at Church's Fried Chicken. My promotion provided me with more than enough work and responsibilities to keep my mind preoccupied. I had to juggle the weight of college and my managerial duties at CFC, and one of them was about to take the back seat.

My store was achieving record-breaking sales, and I was earning more money than I'd ever seen. My focus was now on keeping the momentum going on that job and increasing business. I began to feel important as a result of the success I was experiencing in my career; it began to overshadow any failures I experienced in other areas. I was able to shift my attention from my seemingly failed college sports endeavors to my job. One of the best feelings I experienced was after giving my mother money every week. I would give her between $100 to $150 each week. The feeling of being a responsible, hard-working provider was kicking in. As my career began to shape up, my brother's (WiLewis) life was heading in the opposite direction. While I was moving on, making my own money and paying my bills, WiLewis had to move back in with mom and dad. I always maintained that he was too grown and too old to be in their house. And just as I suspected, my fear would later be confirmed when WiLewis and dad came to blows one day.

It was just another day at the store when I received a disturbing phone call: *Ring! Ring!* "Good evening. Church's Fried Chicken. How may I help you?"

"Hey, Joe, it's me, James (Robert)!"

"What's going on?"

"There was a problem at mom's house. She and dad had an argument and dad hit her."

"What?! When did this happen?!"

"Two days ago."

"And you just now calling me?!"

"Mom didn't want to get you upset."

"Is mom okay?"

"Her face is red and swollen. Dad just walked out the house, but WiLewis went searching for him, he approached dad and threatened to kill him. It happened in a public place. WiLewis walked away backward with his hand in his pocket. You know they never saw eye-to-eye and that WiLewis will do it. He's that out of touch with reality. But, Joe, I must say that I agree with WiLewis because dad has no reason putting his hands on mom."

"You're right, but what provoked this?"

"Mom said that dad got jealous. Dad is always

thinking crazy stuff."

"Let me call mom and see where her head is. Later."

After I got off the phone with James, and immediately called my mom. *Ring! Ring!*

"Mom, it's Joe! James Robert told me what happen. Did you want to stay several days with me until things settle down over there?"

"No, Joe. My place is here with your father."

"But he hit you!"

"He just got upset. Your father doesn't see what he sees."

"That's no excuse, mom!"

"I know this. Your father and I got married when we were teenagers. Joe, you're my baby boy. Don't let this make you bitter about your father. These are things that happen in a marriage, things that only we can work out together. Just remember what I taught you: Let God fight your battle."

"But mom, I remember in Sunday School that Jesus got angry and mad, and God also got so upset that He wiped out an entire generation!"

"That is so true, Joe. But always remember that you must love first, and I do love your father. Jesus planted me here. When He wants me to leave, He will tell me, not you! Okay?!"

"What about WiLewis?"

"Just pray for him."

"He needs to leave your house."

"Your father told him to pack his things and

leave, and he did so today."

"Well, I'll see you tomorrow, and I'll talk to dad when the time is right. Love you, mom."

"Love you too, Joe."

The CFC Regional Manager, Peggy, came to me and gave me some outstanding news, our CFC store made the highest store sale percentage in the last four months of all of the CFC stores. Peggy also told me that I was the talk of the town for outstanding customer service, and she revealed to me that there was a strong possibility that I would be receiving another promotion much sooner than I thought.

"A promotion! Are you sure, Peggy?!"

"Yes! I think that you're ready to climb the corporate ladder. Just remember that in this line of work 25% is 'BS,' and 75% is business. If you can keep this in perspective, you will be successful. Oh, congratulations! You moved to the $25,000 bracket."

"I don't know what to say."

"Curtis, your performance speaks for you."

"Thank you so much!"

After hearing this news, the only thing I could think to myself was "Money, money, money, money, money…MONEY!"

I was excited about climbing the corporate ladder. I knew my future with the company was bright; it was brighter than ever now. All I had to do was continue on the path that I was on, and I'd be living the dream:

the American Dream.

It was approximately one year after Peggy's announcement that the company presented with an astounding opportunity. The District Manager came and offered my own CFC store. I was elated! Excited! But I was also saddened because I knew that the responsibility would prevent me from focusing on my education. I was at a fork in the road: Corporate Success vs. Education. I told the District Manager that, although I was honored to have such an opportunity, I would have to decline since I needed to finish college first. He responded, "No problem" and then stated, "You can still accept the position, and we will work around finishing your college education. We can give you two assistant managers and one trainee assistant that will free you up to finish college. Oh, and the package deal consists of a $38,000.00 annual salary, three percent of sales, and a stock option. Sounds great?!"

"Let's do this!" I said. "This is just what I need—it's the kind of power to do something in life," I thought to myself.

෴

My priorities have changed since the day I met with the District Manager for CFC. My priorities now were: get the money first; finish college second. Before that day, I was more focused on finishing college than getting money. But the offer and the possibility of climbing the corporate ladder seemed too good to be true, and I certainly didn't want to pass it up not knowing if I'd ever get that opportunity again.

I continued for a while working and going to school. I had reached my senior year at Morris Brown College with only one semester to go when I committed the unpardonable sin according to my family: I dropped out of school. I remember the day it all happened. One day, while sitting in a Sociology class, my mind started to wander. I started thinking to myself, "Why aren't you breaking store sale records? You can't do it in college. You need to be at the store training all your employees, but you are sitting here in this class with all these students when you're already ahead of them. You make more money than the professor who is teaching the class, and you can make even more money with your new ideas! You don't need college! It's only holding you back!" The next morning, I woke up, got dressed, and instead of going to class, I went straight to my store and didn't return to college at all. Dwight and Jerome, two friends of mine, called me and asked,

"Whats up, man. We haven't seen you on campus."

"Man, I walked out. I don't need college. I'm making money like crazy."

"But Love, you need something to fall back on just in case . . ."

"In case *what*? That's why I'm banking my money now. Tell you what: you go your way and I'll go my way. I got everything under control here. Just send me a graduation invitation."

CHAPTER 9: THE UNPARDONABLE SIN

"Man, that's bull coming out of you."

"Later, man."

My play mother, Mrs. Helen Ponder, found out about me quitting college and she called me and gave me a serious lecture on why I was making one of the biggest mistakes of my life, but it didn't do any good because my mind was made-up. She then called my mom and told her what I had done, at which point my mom wanted to talk with me. I met up with my mom and listened to everything she had to say, but I somewhat tuned her out, that is, until she made this statement: "Go ahead and make all of your choices while you're very young in life. Some people don't get a second chance, but I'm praying that God will do it for you because you're spoiled, stubborn, selfish and cheating yourself out of something that you'll need someday."

"And what is that, mom?"

"An earned degree and self-blanket security."

I was speechless when she said that. My mom knew she had gotten her point across; but still, my mind was made up. My mind was on the money. I was making lots of it. I was banking it too. I was making financial moves. One of my first big move was investing $25,000.00 in a tax shelter program that would give me more of a return through a Wall Street stock option. After all of the telephone conversations with the company, I finally set up to meet with the agents to invest, and that's when the trouble started. I faced with a bombardment of questions from the agents there: "How old are you, and from where did you get so much money? Is this drug money?"

"NO!! I earned every dollar! My age has nothing to do with this! Do you want to do business with me? Yes or no?"

"Well, Mr. Lovejoy, we need to do some more background checks on you."

"I tell you what: you all can kiss my ass! I don't need this! I'll take my business someplace else!"

After that, I decided to invest in mutual funds, CDs, retirement options, in a money market, and Eastern Airlines stocks. I had a plan and was sticking to it. But things were getting ready to take a detour in my life, one for which I couldn't prepare.

Dear: Toney, we've been blessed with each other's love and friendship. Neither I, nor any card I have read are found, nor any words I have ever written can, express the changes you've wrought in my life; The happiness you've given me, or the deep love, appreciation, and understanding I feel for you. You asked what I would like to do with you. I would like nothing more than to be as important to you as you are to me... Thank you for being my lover-but most of all for being my friend. I trust you so completely, admire and appreciate you so much, that whatever time has in store for us- I look forward to our tomorrows, and lovingly on our yesterdays.

I Love you,
Melissa Lennece

101

CHAPTER 10
THE BALLAD OF JOE AND MELISSA

I MET MY FIRST TRUE LOVE DURING MY FRESHMAN year in college. She was the girl of my dreams. Her frame was sultry. Standing at five feet five inches, she had beautiful brown shoulder length hair and beautiful brown skin that seemed to glisten in the sunlight. A stunning smile displayed her succulent lips and pearly white teeth. Her smile captivated me to my soul and the first moment I laid eyes on her I knew I had to make her mine.

I met Melissa one day when she came into my store. When she walked through the door, I dropped everything I was doing to wait on her. She always came to the store with her mother, Mrs. Evelyn Battle. My infatuation with Melissa was noticeable. For example, I overheard Peggy one day asking Melissa when she came into the store why did I always act like a nut whenever she came around. Frankly, I couldn't help myself. Of all of the young ladies I had dated before, I never felt about them the way that I felt about Melissa. My mind was blown away the day that she walked into the store wearing a pair of daisy dukes and a tank top. She possessed the poise, charm, style, and sense of humor to match her physical attractiveness. Her intellect challenged my mind. I truly adored her.

The day finally came when I made my move on Melissa. She came into the store this particular day all by herself; thank God Mrs. Battle decided to wait in the car. That was my opportunity. I immediately asked Melissa for her phone number. At first, she played hard to get, but desperate times call for desperate measures, so I did the unthinkable; once she turned to head towards the door, I rushed into the lobby and asked her again for her phone number, not caring if I looked like a fool in front of everyone. She seemed to be enjoying seeing me act so desperate, but I was determined to get her phone number. I locked the lobby doors and told Melissa that she was not leaving until she gave me her number. Fearing that her mother would suspect that something was going on and come into the store to investigate, Melissa hurriedly shouted out her phone number and then insisted that I unlock the doors and let her out, which I did.

I didn't call Melissa immediately after getting her phone number. It actually took me several days to build up the courage to call her. When I finally called, her mother answered the phone but thought I had the wrong number since I couldn't remember Melissa's name. I then called back and told Mrs. Battle who I am; that I was the guy at Church's Fried Chicken who was interested in her daughter. That's when she finally handed the phone to Melissa. In the meantime, I overheard Mrs. Battle saying, "Here, Melissa. Some idiot is calling you who cannot remember your name." Sure, the insult stung, but being able to get to know the girl of my dreams was worth her insult.

Melissa and I would spend hours on the phone talking. We also began spending time with each other at Mrs. Battle's home. There, Mrs. Battle would sit in the living room with us the entire time and find reasons to throw insults my way. She truly intimidated me, but I kept my eyes on the prize. Back at my house, however, things were a lot different. My mother just loved Melissa and treated her like a daughter. Everyone in my family fell in love with Melissa except for Rosa. Maybe the reason was out of some jealousy because Rosa perceived Melissa as thinking she was all that and a bag of chips. But I didn't care. I wasn't going to let anyone disrespect and hurt my girl.

Melissa and I preferred to spend time at my parents' house because they would give us our privacy. Sometimes, Melissa would fall asleep on my lap while we sat and talked. Those days and nights felt like heaven to me. We had fallen in love with one another over that summer. We couldn't stand the thought of being apart. I especially couldn't stand the thought of having to drop

Melissa off at her mother's house because Mrs. Battle had no qualms with expressing her disapproval of me in the most insulting ways. But what Mrs. Battle didn't understand was the more she tried to drive Melissa and me apart, the more determined we were to be together. Our hearts had intertwined and fused together; they became inseparable. I couldn't see myself with anyone else. I found my angel; the girl whose beauty was unmatched, whose voice was as melodious as a songbird, and whose very presence would melt away all of my worries and cares. Nothing else mattered while we were together.

⚜

A storm sat on the horizon. The winds were picking up. You could smell the storm in the air. That evening, the weatherman confirmed it on the news that Atlanta was under a tornado watch until midnight. That day, business was slow. We only made a total of $65 in four hours time. Gushing winds beat against the windows of the store, and whenever customers attempted to leave, they would have to gather up their strength to push the doors open. Peggy had given us permission to go ahead and close up the shop a little earlier that night.

Night had descended. Heavy winds were still blowing. The customers had all cleared out of the store. There were only three of us left, two other employees and me. We were locking up the store, anxious and ready to leave, finally glad to be turning off the lights to call it a night. After locking up, I looked through the peephole of the back door to make sure no one was outside. Then

CHAPTER 10: THE BALLAD OF JOE AND MELISSA

I went to the lobby and looked out of the windows to check the parking lot. Stewart Avenue had a reputation; it wasn't the safest place to be, especially at night. Looking out of the windows and the peephole, I didn't see any movement. Assuming it was safe to leave, we proceeded out of the door of the front lobby. While rushing to my car, two guys approached us who seemed to appear out of nowhere. Faster than I could blink, one of the guys had a gun to my head; the other guy pushed the other two employees up against the car. "Open the back door if you don't want your brains splattered everywhere!!!" the gunman hollered at me. The other two employees, both of whom were females, were crying hysterically.

"Shut the fuck up!!!!" the other gunman hollered at the two other employees.

"Now, take us back into the store and office!!! Open the damn safe!! Hurry-up, motherfucker, before I start shooting!!"

"God, please be with us," I began praying in my head. My heart was racing; sweat was starting to drip, and my hands were shaking while I attempted to remember the combination to the safe. Trying to recall a combination code while a gun-toting assailant was screaming at me and threatening to blow my brains out was nerve-racking. After failing to get the safe open fast enough, the gunmen said,

"You think I'm playing with you!" Just then, the other gunman violently pushed the other two employees up against a wall while pressing their faces into the wall, then indicated that he was going to hurt them both.

"Okay!! Okay!! I got it! Finally, the safe is open!" I shouted. The gunman put his foot on the middle of my back and began clearing out the safe. After clearing out the safe, the gunmen forced all three of us into the bathroom and instructed us to lay on the floor and don't move. After that, they closed the door and left. Although I sensed that the gunmen were gone, I still waited for several minutes before getting up and leaving out of the bathroom. I reassured the other two employees who were very shaken up and visibly cold that everything was going to be alright. I called the Atlanta Police Department and reported the incident. They arrived three minutes later. The three of us recounted the details of the robbery to the officers who took our fingerprints along with our statements. We also called Peggy and explained to her what happened; she then notified all of the area management and informed them as well.

While recounting that event, it dawned on me that those two gunmen had cased the store for some time and from a distance. They knew where our blind spots were and apparently had studied our routine. They were watching us without us realizing it.

After driving the two employees home, I headed home. That drive felt like one of the longest drives of my life because everything that had just taken place kept replaying in my mind. The thought of resigning from my position began to cross my mind; after all, this wasn't exactly the first time I had someone threaten to kill me or shoot me while working at that CFC store. It was getting to be a bit too much for me.

CHAPTER 10: THE BALLAD OF JOE AND MELISSA

Once at home, I talked to my parents about what happened. All dad said was it was unfortunate what happened, but it was simply a way of life. But mom encouraged me by reminding me to ask God to dispatch His angels—those 10,000 angels—over me daily so that they can protect me. She reminded me that she prays for our entire family and me daily. And I can tell because things could have taken a different turn and been a lot worse.

※

I never mentioned the robbery to Melissa. I didn't want to trouble her mind since she needed to focus on school. At the time, she was attending Fisk College. I knew college was tough enough to deal with on its own. We stayed in contact with each other despite being at different schools in different states. We wrote each other love letters the entire time we were in school. I gladly expressed my feelings, my love, my loneliness due to being without her, and my earnest desire to hold on to our love until we could finally get married.

Melissa stayed on my mind. Constantly thinking about her made me stay away from all of the other girls. I would talk to myself whenever I saw another *sister* with a figure like a Coke-Cola bottle. I would say, "Curtis, keep on walking. That's only trouble." And during those house parties where the lights would be dim, and the finest girls would press up against my body, pulling me so close to them that I could feel their heartbeats; when it got hot like that, all I could say was, "Run, Curtis! Run!"

CHAPTER 11
WILL YOU MARRY ME?

THE DAY FINALLY CAME WHEN MELISSA WAS ABOUT to walk across that stage and receive her degree. I wasn't going to miss her graduation for anything in the world. For a brief moment, sitting there in the bleachers, I imagined myself walking across a stage and receiving my degree from Morris Brown. The palpable excitement of the ceremony filled the atmosphere causing me to reflect back on the decision I made. However, I quickly snapped out of it and slipped back into the present, remembering that I was there for Melissa. I was excited about her future; moreover, I was excited about our future. I had big plans, but I can't say her family shared my sentiments.

Me and Mrs. Battle never really saw eye-to-eye. Mrs. Battle still looked for opportunities to throw in an insult or two at me; perhaps, she figured Melissa could have done better. I don't know. But at Melissa's graduation, Mrs. Battle did appear to loosen up just a little bit towards me; she wasn't as cold, although she was still pretty chilly for me to be around. Melissa's father, on the other hand, wasn't cold at all towards me. Mr. Battle was actually quite warm and welcoming towards me. We got along pretty well. He loved to throw riddles at me, something that Melissa picked up. But on this day, things would be different between Mr. Battle and me.

"Curtis," Mr. Battle said, approaching me. "Come and walk with me while Melissa and her mother mingle with their friends." I realized then we were about to have one of those serious talks about the future of Melissa and me. "What is your plan for my daughter?"

"I do have a plan for us, but we haven't talked about it yet because we were waiting for this moment (Melissa's graduation)."

"Oh, I see. Well, Melissa has long known that I want her to come and join the family's funeral home business immediately.

"She never mentioned anything about that to me. Did you ask her what she wanted to do?" I asked.

"No, because there's no other option," Mr. Battle responded vehemently.

"She does have the right to say what she wants to do with her life, sir."

"Curtis, this family business goes back a hundred years."

"I respect that, Mr. Battle, but there comes a time

that every individual has new visions and dreams. Is she [Melissa] the only member of the family? What about the other members of the family?"

"Melissa possesses the intellect to take this family empire to the next level."

"It sounds like a winner to me, but I know Melissa that, for sure, she's not going to do it. I don't want to rain on your parade, but you need to count her out," I said boldly.

Angry, Mr. Battle just looked me in the eyes and asked again, "What are your damn intentions with my baby?!" Maybe I should have been less bold with Melissa's father, but I wasn't going to back down. I answered,

"I'm not trying to be smart, but she's not a baby; she is a grown woman who is ready for a new adventure and a new challenge in life with her new husband!"

"What do you mean 'new husband'?!" Mr. Battle hollered. "She never discussed anything about marriage or marrying you for God's sake. She's not marrying a jack-chicken-leg like you. You can't live off of chicken feed!"

The gloves were off now. All formalities were out the window. I responded to Mr. Battle, "You see, I know for a fact that when I ask Melissa to marry me, I know in my heart the answer will be yes. And I'm hoping that I will have you and your wife's blessings upon our wedding."

"Evelyn said that you're arrogant, selfish, spoiled; but she left out 'a smart-ass little bastard,' and that you think you know everything. But you're wrong. Do you know who I am, that I run this family and tell everybody what to do?!"

"Sir, you may do all of that inside your family, but I do know one thing, you put your pants on with one leg at a time; therefore, you're not God! I can see right now you want to argue, but I'm not the one. Please excuse me. I need to talk to my lady, Melissa, who is only your daughter that's in love with 'Curtis Lovejoy!' Get used to that last name because her last name will be mine. Oh, she will never have to turn to you for nothing because I'll be her sole provider and bank account. You can bank on that, sir. Have a good evening," I said before turning and walking away.

I caught up with Melissa who was busy talking and mingling with her friends. I was concealing the fact that I had special plans for us on that day. "Baby, I'm so proud of you. Give me some sugar," I said, smiling.

"I'm going to give you more than just some sugar tonight," she responded. She then looked at the graduation gift I gave her. "Thank you, baby, for my Saks Fifth Avenue $3000.00 gift card. When are we going to New York?"

"Whenever you choose. Anything for my baby!" Melissa then observed her father who was acting upset.

"Curtis, what's wrong with daddy?"

"Oh, let's just say that he thought that I was very quiet and a pussycat."

"What you talking about?"

"Baby, we'll discuss it later. But for now, let's enjoy the moment."

"Mom said that you looked so good," Melissa commented. "I believe she is coming around, Curtis."

"We both hope so for God's sake."

"Now what do you mean by that?"

"Let's say they're beginning to know me as a man who knows what he wants and who does not accept no for an answer. Ready to go?"

"Let me go and let my parents know that I'm riding with you."

"Well, please make it quick because the limousine is waiting and I have plans for us tonight!"

❧

I had plans to propose to Melissa in the most extraordinary way. Much thought, much time and money went into these plans. I planned to make this day (Melissa's graduation day) unforgettable—truly unforgettable. I had the limousine driver to take us to a very special place in the middle of town where I already had rose petals laid down covering the red carpet. "Each rose petal signifies my love for you and how long I had to wait until you graduated from college. Waiting is an adventure, but you are worth the wait. Anything as beautiful and breathtaking as you must have nothing but the best," I expressed to her. I also had photos of the special moments we shared blown up and mounted on the red carpet entrance. Each photo evoked strong emotions within Melissa, taking her back to the moments of each shot. The first photo was one we took on our first date; that was the day Melissa fell asleep in my arms under a tree. Another shot reminded her of the day we were walking together in the rain with no umbrella, holding hands and allowing the rain to soak our clothes. Caressing and pressing our bodies together with our clothes drenched in rainwater felt as if we were totally naked. I also had a love letter I had written Melissa blown up, and it brought tears to her eyes. I even had a shot from the day that I locked the lobby doors of the CFC restaurant to prevent Melissa from leaving without giving me her phone number. "Your mother would love this shot," I joked.

Melissa and I proceeded from the red carpet to the special dining area I had set up where dinner was waiting. On the menu was fried flounder smothered in a light cream sauce, garlic mashed potatoes, country-style coleslaw, a strawberry shortcake for dessert; and our favorite wine, Paul Manson Sparking Champaign. But I was far from done. I also had a surprise guest waiting in the wings. The look on Melissa's face was priceless when the R&B group, The Emotions, surprised her and began serenading her. They sang, "You Got the Best of My Love." I watched as the tears continued to stream down Melissa's face. All of this was for her.

We slow danced later on that night to our favorite song, "Love Ballad" by Jeffrey Osborne. I could feel her heart beating and overflowing with happiness. During the evening, every kiss we shared packed enough passion to fill a lifetime. It was as if time was standing still for us; as if no one else existed in this world besides us if only for a moment.

"I truly love you, Curtis," Melissa said as she held

me tight. "You have truly made my day."

"But baby, it's not over yet," I revealed. "There's more."

"Baby, I can't take any more surprises because I'm overly elated."

"Just one more. Plan 'C'! We need to drive one mile down the road," I said. We drove about a mile down the road to where there was a large gathering of people.

"Why are all of these people gathered around like they're waiting on someone? Why are we here?" Melissa asked.

"They're here for you, baby," I answered.

"For what?" Melissa asked.

"Driver, what time is it?" I asked our limo driver.

"11:28 pm, sir. You have two minutes," he replied. Melissa was confused about what was going on. I knew what was going on, the driver knew what was going on, and the crowd present knew what was going on. But curiosity was eating Melissa alive.

Sensing the time was near, I instructed the driver to let down the sunroof, then I asked Melissa to look at the huge billboard sign with the countdown light rotating on it: 5, 4, 3, 2, 1 . . . I turned to Melissa and said,

"Melissa, I love you so much. I can't live, think, or breath without you. I need to ask you one question: "WILL YOU MARRY ME?!"

"YES, BABY! YES, BABY!" Melissa screamed, hugging and kissing me with excitement.

"Now, you need to say it so that all of the people gathered here tonight can hear your answer," I told her.

I then had a person from the crowd hand Melissa a microphone. She took the microphone and hollered,

"Yes!! I'll marry you, Curtis!!!!" At that moment, the billboard flashed the word "yes," and the crowd went wild. The crowd then began throwing roses inside of the limousine through the sunroof. Tears of joy and excitement were streaming down Melissa's face. Even the limo driver, Charles, admitted that all of this seemed like a fairytale out of a storybook.

Our last stop of the night was the Hilton Hotel; that's where we would both retire and unwound for the evening. Even there, I had one more surprise waiting for Melissa. When we got to the door of our suite, I blindfold her, scooped her up off of her feet, and carried her through the door; then I laid her gently on the bed next to ten multi-colored, two feet tall teddy bears and a bowl of freshly cut fruit. "Now you can open your eyes," I told her.

"Curtis, this is more than I could ever dream of," Melissa uttered. "I feel like Dorothy from *The Wizard of OZ*—'There's no place like home. There's no place like home.'"

"Baby, I want to spend the remainder of my life with you. You're my first, and you will be my last. You're everything my girl should be." With a hungry look in my eyes, "Go to the closet and choose what lingerie you want to wear for me." We were both ready to end the night in each other's arms, which we did. Because we were too tired to make love as planned; we fell asleep in each other's arms.

CHAPTER 12
WEDDING BELLS

WHEN YOU THINK ABOUT WEDDING DAYS, YOU generally envision wedding bells ringing, excitement ionizing the air, smiling faces and laughter from happy family and friends, handsome young men in tuxedos and beautiful young women in bridesmaid dresses ready to celebrate a new season in the life of a friend. Wedding seasons are supposed to be fun. But in the days leading up to me and Melissa's wedding, a dark cloud of fear eclipsed our joy and excitement. I was more concerned about whether or not Melissa's family would get along with mine. Melissa's mom still didn't fully accept me even though her dad accepted the fact that now grown-up, his daughter should make her own decisions. He also realized that I would take good care of his daughter, which was enough to put his mind at ease.

But my worries were put to rest as our wedding day approached. Melissa's mom, Mrs. Battle, seemed unusually polite to me in the days ahead. She didn't look for an opportunity to put me down as she had before, and she actually appeared supportive of me and Melissa's union. "Melissa, what did you tell your mother? Is she okay?" I asked. "She always attacks me and put me down when I come around."

"Curtis, mom has been praying that this would take place. She never wanted us to move in together without us uniting as one. She does have a soft spot, but you have to find it. She's bossy, so I know that we're going to bump heads. She already gave me her input on the colors, flowers, and the walk down the aisle. Don't worry about dad. I'm his baby girl. He won't give us any problems what-so-ever," Melissa explained. "What about your family? I know that Rosa doesn't want to be in the wedding."

"Well, I asked my siblings if they wanted to participate, and they all answered yes except for Rosa Lee," I explained. But regardless of Rosa's attitude, Melissa and I were going to make the best of our moment and enjoy every second of it.

It was three months until the wedding day. In the days leading up to the wedding, we met with Rev. Cornelia Henderson for premarital counseling, prepared wedding invitations, and sat back and watched our mothers plan the entire wedding. We went through the motions: tuxedo fittings, wedding rehearsals, wedding party dinners, etc. The night before the big day arrived.

CHAPTER 12: WEDDING BELLS

On that night, my friends Dwight and Jerome came over to my apartment to spend the night. We shared a lot of laughs and flashbacks before they hit me with the big reality. "Love," Dwight said, "at around 5 pm tomorrow you'll be married. Just pass your player card over to me because you won't need it anymore."

"Love," Jerome jumped in, "it would be best if you put that card in my hand because Dwight isn't going to bust a grape!" Just then, it hit me: I WAS ABOUT TO GET MARRIED THE NEXT DAY!

"Man, I don't think I'm ready!" I confessed.

"You picked a fine time to say something," Dwight replied.

"You got cold feet?" asked Jerome. "Listen, Love; you're doing the right thing. Everything for tomorrow is ready and set. Do you want to call it off?"

"Um... Um... No. I better go with it. It's way too late now."

"Alright, man. I'll see ya'll in the morning," Jerome said. "Good night. If you need any one of us, we'll be here."

❧

It was April 24, 1982, and it was the big day, one of the biggest days of my life. Dwight and Jerome were driving me to the church for the wedding and singing to the music playing on the radio. Because I was so nervous and facing the reality of marriage, I didn't hear any music at all. My mind was pondering one question: "Do you take this woman to love, keep, protect, and cherish...FOR

THE REST OF YOUR LIFE?"

We finally arrived at the church. I was sitting in a room with my best men; butterflies were fluttering around in my stomach. I was somewhat in a daze, feeling both nervous and excited at the same time, not knowing what the future held. "You ready to do this?" asked Dwight, snapping me out of my stupor.

"Yeah, man," I said.

"Man, you don't look so good," Jerome commented after noticing my appearance.

"I'll be fine. Hey, man, peek out there and tell me how many people are out there."

"Love, the church is packed. People are standing along the walls," Dwight said. Suddenly, the music began to play. Jerome anxiously exclaimed,

"Well, there goes the music! Give me a high-five, man!" I took a deep breath, then exhaled slowly. I opened the door and walked into the sanctuary and got into position. My heart was beating faster than it did on the day I got into trouble at Sylvan High School with the police.

"Calm down, Curtis. Don't hyperventilate," one of my best men said. "Just breath slowly." Suddenly, my dad walked up to me and asked,

"Are you okay, son?"

"Yes, dad. I'm just short of breath." He then put his hand on my shoulder and said,

"See yourself through it, son."

"Yes, sir," I said. Then I muttered to myself, "I'll try to keep my composure and avoid embarrassing Melissa, my parents, and myself."

All of a sudden, the musician started playing the wedding song. I looked up and noticed Melissa at the back of the room making her grand entrance. All eyes were on her as she made her way down the aisle. Everyone was smiling. I made eye-contact with my dad who was smiling. He gave me a thumbs-up. Nervousness still pestered me even as I watched Melissa make her way down the aisle. She wore a beautiful cream wedding gown that covered the floor as she walked and a country style cream hat which matched the wedding gown. It felt like stars were floating around my head and, at one point, I began to feel faint. But I kept my composure.

As I stood there facing this beautiful young veiled lady, I thought to myself, "Who is this woman?" She was breathtakingly gorgeous. I felt that I would gladly spend my life exploring the endless depths of her essence.

Finally, Melissa and I face at the altar. She removed her veil. At that moment, I gained my strength. Seeing her face, her beautiful brown eyes and pearly white teeth dissolved the pressure that was on me. I went from nervousness to being entranced.

"Curtis, do you take this woman to be your lawfully wedded wife, to have and to hold, from this day forward, for better, for worse, for richer, for poorer, in sickness and in health until death do you part?" asked the officiating minister, Rev. Henderson. I took one last glance over my shoulder to see the room filled to capacity with smiling and anxious faces. Everything felt like it was in slow motion. Then I looked back at my beautiful bride and said those two magic words:

"I do."

After the exchanging of vows, the minister pronounced Melissa and me husband and wife and permitted me to "salute my bride." Melissa and I kissed for every bit of 45 seconds with our eyes closed. That was our first kiss along the new journey we embarked together. A journey that would be filled with the sweetest of times and the worst of times that would bring out the best in me and the worst in me that would greatly shape me into the man I am today.

We were in paradise. Our honeymoon is in the beautiful, spectacular Jamaica. We escaped to a private beach hideaway at Coral Cove; where we had the best time of our lives walking the beach, feeling the breezes, enjoying the gardens, the music, the hammocks, the unbelievably delicious food, and the people. It was perfect.

Our assigned driver showed us the main street in Little Bay. He drove us to whatever site Melissa wanted to visit. He had an unforgettable personality and a great sense of humor. On our 3rd day there, we journeyed to Negro and then wined-and-dined later at the 1,500 square feet Cliff Side Sun Deck. We'd heard so much about this spot, but we couldn't wait to get back to our little paradise in Little Bay.

They say that a picture is worth a thousand words. We took photos of Coral Cove and all of the beautiful sites. We wanted to be able to remember the magic, to

look back in our later years and be able to remind ourselves of the time we experienced perfection and passion
like no other; to remember the peace and the tranquility
of that extraordinary moment together.

We stayed four days in Jamaica. We got choked
up when it came time to say goodbye to the Coral Cove
Resort. But it was time to return to Atlanta, Georgia; it
was time to face the city air, the traffic, the long work-
days, the hustle and grind that comes with living in the
city; and most importantly, it was time to face the reality
of being married.

The wedding was over. The marriage had begun.

CHAPTER 13
POWER

I HAD A GOAL IN MIND AND I WASN'T GOING TO ALLOW anything, and I do mean "anything," to get in my way and stop me from accomplishing it. I was willing to sacrifice the more important things for the lesser.

Being a store manager changed me in many ways. I became more aggressive and domineering, even more dogmatic. I developed a "my way or the highway" attitude. I had a reputation for firing employees. I fired so many employees during my time in management that the company headquarters sent me a letter telling me to stop firing so many people. But my layoffs were well-founded. I always kept proper documentation of every case. Among the employees I fired was individuals that stole money, gave away merchandise, assistant managers who didn't make bank-drops properly and on time and didn't open up the store on time, etc. I was the one being held responsible for store operations, so I made sure that I ran a tight ship.

Many times, people who operate in management within a company or organization will experience difficulty adjusting to life at home. Bossing all those employees around was beginning to affect my communication with Melissa. She'd occasionally remind me that she was not my employee. Another problem I experienced was the tendency to take my work home with me, literally. Whenever something went wrong at the store, my house phone rang, and I had to be there—I was, after all, the manager. My phone rang a lot. I was always solving problems. But my hard work was also paying off.

Eighteen months later, CFC promoted me to Store Training Manager for the company. My new responsibility was to train the entire eastern regional management staff. Shortly Afterward, the company promoted me to Master Merchant. I was only 26 years old, making me the youngest employee to obtain this position with CFC. It was now my job to inspect the CFC stores and quiz their employees in the areas of store operations, quality product and service, quality appearance, and cleanliness. Stores were required to score not lower than 87%. The inspection process would take 5 to 8 hours. Store failures had a 120 day wait for another inspection; if they passed, maintaining a 90% score in all store operations complied. My store passed the inspection with a score of 99%, the highest score in company history. But the climb didn't stop there.

CHAPTER 13: POWER

In 1983, CFC entered me into the Area Manager Program for the company. I now had three stores under my supervision. These stores' management staff had to report to me. I had to evaluate their management teams, monitor their operations, and control profits and losses. I was busy, but I was reaping the benefits financially. By now, I was making $60,000.00 annually with a 10% stock option; two weeks paid vacation and a second option to buy into the company's franchise when retired. The next level up was the Master Merchant District Area Supervisor position which would be my next goal.

I quickly became one of the most popular Area Managers for Church's Fried Chicken. I incentivized area stores by awarding cash and prizes to the store managers who broke store records, increased store profits and decreased store losses, and I awarded employees who provided correct answers to questions and who gave outstanding service to customers. I organized a softball league among the stores, and more. Life was looking good at work. There, I had everything under control; but at home, that was a different story. Things were already beginning to unravel and come apart.

❧

"Listen, son, just make sure that you take your vacations and spend more time with your wife while you're young and full of energy. Curtis, love your wife." Mom said to me. Then she turned to Melissa and said, "Melissa, obey your husband."

"Yes, ma'am," we both replied. From time to time,

129

married couples, especially young couples who are so full of zest and zeal when it comes to their careers, need to be sat down and reminded of the importance of making each other priority. We were starting to require plenty of these talks considering that it had been over three years since I'd taken a family vacation. Work consumed me.

I needed to spend more time with Melissa; so one day, I told her to put something nice on because I was going to take her to the Sun Dial Restaurant located at the Westin Peachtree Hotel downtown, the lavish restaurant that spins around allowing restaurant patrons to see the entire city of Atlanta. While at the restaurant, I decided that this was the best time to bring up a topic I had meant to discuss with Melissa. "Listen, baby; I need to know if you're getting bored at home. I'm wondering if you need to get a hobby or a part-time job?"

"No, baby. I'm fine with helping you out," Melissa responded. "I enjoy going to the gym to work out, and I love shopping."

"You know, Melissa, it has been almost two years now, and there's no sign of you being pregnant yet. It is on my mind."

"I have a doctor's appointment next week. I'll know for sure then what is going on. But baby, there may be a possibility that I may not be able to conceive a baby," Melissa stated.

"What do you mean by that? And what are you trying to say to me?"

"I was told this about five months ago: that there might be complications with me having a child; but through surgeries, there might be a 75% possibility that I can have a child."

"Baby, why didn't you share this with me before we got married?"

"I would think that it wouldn't be an issue, and I was already contemplating an operation."

"You should've told me before now."

"When I went into this marriage I had no hidden agenda or secrets! I was upfront with you!" Melissa said, clearly growing agitated.

"Listen, baby; your voice is getting too loud. Let's just leave and discuss this at home. Check please!" I said, tabling the discussion for the time being.

As a Store Training Manager, I chose one particular CFC store, store #87, to be my contact store. I had a Training Manager under me named Adrienne. She was a no-nonsense manager who also ran a tight ship. She was honest and trustworthy. We worked well together.

One particular day, a group of trainees from Florida came to the store; they wanted to visit a Master Merchant Training Store. I conducted the tour, where I met Demonna. I honestly couldn't wait until the tour was over so that I could personally go and introduce myself to her. I felt a strong attraction to her. She was very articulate; had long, sandy hair; and had a model's body with beautiful skin. I asked her how long she was going to be in town and she replied for only one week. I had no intentions of letting her slip through my fingers.

A few days later, Demonna and I ended up going out to dinner. She began telling me all about herself; she's married with two kids (a 5-year-old girl and 6-year-old boy), and she and her husband were schoolteachers. She revealed that she was unhappy at home because all her husband's interests are teaching, coaching sports, and lifting weights. I started to talk about my life and marriage to her. We connected quickly. I had other plans, however, to end the evening. I had plans to have more than just an interesting conversation. I looked at Demonna and said, "I wish we never met."

"Why did you say that?"

"Because of what I'm feeling right now for you. I'm willing to see what will happen in the long run."

"I don't understand. Explain that to me."

"Everything you shared with me is like a dream. It seems like I've met you in another life; your soft voice is from another life. And when you were upfront about your marriage, I respect that. But if tonight has to end like this, I'm still glad that we met. All I want from you is one kiss."

"Just one kiss? Why one kiss?"

"One kiss will put an end to this dream."

"I feel safe doing that with you," Demonna said. We kissed. That one kiss lasted five minutes.

While walking Demonna back to her room, we continued to talk. As she put the key in her door, I asked her for a hug. We embraced up against the door and the door shut with me inside her room.

I woke up the next morning at 4:30 a.m. in the

bed with Demonna. I panicked, thinking to myself this is really happening. *This is not a dream. What do I do now?*

JUST A LITTLE LOVE & JOY

Chapter 14

OUT OF CONTROL

My assistant, Adrienne, called me to go over my schedule for the day. "Don't forget you have an interview with Ms. Lynda G. today."

"What's her last name?" I asked.

"I can't make it out. The application got wet."

"Call her and reschedule for the next day."

"She stated that she would be out of town. I think she will be excellent," Adrienne stated.

"Alright," I said, reconsidering putting off the interview. "I'll be there."

"Oh, I almost forgot, Mrs. Demonna Warring, left her phone number."

Later at the office, I sat down and met with Ms. Lynda G. for her interview. "Hello, Ms. Lynda. I looked

135

over your application, and everything looks okay. Tell me why you want to become a manager for Church's Fried Chicken, and why you think that I should hire you?"

"Well, before I answer your question, let me say I'm not here to waste your time because time is money. I don't want to be cooking chicken or cutting the chicken in a walk-in cooler. I don't mind doing these things if it helps to climb the corporate ladder. My appearance says one thing, but my ability to do the job will speak for itself."

"You said a mouth full," I responded. "I can start you at $375.00 weekly, a five-day work period, ten hours a day. When can you start?"

"I can start two weeks from now."

"Okay. The store will fill you in on the paperwork and uniform."

"Thanks so much, Mr. Lovejoy."

"No, thank you." In my mind, I was thinking that Lynda was too fine to be cooking or cutting chicken; she needed to work at the division office. She was very assertive, made eye contact, wore a beautiful sundress to the interview, had bouncing hair, pretty white teeth, and a classic Wall Street walk. For a second, I was wondering if she was in the wrong line of work.

I had a lot on my plate at this time. I was busy running stores and fulfilling my duties as an area manager. I was in the middle of dealing with a legal situation involving my mother and a contractor who was ripping her off on a job he was doing at her house. I was troubled by the news of my wife's barrenness. Now, I was bearing the weight of an adulterous affair. Secrets become heavy after a period. Subtly, secrets place stress on one's mind. Now, things were getting ready to become even more complicated in my life.

When Lynda didn't show up for work, I decided to give her a phone call. She stated that she left a message at the division office claiming that she found something that was better and paid more money. "That's very good for you," I said. My attitude surprised her. "Don't be [amazed]. I felt that you didn't need to be working at Church's Fried Chicken because of your excellent office skills and because the work here can be very hard. It seemed like this type of work isn't cut-out for you."

"Thank you, but don't get me wrong. If I have to do it to make ends meet, I will."

"I can see that you have lots of pretensions and I wish you the best."

"Thank you, Mr. Lovejoy."

"Perhaps we can have dinner soon?"

"That might be possible. You have my phone number. Just give me a call."

"Will do."

❧

I had been speaking with headquarters about incentivizing employees more to increase their performances when something big that I could use fell into my lap. There were over thirty bonus checks that I call "ghost payroll." These were checks made out to store managers terminated by the company or managers who resigned from the company but still existed on the payroll. With these extra funds, I was able to fund my incentives program for my area on my own. I decided to sneak and do this against the company's wishes. You see, each time I approached the company with my proposal about an incentives program, they would reject it. But now, I could fund my program without their knowledge and their consent.

I was quite busy with work. I was forming relationships with companies and organizations on behalf of CFC. I knew all of the bank managers in my area, and I had become very well known in the community. Civic groups and organizations such as the Southern Christian Leadership Conference (SCLC), the MLK Jr. Center, and others, I supported with donations of fried chicken they needed at any given time. I supported the homeless and battered women's shelters also by donating chicken. I visited high schools for their Career Day programs where I'd recruit students from their senior classes for my Managers Candidate Training Program.

To regroup and refresh myself and think of new ideas to get the company brand out there and while figuring out what to do about my marriage and life, I would go to Greenbriar Mall and sit by the water pool and stare into the water. There, I would daydream and brainstorm. Much rested on my mind. I thought about my incentives program a lot, convincing myself that what I was doing was for the best of the employees. I figured that as long as I could keep things in proper perspective, I could see my way through anything.

I would stop by my parents' house once a week to drop off some money, check on mom and dad, and pick up my mail. One day, I received a letter in the mail from Demonna. It read:

Dear Curtis,

I decided that I and the 2 kids would be moving to Atlanta, GA. in two months because the market is really booming there. I've made contact to be transferred to a local high school. I'll keep you posted when I arrive in Atlanta so you can show me the hot spots and take me all around.

Demonna

Things were about to get even more interesting for me. I would have to tread a lot more carefully now. I picked up the telephone and called Lynda and invited her to go out with me to Mr. V's Nightclub during happy hour, and she agreed. At around 6:30 pm we met at the club. When she arrived, I observed her from head to toe, noticing how fine she was. I looked at her car's tag, which read "Dark & Lovely." We began talking about ourselves.

"I guess you get teased about your last name all of the time?" Lynda asked me.

"What brought you to Atlanta?" I asked her.

"The opportunity to better me because there are no opportunities in Savannah, GA. Everything is going down. I left two wonderful people back home: my mother and my father. I have one brother who plays the drums for the singer, Jeffrey Osborne. I was born and raised in Savannah. I have no kids. Now tell me something wonderful about you."

"What do you want to know?" I asked.

"Are you married? Do you have kids? Are you a sex-maniac?"

"I know you're kidding about that last question?" I said.

"No, I'm not," she replied. "Because I don't need any crazy drama."

"Well, I come from a large family with two loving parents, and I'm single," I lied. "I do love sex. I'm not a sex-maniac, but I do love women. Do you have a special man in your life?"

"No, I don't. I finished college, and then I decided to move to the city they call 'too busy to hate,' and you're the first man I'm comfortable with going on a date with."

"Well, thank you. I hope this won't be the last."

"Time will tell."

"Thanks for a wonderful evening."

My personal life was becoming chaotic. At work, I was doing things on my own that could land me in hot water; and now, I was digging a ditch in my personal life that would be difficult to crawl out of, if not impossible. I was simply out of control.

DIGGING A DITCH

THE COUNTDOWN HAD STARTED: 5, 4, 3, 2, 1. Happy New Years!! It was 1986. All I wanted to do was call my mom to wish her and dad a Happy New Year. I got to a phone and called my parents' house. Mom picked up the phone and said, "Hello."

"Happy New Year, mom! Is dad there?"

"You know that he can't be still. You two are just alike."

"Why do you say that?"

"Because it's in ya'll's blood. Your father always holds things inside too long, but you're just the opposite. You prefer showing your feelings, and that's a good sign. You release it. How are Melissa and the marriage doing?"

"Everything is fine."

"Are you spending time with her like you're supposed to?"

"Yes! As a matter of fact, we're leaving tomorrow to spend five days with her parents in Columbus, Georgia. Mom, you know that my job requires me to spend a lot of time in the field."

"Yes, I know that, Joe. But remember this; I carried you in my stomach for nine months and I know your desires and wants. I'm just going to say this, and I'll be finished nosing in your business; if you ponder God's Word in your heart and keep His Commandments, He will order your footsteps and bless your marriage and home."

"Mom, if anything happened to me and you need to know my whereabouts, please search my black book and see everything recorded on a daily basis."

"Are you in trouble?"

"No, mom. Just promise me that you'll do that."

"Yes, son."

❦

l After receiving a voice message from Demonna on my answering machine, I called her back. "Demonna, I got your message. How can I help you?"

"I don't know anyone here just yet, and I have to attend this orientation class. I was wondering if you can drop the kids off at school over the next two weeks?" she asked.

"Yes, I can do that. I'll drop by your apartment tonight. Anything else?"

"Yes. There's one more thing."

CHAPTER 15: DIGGING A DITCH

"What's that?"

"I need you, baby."

"I'll see you later. Just hold on."

I had gotten myself entangled in a real love triangle. I was juggling three women. On special days, I had to figure out a way to accommodate all three: Melissa, Demonna, and Lynda. For example, for Valentine's Day, a day that was special for me because it is my mom's birthday, I'd take my mom out for lunch then take Melissa to The Boston Sea Party Restaurant, and send flowers and candies to Lynda and Demonna.

As far as my career was concerned, I was still attempting to climb the corporate ladder. My goal was to land the Master Merchant Area District Supervisor position. I had my assistant Adrienne call all of the store managers in the area and let them know about an area meeting that was being held at the Hilton Hotel downtown on Sunday at 11 am. I iterated to them the need to keep a 95% efficiency rate and that I was submitting my Master Merchant Area District Manager application. My stores would have to be inspected by the company's inspector for me to qualify to receive the position. The inspector didn't give me a specific date when they would show up and conduct their inspection, so I stressed to the store managers the importance of keeping their stores and efficiency rate up. After the inspector inspected the stores in the entire area, the next step was for them to call me and inform me of the results. These results, determined whether or not I would get the position.

The anticipation was killing me. *When is the in-*

spector going to show up? Will the stores in my area be prepared? Are they going to let me down? Am I going to get the position? All of these thoughts plagued my mind day after day. I felt anxious and nervous. I tried to overcome my anxiety by keeping myself busy, and trust me; I had plenty of other concerns to keep me preoccupied.

Out of the blue, I received a phone call from Lynda. "Curtis, it's Dark and Lovely (Lynda's nickname)."

"Who?"

"Lynda!"

"Oh! What's up?"

"I want to know if you would like to go home with me to meet my parents for the weekend?" she asked.

"I don't know about that. I probably need to hang around in the city," I replied.

"You work too much, and you need to take a break. My dad can get some crabs and fry some flounder with some old-fashioned coleslaw, and we can take a stroll down The River Walk. What do you think?"

"Um... Um..." I paused, contemplating my answer. I thought about the importance of being at home so I could be there to meet the district manager inspector; I also thought about Melissa and what I would tell her. Suddenly, without considering the consequences of my actions fully, I answered, "Okay. It's a done deal. I'll see you at your place on Friday morning at around 8 a.m."

Right after getting off of the phone with Lynda, I noticed another message on my answering machine:

"(Beep) Hi, it's me; only me, Demonna. Just want

to give you an update on what's happening. The kids' father moved to Atlanta, and he's staying at my place. The kids know that Uncle Joe won't be coming over. I've enrolled at Columbus College for a semester and will be living on campus. I'm hoping that we can see each other. Check your mail because I will send you details of where I'm staying. I hope that your mother isn't reading your mail. Here's my number. As I always say, until I see you, please be discreet. I love you!"

Shortly after receiving that call from Demonna, I received a call from Melissa: "Hi, baby. Let's go and see the new movie Thief of the Heart. We can catch the eight o'clock show tonight."

"Yeah, okay," I said. Then I thought of something to say to Melissa so that I could cover my tracks for my getaway with Lynda: "Melissa, I got a company meeting in Savannah this weekend. Do you want to go with me?"

"No, because there's nothing for me to do while you are in your meeting," she replied. "Anyways, I have something I want to check out for the house."

"Okay. Good," I responded, feeling relieved. I set everything for my weekend getaway with Lynda.

The day arrived when Lynda and I were scheduled to get on the road to head to Savannah, Georgia. We talked on the phone for a brief moment. "Good morning," Lynda said. "I see you're not ready to leave. Can you please be on time?"

"What's the hurry?" I asked.

"Nothing. I like to leave on time. You forget that I'm analytical. Don't start getting technical with me. Let's just have some fun! We'll stop in Dublin, Georgia. That's halfway. Curtis, why you never invite me over to your place?" Lynda asked suddenly.

"When do you want to come over?" I responded quickly. "I'm never there. Did I tell you that my area is going up for inspection? That's the reason why I hesitated when you asked me to go home with you. If it seems like I'm somewhat preoccupied, it's because I'm on pins and needles about the unannounced outcomes of the inspection."

"Well, it's my mission to take your mind off of work."

"Did you make a reservation?"

"For what? We're staying with my parents. They have five bedrooms. We both have a room."

"Okay."

"Once my parents are sleep, I'll slip into the bed with you."

"Please don't be making too much noise," I said. "You know that you can't keep your mouth closed."

"I'll try."

"Come on, Lynda!"

Lynda and I drove down to Savannah, Georgia, and Lynda introduced me to her parents. Her dad seemed very hospitable, unlike her mom. Her mom seemed a little aloof, and wary; even suspicious. I could tell it would take her some time to warm up to me. Lynda's parents accompanied Lynda and me to the River Walk where

146

all of the restaurants and night spots were. Savannah is known for its seafood and its jazz and blues. While walking around, enjoying the fresh breezes from the ocean blowing and listening to the superb sounds of the jazz and blues music billowing from every little joint on the strip, I received a beep on my beeper. I looked down and checked the number. "It's one of my stores," I said to Lynda and her parents. (It wasn't one of my stores; it was Melissa.) I'll wait to call her back when I can get to a bathroom, I thought to myself. I continued enjoying my time with Lynda, experiencing the sights, sounds, and the midnight pleasure. While her parents were asleep in their beds, Lynda was in mine.

The following week after my getaway with Lynda, I drove down to Columbus, Georgia to visit Demonna. I was so anxious to see her. And from the greeting she gave me when I arrived, she was anxious to see me, too. When I arrived at her apartment, she met me at the door wearing a sky blue three-piece lingerie that complimented the curves on her perfectly shaped body. She had the place fixed up just for me: candles lit all over the place; the sweet smelling fragrance of wild strawberries filling the room; a hot jacuzzi; a bottle of red wine, and my favor Chinese dish. Everything was perfect; just perfect for now.

Chapter 16
BUSTED

I stopped by mom's house for some good cooking, and while there, she gave me a good verbal thrashing.

"How are you doing, mom?"

"Just fine. Trying to stay warm," spoken in a calm voice, concealing that she was bothered by something.

"When I got out of the car I smelled those collard greens and homemade fried chicken. Melissa can't cook like you, but she's getting better," I stated while gobbling down my food.

"Slow down before you choke!" mom uttered.

"But it just tastes so good," I replied.

"I know, but take your time. And don't forget the mail in your room on the nightstand. Have you all taken that vacation yet?" mom asked, finally getting around to what was bothering her.

"You know that we spent three days down at Melissa's parents' home."

"I'm talking about only the two of you alone with each other and away from Atlanta," she responded.

"No. Not yet."

"What are you waiting for?"

"Mom, I have so much on my plate," I said.

"Make time for her," mom stressed passionately. "And stop using that job as an excuse, Joe!"

"Well, Melissa just started a part-time job. She wanted to work," I said.

"When was the last time you went to church?" mom asked, shifting the subject.

"Mom, why are you all over me? I just came by to get a home-style meal from my mother, and you are giving me the third degree!"

"Your father and I have done our job. God said to raise up a child in the way they should go and when they get old, they won't depart from it. You'll come around in due time." I was trying to understand what she meant by that.

"Okay, mom. I heard everything you said. Let me get back to work. Love you both. Tell dad I said hello."

"Don't forget your mail," mom reminded me.

"Thanks, mom." I went into my old bedroom and picked up the stack of mail sitting on the nightstand and began going through it. Bill. Junk mail. Telemarketer. Oh, a letter from Demonna. I'll read it later. Need to get to my contact store and check on the inspection status.

While leaving my mom's house, her words played through my mind like a broken record. I began to wonder if she was on to something if she knew I was keeping a secret. Why was she on me so hard about my marriage to Melissa? That seemed to be the main thing she wanted to talk about, that and the special emphasis she placed on "living in sin." She did receive my mail, so she certainly noticed the letter from Demonna that came to me. But maybe it's nothing. Maybe I'm just over-reacting. So, I shrugged her stern warnings off and figured that she was just a mother; overly curious and nosy, wanting to be involved in my affairs. In my mind, I had everything under control, and I was not about to get caught. Or so I thought.

✢

Arriving home from my visit to my mom's house, Melissa met me at the door and noticed I wasn't looking well. I was exhausted as a result of doing so much. "Hi, baby. How was your day?" Melissa asked.

"It was fine."

"Curtis, you are not looking well. You need to slow down and get some rest. I'm going to run you a hot bubble bath."

"Okay. Just let me check my messages first."

"No," Melissa interrupted, "don't check anything. Just put your briefcase in your office and go straight to the bedroom and undress."

"Okay, baby."

"Are you hungry?" she asked.

"No. I ate over at my mom's house," I answered her while sitting my briefcase and my mail on my desk. I got undressed and then soaked in the hot bath Melissa prepared for me. She started washing my back and my legs while singing her favorite love song; You Got The Best of My Love. After bathing me, we went to the bedroom where she oiled me down while gently kissing all over my naked body. I dozed off to sleep, forgetting that I left my mail on the desk in my office.

The next morning I felt well rested and ready to tackle another day of work. Everything seemed normal. There was no indication of any trouble. It was just a normal day like all the others. Melissa seemed normal. I had to drop her off at work, so we got in the car to take her to work. While driving, Melissa suddenly began asking questions. "Curtis," she said in a gentle voice, "do you know where Cody Road is?" At first, I was wondering what she was talking about, and then it hit me: I am busted! But I still had to play it off. So I answered,

"No."

"I mean, Cody Road in Columbus, Georgia?"

"Oh, yeah," I said.

"So, during this past month, on Tuesdays, you are on Cody Road?" she continued.

"Now, you're aware that I got business in Columbus?" I replied. "A Church's Fried Chicken store is on that street. Why are you asking me all these questions?" Then she hit me with another question:

"Who is Demonna?"

"Demonna, who?"

"Demonna Warring who is attending Columbus College; the one who be with you in the Jacuzzi; the one who has candlelight around the apartment . . . THE BITCH WHO YOU BE MAKING LOVE TO ON THOSE TUESDAYS WHEN YOUR ASS NEED TO BE HOME WITH ME?!!!! You got me fooled, thinking that you're working all these hours non-stop at Church's Fried Chicken!!! Curtis, are you fucking her?!! That's who you want to be with?!!!"

"Um..." I uttered, lost for words. "Listen, Melissa; I have no idea what you're talking about!"

"Oh, so you deny all of this?!!"

"Yes, I am!"

"Curtis, she wrote you a letter! I read the letter last night while you were asleep! I was in your office! My intuition told me to pick up that letter, so I did!"

"Why did you open my mail?!!" I fired back. "It was addressed to me, 'Curtis!!'"

"I'm your wife!! I got the right to do that!!" she replied. "She is expressing her pleasures of having you and wanting all of you—and she loves you!! What the hell am I supposed to think?!"

"Okay! Okay! I do know her! She's crazy, and she wrote that letter just to get back at me because I wouldn't give her any play! And that's the truth!"

"You expect me to believe that?!" asked Melissa.

"Yes, I do!"

"Don't say anything else to me!! And don't worry about picking me up! I'll get home on my own!" she said angrily.

"You don't want me to pick you up?" I asked.

"What did I just tell you, Curtis?! See you to-night!"

After my confrontation with Melissa, I immediately rushed to a telephone to call Demonna. I looked for her phone number in my little black book, but Melissa had scratched it out. I checked my beeper and noticed that Melissa had deleted all of my phone numbers. I had no way of contacting Demonna. But suddenly, my beeper beeped, and it was Demonna. I immediately called her and explained to her that Melissa found out about our affair, to which she replied, "Dammit, Curtis!! What do I always tell you when we're finished?! 'Curtis, be discreet!' But nooo! You had to take my letter home, and Melissa read the letter!"

"I didn't think that she would open my mail because that's my business," I responded.

"Curtis, she's your wife! If it was the other way around, I could care less because I don't want Wilbert [Demonna's husband] in my life. I stopped loving him over a year ago. But your wife does love you, Curtis. She told me if I can wash your clothes, lay your clothes out each morning, have your breakfast and dinner waiting on you when you get up and when you return home, and wash and fold your clothes each day, then I'm welcome. But if I can't, I need to keep my ass where I am and take care of my old man and leave her man alone. And if she ever suspects that I'm still involved with you, she will call my husband and spill the beans on me."

"What did you say?" I asked Demonna.

"Curtis, in the beginning, when she was talking, I denied everything I said in that letter, but then she broke things down to me. And, no, Curtis, I can't do all of those things for you right now because of my kids. So I admitted the truth: that everything in that letter was correct."

"Why did you do that? I didn't agree to anything. I said that you had a crush on me and that I didn't give you any play."

"Curtis, admit it: you got busted. I'm very sorry that this happened. I do love you, but I can't do for you the things that Melissa is doing for you right now. So take this time to pamper her. Remember that she will hold this against you and she won't forget it unless she has a forgiving heart. Only time will tell. I'm here if you need me. I'll be returning to Atlanta in three months. I still love you. Bye."

CHAPTER 17
ALLEY RAT

"PLEASE LET MELISSA BE AT HOME WHEN I GET there," I said to myself. When I arrived home and entered the house, I was so relieved to see Melissa was there. She could have left me, went to stay with her parents, separated, or even filed for divorce, but she was there. Still, things weren't the same, and they would never be. The house was so much quieter, and the mood was somber. Melissa didn't talk much; at least, not to me. When she did talk, she was very short with me. She still cooked and cleaned and washed the clothes, but she basically avoids me as much as possible. She even began contemplating joining the Army Reserves undoubtedly to get away from me so that she wouldn't have to see my face. She was this way for several months.

Rather than learning to be wise and cutting my

crap out, I did the dumbest thing anyone could do during this time. I began spending more time with Lynda, pouring my attention on her. I figured the less of me Melissa saw, the better; and that she just needed more time to recuperate from the pain I caused her.

One night, after Lynda and I had dinner together at her place, we decided to top things off with a romantic bubble bath while listening to some Freddie Jackson, but I couldn't stay the whole night. I needed to get home. Up until this point, Lynda was still under the impression that I was single. But the moment that I began getting dressed to go home, Lynda grew suspicious. While putting on my shirt, I noticed that I had a red lipstick stain on it. Immediately, I asked Lynda if she would get a wet towel and remove the stain. After discovering that wasn't working, I asked her if she wouldn't mind washing the shirt for me so I could get the stain out. She did. But while doing so, she became suspicious as to why I was so adamant about removing her red lipstick stain from my white dress shirt. After the shirt finished washing and drying, she laid it flat on the ironing board and began to press it out. While pressing out my shirt, I could see the revelation come over her. Suddenly, she looked up at me and said, "Your ass is married!! Please tell me you're not!!" I looked up at her, seeing the confusion and disappointment on her face, and confessed,

"Yes, I'm married. Been so for the past 3½ years."

"Why you never said anything?! It's best just to tell the truth! That's why you never invited me over and never would spend the entire night with me; but on the other hand, we hang out in plenty of places! Mom said you had that sneaky look and that there was, something about you she couldn't figure out." At that moment, tears began to stream down her face.

"I'm sorry, Lynda. I wanted to tell you, but I was too far ahead," I said.

"You used me!!" she cried.

"It was not my intentions for this to happen. I just got caught-up, wanting my cake and ice cream all at the same time."

"That's selfish, Curtis!"

"I can't help it."

"Yes, you can! Just say no or walk away!"

"Easily said, but hard to do. Well, let me leave."

"It's best that you do that," she said, walking me to the door. Before I could leave, Lynda stopped me and said, "Curtis, I have one question: Why did you let me fall in love with you? My father gave you high praise. He really likes you like a son. I shouldn't say this, but I'm in love with you."

"Please don't say that."

"It's the truth!"

"I've got to go! Take care. Bye," I said before turning and walking away.

My personal life was certainly falling apart. Melissa had Demonna nervous and paranoid. Demonna called me one day and asked me to describe Melissa to her. When I asked her why she wanted a description, she said that her boss informed her that a light-skinned woman stopped by her job and inquired about her. She was extremely nervous, feeling as if Melissa knew where she worked and was now stalking her. As Demonna expressed to me over the phone, "Curtis, you don't know what women are capable of doing." I could hear the fear in her voice. Melissa was still not talking to me. Lynda, on the other hand, was still in love with me and wanted to try to make it work out for us somehow. And Demonna didn't know about Lynda.

While my personal life was spiraling out of control, my professional life was facing its own set of challenges. I had to start carrying a gun for safety. There were three CFC stores I absolutely hated visiting. These were the worse off of, the worse stores. They were plagued by incompetent management, crooked employees, crime, and drugs; and it's no surprise that they reported the greatest losses and lowest profits. One of the stores was on Prior Street: it was store #106. When you pulled up, the drug dealers were across the street selling drugs openly. The store got robbed every week, sometimes twice a day. Disgruntled customers would throw rocks through the windows; some would even do drive-by shootings on the store. It was a hell-hole. The police wouldn't do anything to get rid of the crime, arrest the robbers, nor protect the store patrons and customers; they would show up, take a report, and then leave; never following-up with anything. Customers complained that the store was never open on time and had horrible customer service. One night, I decided to ride through my area without the managers knowing it. I rode by that particular store, knowing that it was closed, but I noticed that the assistant manager's (a female) car was still there. I decided to check out what was going on. I unlocked the front door, walked through the lobby, entered into the office, and caught the assistant manager having sex with one of the employees. The male employee was shocked. He tried to move her off of him, but she just glanced at me, pushed him back down, and kept right on riding him as if I wasn't even standing there. I politely took a photo of them and closed the office door. I arrived the next morning to audit the store and personally hand her termination papers.

One day, I was sharing with some of my other store managers the problem I was having with that particular store concerning repeated robberies. Two of these managers, who had come down to Atlanta from Chicago, advised me to buy a pistol and keep it on me. They explained that they always keep their guns on them. So, I started carrying. I had a permit. And sure enough, the store got robbed again. I can remember it clearly. It was on a warm night in July when I noticed this car parked at an angle where the employees couldn't see it. It was around closing time, and thankfully there weren't any customers in the store. I was sitting in my car in the parking lot just waiting for the robbers. I saw one guy get out of the car, put his ski mask on, run into the store, put a gun to the cashier's face, get the money, run back out of the door and jump into his car and sped off. I took off in hot pursuit of the robbers in my car, following them for miles. One of the employees in the meantime called the Atlanta Police Department and reported the robbery. While I followed the car, I could hear the sirens in the background. Still, I was determined to catch these robbers myself. Unfortunately, I didn't catch them. I ended up crashing my car. But I was determined that these robberies, among other things, was going to stop attacking my store.

After I took over that particular store, within the first forty-two days, the store experienced twenty-four robberies. Thieves broke into it ten times. It acquired eighty-six customer complaints, fell $386 short in cash, over $950 worth of merchandise vanished and had eight employees terminated (including the assistant manager that I caught having sex). Also, I had two tires cut on my company vehicle and ended up missing three deposit slips for $455, $1,289.00, and $661 (Deposits made by the store's manager, Travis.) After investigating the matter, I discovered that Travis had been taking the money over the weekends gambling with it, hoping to win big over the weekends so he could replace the money by the following business day. CFC ended up taking out a warrant for his arrest. This store caused me headaches.

There were two other stores similar to the Prior Street location that I had to deal with; one of those stores was store #244, which was on Alabama Street in Downtown Atlanta. This one was one of the nastiest and filthiest stores in Atlanta. It was rat infested; the lobby was dirty; flour all over the floor in the kitchen, and employees were out of uniform. I snuck into the store one day in street clothes just to observe it. I noticed employees buying drugs when they should be working. The store manager was out of uniform and, a female cashier had her breasts out (her line had all of the men in it). There was no supervision and, upset customers asking for the store manager and told that he wasn't there (although he was upstairs in his office). Friends of employees were entering in and got free chicken and walking out of the door. And a female cashier is pocketing money out of the cash register. Amazingly, the food and health inspector gave this store a 95% passing rate. I later returned to this store with all of my store managers and the police to straightened it out, and I had the young cashier who was stealing money arrested. She eventually gave back the $3000 she had stolen from the store over the last four months and offered to divulge information on some of the other illegal activities taking place in the other stores in exchange for a lesser penalty.

Lastly, there was the store that gave me the most headaches and sleepless nights: the Auburn Avenue location (store #133). Aside from being located in the same area as the MLK Jr. Center and Dr. Martin Luther King, Jr.'s house, there was nothing else good that came out of this area and this store. Here I had to deal with stealing employees (they'd work just long enough to steal money and then quit). A thieving, crooked manager with a boom-box turned up to the max. People just hanging out in the lobby with all types of conversations taking place but no one buying food. Thugs are arguing in the lobby. Homeless people covered in urine asleep and lying on the tables. A prostitute in one corner of the store turning tricks right in the lobby and bouncing up and down on a male with her skirt pulled up. And lastly, guys rolling dice on the tables. While there, a pimp walked into the store and grabbed one of his girls by her hair and told her to "get your ass back on the street and make me some money!" She was screaming and hollering, and no one was paying her any attention. The whole time I was there I had my hand on my pistol concealed beneath my coat. Not too much later, the store's manager, Alex, walked in. Around that same time, I noticed a pimp pistol-whipping his girl in the lobby area heading towards the restrooms. I couldn't just sit by and watch that happen, so I got up and told him to leave before I called the police. The girl ran out of the store and the pimp went running behind her. There were sounds coming out of the restroom at that moment. When I opened the door, I saw a girl performing oral sex on a man. I made them leave. I continued to look around and I found employees in the back dancing to music while there was only one employee waiting on the customers; the manager was just sitting in his office with his feet on his desk, smoking a cigar. I had to return with the police after that to sort things out and try to clean up that store.

One day, while at that store, a young woman approached me out of the blue. "So, you must be the 'big man' who calls the shots now?" the young woman asked.

"Yes. Who are you?" I asked her.

"Everybody calls me Rat."

"Rat? Why Rat?"

"Because I'm always moving fast. I see and hear everything around here."

"I need to ask you some questions," I said. "Meet me on the other side of the store, please." I wanted to get the full scoop from her on the store's manager.

"Oh, sure. No problem. I'll be waiting," the young woman said. A few minutes later, Rat came to the car.

"Hi, Rat. Get in the car," I said. She got in. "Let me introduce myself. I'm Curtis Lovejoy, the area supervisor. Can you give me the scoop on the manager, Alex?" I asked.

"Yes, I can. But what's in it for me?" she asked.

"For right now, $50."

"What do you want to know?" she asked.

"I believe Alex has been lying about everything that's happening inside and outside of the store."

"Well, first of all, I can't stand that low-down bitch," Rat stated. "He's been setting up all the robberies with two other guys who stay in the projects, the pimps been giving him money so that we can run our business inside the restrooms when the weather is bad; and sometimes, the girls will give him all of the blow jobs he wants. He had one of the girl employees jumped by three of the bitches working the block because she spilled the beans about him to other area managers before you."

"So, you mean to tell me that you been doing this and paying him? How long has this been going on?"

"Ever since Alex took over down here about two years ago. You see, the pimps got some dirt on Alex, and they're using that against him. Me and Alex fell out because I refused to pay him. I told him a blow job is more than enough. He got angry with me and pinned me up against the wall, put a gun to my head, and told me to stay off the property. So, to keep down mess, I just stay out of his sight. I told the police, but they don't believe us hoes. I can't stand the pretty mother-fucker. He got his own little rackets going down here just like all of the pimps, thugs, and hoes, and that's the real deal!"

"I need you to be my eyes down here. When you see anything suspicious or out of the normal, get to the nearest phone and call this number and tell what you see to Adrienne. She's in my contact store. Only use this number when a robbery takes place."

"Okay. What's in it for me?"

"I'll spot you $30.00 a week. Remember, this is between us."

"Sure, boss. Oh, by the way, can I do anything for you?"

"Rat, don't try that. I don't go down that road."

"Okay. We're cool. I'll give you the lowdown on everything that don't look good."

After a few days had gone by, Rat called my office with some tips about Alex and the robbers who had been robbing the store. She became very helpful in my fight to clean up not just the Auburn Avenue Church's Fried Chicken location, but also exposing a racket in that area. Over the course of working with her, I began to question her about her personal life—asking her why she chose to prostitute herself on the streets. She was a very fine woman and one of the best hookers on the block. Other girls often resented her due to her high clientele. She knew how to drive men insane with some of her tricks in the bedroom. Her response to my question was both enlightening and heartbreaking. When I questioned her why she was a prostitute and if she wanted a better life, mentioning to her that this life was not the best way and that it would eventually come to an end, she responded, "I know that, Mr. Lovejoy. And I respect you because you gave me your word and you trusted me. My entire life, I wanted others to trust me. My mother, she was a hooker. My daddy raped me at an early age. And throughout my teenage life, my mother would turn the other cheek. When she wanted to say something, dad would beat her over and over. Finally, I ran away after high school, looking for someone to listen to me and love me. But that day I approached your car and you asked me to meet you on the other side and you said 'please,' that did something to me on the inside because no one has ever used the word 'please' to me. And when I got in the car with you, you never asked me to do anything. You never made a move on me. You never asked me to do anything. That's why I respect you, Mr. Lovejoy. You have constantly told me it's time for a change in my life, but I must make that move and put the past behind me. I think I'm ready to do that because these streets lead to death. I want to say thank you for all you've done for me; of all the little pep talks and telling me that 'shrink doctors always tell their clients that they must find themselves, but they got it wrong. When a person finds JESUS, JESUS will help you find yourself!'"

Eight months later, someone found Rat dead one block from a church at around 9 pm. Her body discovered cradling a Bible in her arms. A member of that church claimed that Rat had given her life to Christ during an evening service before her murder. She had not been long leaving the church that night. I believe she ran into one of her old clients and she refused to surrender her body to him, and he killed her. On the one hand, my heart crushed by the news of her murder, but on the other hand, I was happy to know that she had surrendered her life to Christ before the murder; therefore, she made it through the pearly gates of heaven. I know I will see her again one day.

Rat's death gave me the strength to finish the job that I started, which was to bring creditability, leadership, respect, and dignity back to a dying community. And within ten months, due to the fire she lit under me, I restored all three of my problem stores back to rank #1, #2, and #3 in sales and profits. Four months after that, stores #106 and #133 became Master Merchant stores with passing scores of 98.3% and 91.8%. Whenever I visit those three stores to this very day, I can feel the spirit of Rat, whose real name was Mona Lisa B.

CHAPTER 18
THE DAY MY LIFE CHANGED

THE FORECAST FOR THE DAY SAID "PARTIALLY rainy." It was cloudy and wet outside. On that morning, Melissa wasn't feeling so well. I asked her if she wanted me to take her to the hospital. She told me that she'd be okay and that she would call in sick and take that day to get some rest. I told her that I needed to run an errand that morning and that I'd be back to check on her afterward. I hit the road to take care of transporting a cash register from one store to another. While I was out doing business, I stopped to call Lynda and inform her that I might need to adjust our plans for the day. We made plans to spend some time together that day while Melissa was at work, but since Melissa wasn't feeling well and had decided to remain at home, I would have to push our plans back and stop by her house later around

11 am should all go well. I needed to make the drop at one of my stores then head back home to check on Melissa, and I'd be heading out her way. That was the plan.

I had driven this stretch of road seemingly a million times; but this particular morning, however, things would be different. The road was wet. I had decided that I didn't need to wear my seatbelt. Everything seemed to be normal—no ominous signs; no bad omens; nothing out of the normal; just a little rain. I had finished making my drop and was on my way back to the house to check on Melissa. I was traveling down Highway 166 heading towards Greenbriar Mall when suddenly, out of nowhere, a car merged onto the expressway traveling extremely fast and cut right in front of me. I was in the right lane, and there was another car on my left-hand side. I quickly hit the brakes to avoid getting hit by the speeding car on my right and also to avoid hitting the other car on my left. My car began to skid, then it hydroplaned. My heart rate accelerated. Everything happened so fast, so unexpectedly, so suddenly. Before I knew it, I had slammed into a guardrail. My head slammed into the left door window knocking me unconscious.

There was peace. Quietness. Silence . . . . And then, my eyes opened, and all I saw was everything spinning round and round. It was surreal like I was in a dream like I was in *The Wizard of Oz* with Dorothy, trapped in a tornado, feeling powerless and vulnerable. There was nothing that I could do at that moment. The car was spinning out of control. I can remember reaching for the passenger door right before the car violently crashed into an electric pole further mangling it. I hadn't yet realized the damage done to my body.

As I laid in the car motionless and still, completely pinned in, the only thing I could feel was the raindrops falling on my face. Again, everything seemed like a dream. Suddenly, as the serenity started to wear off, I began to feel intense pain in my lower back; it felt like someone was applying a blowtorch to my lower back. I tried to move but realized that something wasn't right; something had changed. I began to go unconscious again. My vision faded to black, and everything around me grew silent.

The saying is that our lives will flash before our eyes just before we take our last breaths. I saw Melissa's face. I saw my mother's face. Their love, their warmth, and affection, their passion, these are what flashed before my eyes before darkness took hold. Would I ever see their faces again, feel their love again, hear their voices again? Would I ever get the chance to tell Melissa I love her and embrace her the same way I did on that magical night that we, enraptured in the euphoria of genuine love, and fell asleep in each other's arms on our wedding night? Or would I ever hear my mother's sweet voice in my ears? I would appreciate her sweet chiding, her admonishment, those motherly praises one more time.

"Everything is going to be alright!!! Just hang in there!!!

The ambulance is on the way!! Open your eyes, sir!! Don't leave me!!! Talk to me!!!" That's all I could hear as I laid motionless. It was a man's voice, a good Samaritan's voice pulling me back into a state of consciousness. I could hear the sounds of sirens in the background. As they approached, they got louder and louder, then they stopped. I could hear doors opening and closing, then I heard another person's voice in my ears saying,

"We're here to take good care of you! What is your name?! Do you know what day it is?! . . . . *He's fading quickly!!* Sir, stay with us!!! Don't close your eyes!!! Keep them open!!!"

I couldn't feel my body. I heard one of the paramedics instructing the other one to stabilize my neck. At that point, I realized that the damage was more severe than I had previously thought. As paramedics strapped me to a spinal board, I could overhear them discussing my injuries further. One said that my left wrist was fractured and the bone was sticking out. While we were in the ambulance, one of the paramedics was having trouble placing the needle into my arm so that he could start the IV because the ambulance was going at such a high speed. The paramedics kept talking to me the whole time while on our way to the hospital.

We finally pulled up to the Emergency Room entrance. The paramedics quickly disembarked me and rolled me into the Emergency Room. Unable to move my head and feel my neck as well as the rest of my body, all I could see were lights. I could hear screams, cries, and hollering. At that time, my only thought was, *I wonder if anyone contacted my wife?* I wanted Melissa; I needed her. Fear and panic began to grip my soul like never before. My life had seemingly been plucked up and thrown into a whirlwind of chaos, and I was powerless and afraid. At that moment, I heard the gentlest, sweetest, most soothing voice in my ear; it was Melissa saying to me, "I'm here, baby. Everything is going to be alright. You had a very bad car accident." She then laid her hand on my forehead and said, "God was with you." I could see the tears streaming down her face as she stroked my face lovingly. Her touch was so gentle that it was angelic and angelic was her face too.

Shortly afterward, I heard my mother's voice. She was hollering, "Let me see my child!" Suddenly, her face came into my view. I could see the tears flowing down her cheeks as she beheld my condition. But she realized she had to be strong. "God is good, Joe. He will see us through it all! You're in a position, lying on your back, which is bad but good in God's sight. Now, you can focus and lift your eyes towards heaven where only God can give you strength." Her words were comforting; although inside, all I could feel was fear.

❧

"Mrs. Lovejoy," the doctor said to Melissa while she and my mother were in separate rooms, "Mr. Lovejoy has a serious spinal cord injury and a fractured left wrist. We need your consent to amputate his arm."

"No way!!!" Melissa yelled. Melissa and my mom continued to talk with the doctor while I laid in the bed

173

wondering where my life was heading, wondering what light could exist at the end of this tunnel. Tears were flowing from my eyes. Fear, sadness, and anger filled my heart. The realization that I was not in control of my own life and of what would happen to me was beginning to sink in. I understood that I was entirely at the mercy of others and God; it was a sobering and humbling revelation.

I spent most of the day in the emergency room, fading in and out of consciousness while hooked up to machines. I spent most of my time unconscious. Melissa was there by my side the whole time. She was my angel, along with my mother. Melissa would update me on my condition and inform me of what was about to happen to me; she also began contacting local pastors in the city, asking them to pray for me. I was informed of the call made to the Shepherd Spinal Center on my behalf and that they were receiving me to their Critical Care Unit. Melissa told me that this was the best spinal care center. When talking to other people, they also highly recommended this facility.

The doctor explained to me that they were keeping me on the board until I arrived at the Shepherd Center. I had sustained severe head trauma, had a cast on my left wrist, fractured my distal radius, and I couldn't feel anything because I was paralyzed from the neck down, having broken seven bones in my cervical.

By this time, news of my accident is circulating around the city. A news bulletin flashed across local television stations reporting the accident. CFC management and personnel has begun receiving details about the accident. Time had come for transporting me to the Shepherd Spinal Center. It was a smooth ride; perhaps, the smoothest ride I'd ever experienced. Upon arrival, Melissa and my mom were already there waiting for me. Dr. McDonald, the man who recast my left wrist, met with Melissa and my mom to give them an overview of what would take place over the next 36 hours. "Curtis has a subluxation of C5 on C6 and also a grade-one open left distal radius fracture along with numerous minor lacerations and abrasions," he revealed. "He is in traction. He was placed in traction through a halo. In traction, the C5 on C6 subluxation reduced. An Axillary block was also done on the left side, and the grade-one open fracture was copiously irrigated and reduced and placed in a sugar long splint." He went on to share this report with them:

- HEAD: Normal cephalic and paralyzed from the neck down.
- NECK: He is tender to palpation posterior and thyromegal is appreciated.
- CHEST: Clear to auscultation and percussion without rale, rhonchus, wheezes. Bilaterally equal expansion.
- CARDIOVASCULAR: Slightly normal sinus rhythm. No murmurs, ribs, or gallops.
- ABDOMEN: Non-tender; non-distended. Without nasses or organomegaly. Bowel sound positive.

- GENITOURINARY: Patient has a Foley Catheter in place. He has normal uncircumcised male genitalia. Scrotum has both testes descended.
- RECTAL: The patient has no sensation, only deep pressure discriminatory in the anal area. Lack bowel and bladder control.
- PARALYZED: Upper and lower extremities. He probably will never be able to walk again. Right now, he is Quadriplegic.
- The seven bones in his neck and up has lots of swelling. In order to operate on his neck, we need to let the swelling go down. We'll keep a close eye on his vital signs; therefore, he must be stabilized now until surgery.

Chapter 19
LOOKING UP

WHEN I FINALLY OPENED MY EYES, THE ONLY direction I could look was up. My eyes were the only thing I could move. I couldn't move my hands, my arms, my legs; I couldn't feel my body. As I laid on my back in the clutches of helplessness, tears began to stream down my face; and yet, I couldn't even lift a hand to wipe them away. For the first time in my life that I can remember I was at the complete mercy of others.

Besides the drugged up body, my mind was coming and going. At times I would be coherent and talking, and then, the very next moment, I would be dead asleep. At times, I would talk out of my head; at other times, I'd be aware of what I was saying. Everything was hazy.

While I was at the Shepherd Center, the nurse

informed me that I had many, many visitors who came by to see me putting the number at around one hundred people per day. She said there were so many that came the center had to turn many away. Melissa played a major part in directing the flow of visitors. She dealt with CFC employees coming, making sure that everyone was informed and accommodated. Melissa was calling the shots and maintaining the order. Of course, there was my family. My mom stayed by my side. My other family members were there for me: Diane, Anne, Rosa Lee, Sallie, WiLewis, Carl, and dad. It was difficult for some of them to see me in the condition I was.

Not all of my guests were known to Melissa and my mom. During the midnight shift, I was being taken care of by a nurse named Mary; her shift ended at 7 a.m. One day, after arriving to work, Mary noticed a young lady sitting all alone in the waiting room. Mary passed by the young woman at least three times before stopping to check on her and to offer her some assistance. Mary asked the young lady her name. The young woman answered, "My name is Lynda. I want to know if I can see Curtis Lovejoy." Mary, being quite perceptive, responded,

"His wife is in there."

"I'm just a close friend of Curtis'. I'm willing to stay all night until I see him," Lynda replied.

"Let me see what I can work out," said Mary. "Wait here. I'll be back." Thirty minutes later, Mary returned to the waiting room, got Lynda, and then escorted her into my room. Lynda and I talked. I remember her rubbing my face gently, wiping away the tears from my eyes as they strolled down my face, and telling me about how the news of my accident affected her and her dad. Her dad still considered me to be his buddy. She explained that she arrived at the Shepherd Center the moment she found out about the accident, but when she arrived, she noticed that my wife was controlling the flow of traffic into my room. Knowing that I was married, Lynda didn't want to create a situation with my wife and family, so she left with plans to return when things settled more. Lynda waited nearly seven hours in that waiting room to see me. She told me about how Melissa and my sister, Rosa, nearly got into a fight in the lobby. Rosa could be heard yelling,

"I'll be damned if you're going to stop me from seeing my brother!!!" Mom had to step in between the two of them to stop them from ripping each other apart. Lynda still loved me and wanted to be with me. She was even willing to look past my current condition.

Demonna didn't visit me until November of that year. She explained to me why. As she explained, she wanted to find the best time to avoid bumping into Melissa. Unlike Lynda's situation, Melissa knew how Demonna looked. Demonna was paranoid as expected. I explained to her that she needed to come by after 10 p.m. if she wanted to avoid running into Melissa.

When Demonna arrived and saw me lying in bed paralyzed, she started to freak out. She was so scared of me and nervous to be around me. She started blaming herself for what happened to me. I explained to her that none of it was her fault and that I was in the wrong about everything. I expressed to her that something had to give concerning our relationship. I told Demonna, "I was on my way to Hell, and I was wondering how would I get out of this big mess. Every day, I was sinking deeper and deeper into quicksand."

"Curtis, what are you going to do?" Demonna asked.

"I must bounce back from of this. I need to start walking and getting my head together," I answered.

"Will you be able to walk again? How is your mother handling all of this? Can you even feed yourself?" Demonna asked firing off a series of random questions.

"Pull yourself together, Demonna!" I urged.

"Curtis, would we be able to do it again?" asked Demonna.

"What are you talking about?"

"You know, make love?"

"I don't want to talk about it," I said upset. My condition was too depressing for me to think about the subject of sex. It was too much for me to think about and too much for me to bear. The more I thought about my condition, the more bitter I became. Demonna continued to come to see me twice a week.

My dad came to see me right after the accident. When he and mom came into the room, it was tough for him to look at me. The sight of me in my condition was unbearable for him. He couldn't stay in the room too long. To avoid letting me see him cry, he simply turned and walked out the room. "Is dad ashamed of me?" I asked mom.

"No, Joe. He's hurting pretty bad on the inside. He wishes that he could trade places with you," she said.

"Why dad don't cry, mom? Is it a man thing?"

"No. Your daddy cries on the inside. He can only go so long before he busts wide open. The day will come when it will happen. But for now, he talks about you all of the time, saying that you got something inside of you that is burning and just waiting to explode; It's something very good. Joe, remember this, that everybody in the family can't see you like this. Diane, Anne, Rosa Lee, and WiLewis, they are all taking this accident very hard. Carl and Sallie are doing fine. You know, your brother Carl will always be praying for you and every day he'll be by your side; he may fall asleep, but he loves you. And if you don't see the other members of the family, just remember that they're taking it very hard."

"What about you, mom?"

"Joe, you're my last child, my baby boy. You're a special child because you stick to me like glue. I love every one of you, but because God made you the chosen one in this family, He is preparing you for something great in this life. He'll let me and your father live long enough to see His will done through you. God is going to give you a very long vacation."

"What do you mean by that?" I asked.

"You will see in due time," she responded.

"But mom, why did this happen to me?" I asked.

"Joe, get some rest. Just be still. God will see you through it all. Close your eyes and go to sleep."

The first two months at the Shepherd Center were a big eye-opener for me. I couldn't do anything for myself. I had to rely on others to do for me everything I used to do for myself. I remember the first time a nurse had to use a catheter on me; it was humiliating and embarrassing. An act done in private was now a total stranger's responsibility. Furthermore, some nurses had no compassion at all; they would ram the catheter up my penis causing sharp pain, and when they would pull the catheter out, I would see blood on the tip of it. To extract waste from my bowels, nurses had to stick their fingers up in me. The feeling of powerlessness made me feel less of a man. I would pray to God to help me so that I could regain a sense of dignity and be able to push out my bowels at least and administer my catheter. And He did. At first, I didn't have any feeling in the nerves beneath my neck, but thankfully, the feeling gradually returned to my upper body as time progressed. In two months, I started regaining feeling in my fingers; and then, in my hands. I was relieved that I was gaining strength and would be able to do my catheter. Still, there was one part of my body I was certainly concerned about and hoping the feeling would return in, my penis.

I couldn't get an erection. That bothered me deeply. All my life I prided myself on being a ladies man;

furthermore, I was married. Being incapable of performing sexual intercourse would certainly create issues in my relationship with my wife, Demonna, and Lynda. I couldn't go through life that way. At first, I tried everything that I figured should have worked. I had my girlfriends come to the center wearing mini-skirts, thinking that would heal my condition, but that didn't work; I still couldn't feel anything. I couldn't get an erection. I had Melissa bring me a couple of Playboy Magazines, thinking that would help me, but they didn't. After trying everything I could think of, I cried out loud to God, "Lord, I know I'm not [King] Solomon—he had one thousand wives; I only have one, and I haven't been faithful to that one. I REPENT! If you put me back on the right road, I'll do better; and the next wife you give me, I'll love her with all my heart!" A few weeks after praying that prayer, a miracle happened; a fine, brickhouse, bombshell of a nurse suddenly walked into my room. She was beautiful. She looked like a cross between Hallie Berry and Jennifer Hudson. With a big smile on her face, she said,

"Mr. Lovejoy, my name is Jennie. I'll be your nurse for tonight." Immediately, I felt like I had been reborn! "Will you be ready for you IC's in the next hour?"

"No! I'm ready right now!" I responded excitedly. While she was preparing to take my urine, that's when it happened: I became erect the moment she touched me.

"What's wrong with you?!" Jennie screamed suddenly. "You need to calm down!"

"No! No! No! I've been waiting for this to happen," I told her. "This isn't the time for me to calm down; this is the time for me to rejoice and thank the LORD!" I then explained to her everything that happened to me, and she understood. After that, we both laughed.

Chapter 20
WRESTLING IN THE NIGHT

DEATH CREPT INTO THE ROOM AND overshadowed me like brooding darkness swallowing the light of hope; it was like a shadow hovering over me and staring down at me with piercing black eyes while remaining ominously silent. Suddenly, it struck! My heart stopped beating. I felt my life leaving my body as if sucked out. Coldness crept into me through my finger tips and gradually moved throughout my body until the light in my eyes began to fade. There I was, a cold corpse on a table—a just sentence of a life of immorality, deceit, treachery, and dishonesty. I had died in my sins. I could feel myself being swallowed up by eternal darkness and feeling separated from God. Panic and fear engulfed my soul. Then suddenly . . .

I woke up.

My eyes quickly flung open, freeing me from that nightmare. I'd never experienced anything like that before. I had never dreamed that I was dead and was experiencing God's judgment for my sins before then. I knew right from wrong and that I was living wrong, but this dream really impressed upon me the reality that I needed to change my ways. I could sense that it was God giving me a warning, and I well received it. But I also had an ultimatum of my own to present to God.

‿ℓ‿

"God, I'll give you three days to heal my body; and after that, if I'm still not healed, then there is no God!" I cried out from my bed. I would cry out night after night, clinging on to dear hope. Night after night, I experienced no miracle or supernatural sign of anything taking place or getting ready to happen. It seemed as if when I was at my weakest point, God was more distant than ever.

Night three came, and there was still no miracle. I experienced the most indescribable sense of disappointment and despondency combined with anger, bitterness, helplessness, fear, and frustration. A lot of negative emotions and thoughts flooded through me and left me feeling more paralyzed than my physical condition. I didn't want to speak, think, or feel anything. All I wanted to do was die.

I closed my teary eyes and laid there trapped in the grip of mental, spiritual, and physical paralysis, teetering on the edge of suicide. Perhaps my physical paralysis was both a blessing and a curse since I was too confined to a bed to further trek down the road of self-destruction as I had done for so long. But my physical condition brought me to the brink of suicide; yet, due to my condition, I couldn't act on my suicidal thoughts. It seemed like my life was stuck on a see-saw of actions and reactions, fortunate and unfortunate circumstances. But in the morning, when I opened my eyes and saw my mother's face, it became more pronounced as the blur of sleep began to clear up that I remembered the beauty of life. My mom was standing over me. With a concerned expression on her face, she looked into my eyes and asked, "Joe, what were you murmuring? You were murmuring all morning long." I told her what I said to God in prayer: that if He didn't heal my body within three days, I would denounce Him. After I said those words, she quickly grabbed her purse and said, "You better repent, quickly!! I won't return until you repent!" She then walked out of the room.

I learned later that when mom left the room, she didn't abandon me; she simply went to the nearest place in the center where she could be alone to pray. The closest place she could find was the ladies restroom. There, she went and knelt down in a stall; and not caring whether or not anyone walked in on her and heard her, she began to cry out to God on my behalf, interceding for me. She prayed that God would rebuke the devil out of my mind and asked Him to forgive me for my blasphemy.

As time went on that day, I laid in that bed thinking more and more. I questioned God. I thought about my life. I thought about everything of importance to me during that time in my life. I continued to hope for some divine sign or instruction from God to come, but silence met me. I was determined not to remain in a state of paralysis. I figured that on the sheer power of my will alone I would be able to move my limbs; but the more I tried to move them, the weaker I became. It took a few minutes before I finally realized that nothing I came up with would work. I couldn't get anything I wanted from God, neither could I force my body to work through the power of my mind. I was in a completely powerless state. I was tired. Exhausted. Weary. I was worn out. I could no longer resist the compulsion to do what my bitterness wouldn't allow me to do, surrender to God.

That day, I began to pray differently. I didn't want to fight God anymore. I didn't want to argue with God. I was tired of giving Him ultimatums. I didn't want to walk down that dark and frustrating path. Now, it was time to follow my instincts, to follow the path that I had been taught to walk as a child. So I prayed,

"God of Abraham, Issac, and Jacob, I come to you as humbly as I know. I tried using my power, but nothing is working. Mom told me that you're a healer and a forgiving God. She also said that you loved me before I was born and that you have something great for me to do. I don't know what it is, but I do know I need you to restore me back in one peace, Jesus. What I'm saying is that I'm sorry for all my wrongdoing. Please forgive me, in the name of Jesus! Whatever you want me to do,

CHAPTER 20: WRESTLING IN THE NIGHT

I'll do it! Where ever you want me to go, I'll go!

I want to make this deal with you, Jesus. I'll do what you want me to do, but I need your patience to run this race. Please be patient with little ole' me. Amen."

After praying that prayer, I felt a heavy burden lift off of my shoulders and a sudden peace entered the room; it was a feeling I'd never felt or experienced before. I immediately called for my nurse. Her name was Sandy B. When she came into the room; I said to her the presence of God was in the room, and I asked her if she would get a Bible and start reading to me from the book of Job. As Sandy read the book of Job, I closed my eyes and began to envision every detail. I pictured in my mind how Job lost everything he had; he lost his children, his servants, his money, and his health. Job's body was stinking, covered with sores, and rotting due to his sickness. I then pictured the end of the story where God restored everything Job lost double-fold. Hearing Job's story made my soul feel so at peace. While reading, Sandy just paused for a moment, looked at me, and said she felt chills come all over her body and that she began to feel the presence of God in the room also. We felt the peace that passes all understanding, so much peace. My soul was at ease and was ready to embrace my new tomorrow.

CHAPTER 21
LEARNING TO ADJUST

D URING THIS PERIOD, I LOST OVER 95 LBS. MOST
of my muscle mass was now gone. Feeding is
through a feeding tube. Hooked up to my body
are three IV's. Heavily medicated, and time for me to
undergo surgery. My transfer was to Piedmont Hospital
where Dr. Mack successfully performed the operation.
He took a piece of bone from my hip to complete the
bone fusion between the fourth and seventh vertebrate
and then added two pieces of twisted wiring to secure
the bone fusion, which left a five-inch scar on my neck
and a three-inch scar on my right hip.

Now begins the recovery process after surgery.
One of the toughest processes to go through is physical
therapy. Physical therapy sessions were five days a week
from 7:00 am until 4:30 pm and they were pure hell.

I had to practice feeding myself, which I could barely do considering that I could barely lift my arms. "Keep trying," the therapist would insist. She wanted me to use my right arm, which was in a sling, but I couldn't move it; it was too heavy. I remember becoming so frustrated with trying to use my arm to feed myself that I dropped my face into my plate and started eating. The therapist stopped me and insisted that I try to feed myself the proper way. But I was tired, frustrated and ready to quit.

I had to take several classes during therapy: Life with Spinal Cord Injury Class; Pressure Sore and Weight Shift Class; Leisure Time Class; Sexuality Class; Return Back to Work Class; Home Accommodation Class. Each of these classes was designed to help me adapt to my new life. The Pressure Sore and Weight Shift classes were certainly two of the most needed classes. I had seen photos of bed sores, and it wasn't a pretty sight. They start out as a little red mark on the body, and if the individual doesn't shift their weight consistently, those little red marks will develop into a much bigger problem. Pressure sores aren't to be taken lightly either; they smell very bad; and if left untreated, gangrene will set in, and the poison from these sores can get into your bloodstream. Untreated, these sores in time, cause infection which can lead to the need for amputations. I also enjoyed the class on sexuality for men. When they showed us the different types of penis implant devices, that blew my mind. All I could think about was how incredible technology was... and is. But still, I recalled an old saying: *Ain't nothing like the real thing*.

My body was undergoing the long, slow, tedious journey back to health. I knew that my body would never be like it was, but I was willing to live with the changes—I was ready to accept and live with the reality that I was now a Quadriplegic (paralysis caused by illness or injury that results in the partial or total loss of use of all four limbs and torso). But just like my body, my marriage had taken a major hit; and although I knew my marriage would never be like it was in the beginning, Melissa and I were willing to live with the changes in the relationship. I had done tremendous damage to Melissa's heart through my affairs. I noticed how Melissa stuck by my side through my situation almost like a protector. She fought for me, watched for me, made sure that all went well for me. All I could think about was how much of a sacrifice she had made for me and how selfish I had been towards her.

I had been dealing with a lot on my plate. Besides my physical condition, I was still concerned, believe it or not, about my CFC stores passing their area inspections. I remained in communication with my area store managers. In fact, one day, the entire district area of Church's Fried Chicken store managers stopped by to visit me. They were planning to do something special for Melissa and me. They started taking up money for me. Also, the president of Church's Fried Chicken was working on something big for me. He wanted to have a special day in Atlanta when all of the sales generated during lunchtime would go to Melissa and me. The managers told me about how Melissa was so helpful in getting everything set up; how she took control of everything and was very energetic, upbeat, content, and innovative in her ideas, always thinking about what was best for me. They commented on how she could be both a businesswoman and a wife at the same time, which I already knew.

One day, Melissa came and sat down beside me. I knew it was time to come totally clean with her so that I could clear my conscience. "Melissa, come over here and sit by me. I want to share something important with you," I said. I began pouring my heart out to her. "From this day forward, I'm planning on going to sleep each night with a clear conscience. I want to talk about my extra curriculum activities. Please don't say anything. Let me finish without any interruptions. I believe that this accident happened for a reason. It felt like my world was falling apart. Melissa, I'm so sorry that I lied to you about having an [extramarital] affair and spending time with Demonna in Columbus. That morning, when I was taking you to work, I was in denial about the entire episode. Instead of me spending all of my time with you, I refused to do so and chose to spend time with someone else, which was totally wrong on my behalf; and later on, I got involved with another person also. My selfishness and disrespecting of my marriage vows were down-right against God's principles for marriage. I guess you can say that I wanted all of my cake and ice cream when I chose to do what I did. Please don't cry. I never had any intention to hurt you at all. I just got greedy. Please accept my apology from my heart. I'm asking for forgiveness from you. I'm not asking you to stay with me. If you leave me today, it will be fine. I'll make it. I'd prefer that you leave me now instead of hanging around because you feel sorry for me. If you need time to think about it, then do so. I'll accept whatever your decision is."

Melissa just sat quietly as I explained everything to her. "Curtis," she said with tears streaming down her face, "I am hurt, and that hurt you can't just sweep under a rug like it never happened. I think that you need some help. I'm willing to seek marriage counseling with you. We need to work on our marriage. It will take me some time to trust you again. You're bullheaded, spoiled, and arrogant, but God blessed you with charming dimples that override all of your bad habits. I took my marriage vows seriously. I still love you, and I'm willing to work things out with the proper help."

"Are you sure this is what you want? Because I don't want to get down the road and you flip the switch on me," I said.

"Curtis, I can't promise you that won't happen. We both need to be positive and work together as one."

"If you so happen to change your mind, will you share your feelings with me?"

"Yes, Curtis. I will. I'll remain honest with you," Melissa said. She leaned over and kissed me, and then laid down on the bed beside me. I was still wondering if she would ever leave me. I was also wondering if mom knew about the extramarital affairs. I suspected she did.

✕

It was one Friday afternoon, and I was relaxing when my

mom walked in. "Joe, you have a special guest," she said.

"Who is it?" I asked. She then pulled the curtain back and there was Reverend Timothy Flemming, Sr., the pastor of the Mount Carmel Baptist Church in Atlanta, Georgia. That was the church I was attending. His voice was very uplifting. His smile lit up the room. He brightened the mood in the room with his humor, telling jokes, and lifting everyone's spirit. Afterward, mom left the room, giving us time to be alone. Rev. Flemming started to share these words with me:

"First of all, you're a miracle. You supposed to be dead, but God isn't through with you. The devil thought he had you, but Jesus stepped right in just in the nick of time and told the devil 'Not this one. He is my property.' After seeing the pictures of the accident, you're truly blessed. Brother Lovejoy, it was your mother's prayers that God heard and acknowledged. I won't tell you don't cry, but I'll say this: it's okay to cry because God is collecting all of your tears, and when the time comes, He'll share them with you to let you know that whenever you get down and out He will reveal how you made it over during that difficult time *back then*. Every day, during breakfast, lunch, and dinner, I want you to use all that you have in your body to move your legs. The blessing may take a few days, some months, and even some years, but don't you give up. It won't be easy. You must increase your faith in God. It only takes the faith that is the size of a mustard seed to move mountains. God will take this accident and use it for His glory. Surrender to Him."

"Yes, sir. I will," I said. Pastor Flemming's words

reminded me that there is a light at the end of this dark tunnel and a purpose behind this pain.

"Please follow your doctors' and therapists' instructions," Pastor Flemming added. "The entire church family is praying for you. Remember: you must do your part and believe that God will do what He says. You will walk again." After that last statement, Pastor Flemming laid hands on me and started praying over me; afterward, he resumed telling jokes. Mom finally re-entered the room, at which point Pastor Flemming led all three of us in prayer. Pastor Flemming's visit left me feeling more encouraged to continue to hope and have faith that my situation would improve. I needed hope. That was more valuable than surgery, medicine, and therapy.

*

One of my rehabilitation exercises to help me adjust to my new reality was to go out into the public and get used to being around people outside of the Shepherd Center again. To do this was certainly easier said than done. Several of the Shepherd Center staff members accompanied ten of our patients who used wheelchairs to Lenox Square Mall. I had to overcome a lot of negative emotions just to proceed with this exercise. I was worried about what everyone thought about me in a wheelchair. I didn't like the deformity of my hands among other features on my body. I felt out of place in that mall around all those people, many of whom I could sense staring at me. I had to get used to asking others for help with the simplest things like opening a door. All of this was a humbling experience. I was afraid to ask anyone for help at first out of my fear of being rejected, but my physical condition left me with no other choice. My first experience with asking a stranger for help was when I spotted a middle-aged woman who was having a bad hair day. I rolled up to her and asked, "Excuse me, ma'am, I'm wondering could you please help me with the door?"

"Excuse me?" she asked with a puzzled expression on her face. I realized I was talking too low, so I repeated myself:

"Ma'am," I said, elevating my voice some, "could you please help me with the door?! Please!"

"Oh, yes. Anything for you, cutie," she replied.

"Thank you so much, ma'am."

"Is there anything else you would like for me to do for you, handsome?" she kindly asked.

"I believe that's it. If I come up with something else, I'll let you know."

"You do that. You have a good day," the lady said before turning and walking away. Denise, one of the staff members who had been monitoring the situation, came up to me and said,

"See, Curtis, how easy was that?"

"But Denise, everybody isn't going to be that nice," I responded.

"I know that, but you won't know until you are facing the situation, and that's when you ask yourself, 'Now, what do I do?' Adjusting is a part of life. The one who can make adjustments as they go, probably won't have so many delays or disappointments in life."

"Coming through that door wasn't easy at all. It was hard trying to get over the threshold," I said.

"It takes time, Curtis. You need to build-up your strength, endurance, and use that pretty smile that you have. Okay?!"

The staff members and the ten of us patients spent all morning in the mall getting used to things; but now, it was time for my greatest challenge yet: lunch. Due to the deformity of my hands, it was still difficult for me to feed myself. I was in a position where I had to attempt to feed myself while in a public setting in front of strangers. While in the food court, I thought the staff members were going to order our food for us and bring it to our tables, but they didn't; instead, they made us order our own food and then take it to our own tables. I knew I needed to order something I could easily hold in my hands, so I ordered a gyro. As I was trying to eat the sandwich, it was very difficult; it kept falling apart. I got white sauce all over my fingers. I then decided to lay the sandwich on my plate and spread it out so that I could eat it with my fork, but that proved to be equally as difficult for me—I couldn't grasp the fork with my hands. At that moment, desperation kicked in. At first, I looked around to see if anyone was looking at me. I didn't notice anyone staring at me, so I plunged my face into my plate and started eating my food like a pig. About a few seconds later, I got the sense that I was being watched. I looked up and noticed that there was a couple staring at me with a look of disgust on their faces. At that point, I felt so embarrassed; but then, my embarrassment turned to anger as I felt judged, violated by their eyes, and ugly. I then threw my food and drink at that couple and spat my food at them. Denise got up and ran over to me and hollered, "Stop that, Curtis!!" Then she grabbed me. The couple that was staring at me quickly got up and ran out of the food court. I was fuming mad while sitting there with white sauce and bits of food all over my face. "Curtis, why did you do that?!" Denise asked.

"They turned their noses up at me while shaking their heads! I couldn't take that! I'm a human being just like them! I'm sorry, but if that happens again, I'll do the same thing!"

"Listen, Curtis; you can't do that. That's the wrong way to do things," said Denise.

"Then they shouldn't have given me that disgusting look!" I replied. "Take me back to Shepherd Center now!" I hollered, still angry from that incident.

"No, Curtis! We came together, and we'll leave together! Just calm down and take a timeout. You need to wipe that white sauce off your face. Do you need some help?"

"No. I'll do it myself. Just leave me the hell alone!" I said. Another staff member then came over and asked, "Curtis, are you okay?"

"You all just leave me alone and don't say anything to me!" I said to the other staff members. Thoughts were running through my mind: *These people don't understand me. They don't care about my situation. I just need to get back to the Shepherd Center around my friends.*

CHAPTER 22
OVER THE EDGE

NOT A SINGLE DAY WENT BY DURING THIS TIME when I didn't experience pain in my body. Due to the loss of so much muscle mass, it was difficult for my neck and shoulders to bear the weight of my head. My body would experience continuous muscle spasms that would send very sharp pains all the way from the seventh vertebrae in my cervical throughout my shoulders, arms, and hands causing my fingers to contract. When in my wheelchair, the spasms would travel down my spine, pulling me back into my chair with great force before traveling down through my legs (I could feel some sensation in my legs by this time, especially in my right leg). The spasms would cause my leg to kick up on its own, and they would last for around twenty seconds. The spasms would last for over forty-five seconds when I didn't drink enough water and hydrate my body. During winter only, the spasms intensified. My doctor prescribed me 40mg of Baclofen, which was the maximum dose. This medicine helped to calm my nerves and relax my muscles, but there was something else that came my way that helped to soothe my soul.

It was a cold holiday season. It looked as if it was going to be a white Christmas. My doctor approved of me leaving the Shepherd Center and spending a few hours with my wife and mother that day. I was under the impression that they were taking me Christmas shopping; that's what they said they were going to do. They claimed they needed to do one thing on our way to the mall: they wanted to stop by one of my CFC stores and say hello. They then drove me to one of my stores. Once we pulled up in the parking lot, I noticed that there were a lot of people standing around; some were holding signs that read "We love you Curtis!" and "Today is your day!" while others had balloons. The second everyone saw me they started jumping, cheering, hollering, and clapping. I asked Melissa what was going on and she said, "They're honoring you today!"

"Who?! Me?!" I asked.

"Curtis, just receive it, baby," my mom said. There had to be between three and four hundred people out there that day in honor and celebration of me. I saw old classmates of mine from elementary and high school, coaches of mine, teachers, co-workers, friends, people from the community I had never seen before but whose lives I had touched in some way, relatives of mine; I even saw the President of Morris Brown College, Dr. Threat. Also present were members of the SCLC, kids from the MLK Elementary School, Sylvan High School marching band, Mount Carmel Baptist Church, and the Ben Hills United Methodist Church. There was a stage set up with a podium on it in the parking lot. When we parked the car, someone came to assist me out of the car and onto the ramp leading up to the stage. While on the ramp, I noticed who was standing at that podium waiting for me to arrive: it was the honorable Mayor Andrew Young. I was shocked and feeling as if this was a dream although it was real. When I got to the stage, Mayor Young began to speak:

> "Curtis, today is your day in the City of Atlanta, Georgia. I want to honor you and present this proclamation to you along with a host of Atlanta for your extraordinary work with Church's Fried Chicken and your community service. The proclamation says:
>
>> 'You've exemplified an unyielding spirit of determination and a powerful self-driven force. We recognize you as one of the elite outstanding field executives in Church's Fried Chicken. As the Mayor of the City of Atlanta, Georgia, I proclaim December 13, 1986, as Curtis Lovejoy Day in Atlanta!'
>
> We're praying for you and your family. Get well

because so many depend on you."

Everything was amazing. I hadn't realized that I touched so many people. The President of Church's Fried Chicken, David Hamburger, was present also. He congratulated me on my big day and thanked me for all of the years of sacrifice and hard work I put into the company. In an amazing act of generosity, Mr. Hamburger donated all of the CFC store sales in the company made from 11 am to 1 pm to the Curtis Lovejoy Trust Fund. Mr. Hamburger's generosity, along with the Mayor's proclamation, was an incredible honor.

It was February 13, 1986, and I had another celebration to attend. This one was Church's Fried Chicken's Awards Day celebration and seminar, which I was requested to be in attendance. My physician, Dr. Mack, allowed me to take some time out of the Shepherd Center to attend the event. The event was in Orlando, Florida. The awards were to be on that Friday at a special banquet on a chartered boat.

For this event, it would be my first time to fly on an airplane, and I was nervous. Not only was I filled with the obvious concern that a first-time flyer would have (experiencing a plane crash), but I also had another concern: *What if I needed to go to the restroom?* I was also concerned about how I would be perceived once at the event since I was now in a wheelchair. I didn't want to be overshadowed by the sympathy of people. I didn't want people to view me as a charity case. Melissa had to set my mind at ease about attending the event. "Curtis," she said, sensing my distress, "everything is going to be fine, baby. The company is going to honor you for becoming a Master Merchant Area Manager. On Friday night, we'll board a ship that will sail on the ocean. While on the ship, there will be a banquet and a dinner, and an award ceremony will take place. This occasion is just for you. You deserve it."

"Do you believe that everyone will be happy for me because I know that there are a few people who don't like me? They were opposed to my way of doing things, and they are jealous of my area."

"Baby, don't worry about those people. Nobody can beat you at being you," Melissa responded. "Just remember that a smile will kill all of that. Life is too short to focus on them. That's behind you. Continue to go forward with speed, okay? Okay?! Let's have some fun! I'll be with you all the way." Even though her words were comforting, I still had the situation with the plane ride.

Melissa and I arrived at the airport three hours early. I was the first passenger to board the plane due to my handicap condition. Airport employees had to carry me onto the plane and transport me to my seat. Before the other passengers could board the plane, I was ready for take-off, strapped into my seat. When I felt the plane starting to lift, I closed my eyes, nervous and afraid. Melissa had to help me to breathe properly so I wouldn't hyperventilate due to fear. The pilot came on over the PA system and announced that we were now at 30,000 feet and it was safe to take off our seat-belts and move around. At that moment, my eyes became extremely heavy, and I began to fall asleep. I slept for a good little while before Melissa woke me up and informed me that it was time for my IC (intermittent catheterization). I was wondering how in the world we were going to do this on a plane. Melissa called for a stewardess and asked her for a blanket; afterward, she looked at me and asked, "You okay?"

"Yes, but...this is embarrassing," I said to Melissa.

"Curtis, we can't get you to fit in their small restroom," she reminded me. We had to empty my bladder right there in my seat. Melissa worked it out.

Once we arrived in Orlando, transportation services were waiting for us to take us to the Hilton Hotel downtown. When we arrived at the hotel, the company had a poster with my face on it in the lobby, touting me as one of the honorees for their celebration. Shortly after I arrived at my room, two of my friends, Willie and Derrick, stopped by to check on me. I expressed to them just how elated I was for the honor, but that I really wished I was still back at the Shepherd Center. I didn't feel comfortable with the way I looked, handicapped and in a wheelchair. I wanted people to remember me for how I used to look and not how I currently looked. I knew that for many of the attendees who knew me, it would be a shocker for them to behold me in my current condition. I felt deeply depressed over this; nevertheless, I was there and ready to be honored.

It was time to attend the celebration. Of course,

I was having second thoughts about going, and I was trying to talk Melissa into allowing me to stay behind in the room while she went in my place to receive my reward. Perhaps she could tell them I wasn't feeling well and that I needed to stay in my room, or she could make up some other excuse. But she didn't have it. Melissa was adamant that I attend the celebration, refusing to take "no" for an answer. She picked out my outfit: a red and black tuxedo with a bow-tie. My outfit matched her dress.

Melissa and I arrived at the ship. When I first saw the ship, my initial thought was, "This ship is huge!" Derrick and Willie were there to assist me. They rolled me up the ramp and to the entrance. Upon arrival at the top of the ramp and the entrance, I saw people clapping and whistling in honor of my arrival; many of them were hollering my name. I was glad to see all of my store managers and co-workers present. Melissa and I then proceeded to the ballroom for the banquet. In the ballroom, I was speechless at how many people were in attendance at the event. The room was packed.

The President of Church's Fried Chicken took to the podium and began sharing a few wonderful words about my career with the company: about how we first met, and how aggressive I was when it came to working and accomplishing goals in the company. He spoke about how much of a team player I was and how good I was at team-building. Afterward, he called me up to the stage to be honored. As I made my way to the stage, the audience gave me a standing ovation that lasted for several minutes. I was wondering when everyone was going to stop clapping. I then looked over at Melissa and noticed that her eyes were filled with tears. The love everyone was showing me was overwhelming. On stage, Mr. Richard Trimble presented me with two large golden cups along with a CFC jacket with my name engraved on it and the words "Master Merchant Area Manager" on the back. Although I tried to hold back the tears, I couldn't. A flood of emotions began to overtake me. I broke down in tears. But I wasn't crying because I was happy; I was crying because I felt so loved and so appreciated by people who had no idea what I was going through internally. I didn't want sympathy from anyone, but to see so many faces I knew and didn't know smiling at me and to feel so many hands patting me on the back and expressing their heartfelt appreciation for my hard work, years of service, and the example of excellence I set for them, and to see the look of admiration on their faces and hear them tell me how I inspire them, that really got to me. Even still, in spite of all of this, I still found it difficult to love myself.

Everyone was talking about how delicious the food was at the banquet, but I couldn't tell since I didn't eat anything. I didn't have an appetite. After everyone finished eating, it was on to the dance floor. Suddenly, I became even more depressed because I couldn't dance due to my condition—I would never again be able to grace a dance floor and do the things I use to do. The memory of what

CHAPTER 22: OVER THE EDGE

I once could do and revelation of what I'd no longer be capable of doing was beginning to eat me alive. I just watched as everyone else was smiling and dancing and talking and laughing and having fun. In my mind, I was thinking to myself that the only thing these people have to do is give me a pat on the back, say a couple of kind words to me, show a little sympathy, and then move on. But I'm the one who has to roll around in a wheelchair for the rest of my life and bear the burden of never again being able to experience even some of the simplest movements and abilities, which they enjoy without hesitation. Envy and anger began to consume me fully, and what was supposed to be a celebration in my honor was now a blatant reminder of everything I'd lost that rainy day forever in November.

In my mind, everything was becoming distorted. All of the chatter was beginning to sound like a cacophony of jumbled up sounds bleeding into the music, which seemed to get louder and louder until beginning to drown my internal thoughts. I grew more annoyed as each second passed. Paranoia began to take hold of me. I started to assume that the laughter permeating the room was directed at me and assumed that the people who were pointing in my direction were pointing at me. The discomfort was too much. I expressed to Melissa that I needed some air and that I was simply going outside for a few minutes. I rolled myself out of the room and outside to the deck of the ship. It was windy, chilly, cold outside. It was dark. All you could see was darkness before your eyes for miles and miles around. But even these conditions were preferable to the chaotic scenery I had just escaped from. I preferred the silence and the loneliness. That chaos had my head spinning like it was inside of a toilet. And now, in the stillness and coldness of the night while the heavy winds whistled all around me, I was being tormented by other thoughts: thoughts announcing to me how ugly, helpless, handicapped, and damaged I was. Tears began to stream down my face. Right then, another more terrifying thought crossed my mind while noticing how close I was to the edge of the ship. I thought about how easy it would be to simply end all of my miseries and fears. I began convincing myself that by plunging myself overboard and into the frigid waters below I would be relieving everyone else of the *burden* of me. At that moment, I no longer felt cold. A strange warmth came over me. I became completely numb. All I could hear was my heart beating in my chest. It felt as if the world around me had dissolved and disappeared. There was only the compulsion to keep rolling closer and closer to the edge of the deck. I was giving up and just wanted to die. I looked and noticed that no one else was around. *Curtis, you'll never be able to do the things you use to do*, I thought. *You can't please your wife in the bedroom anymore, no one wants you around, and you're useless now*, I thought to myself. Each thought was like a force propelling me closer to the edge of the ship. *You're almost there, Curtis, I thought. Push! Push! Push! Finally, you're at the edge. All I need to do now is lift these heavy legs off the footrest and place them on the floor. Damn, my legs and feet are so heavy! They're like dead weight. But I finally got it! Now, I just need to grab the rail. On the count of three, with everything inside of you, Curtis, just pull your entire body up and go over the rail. Okay! 1... 2 ...*

"Sir, please don't do it!" someone yelled out of the blue. "I beg you, sir! That is not the way! It can't be that bad!" the stranger yelled while slowly moving closer.

"Yes, it is!" I responded. "It's the only way out for me! Leave me alone!"

"Please, sir! Just wait a minute! Take your hand off the rail," the man said. Once I took my hand off the rail, the man rushed over to me and grabbed the back of my wheelchair and rolled me away from the edge of the deck. "Sir, I don't know you, but I know that God loves you," the man told me.

"Nobody loves me. I'm just a big problem to my family and others," I responded.

"Well, just remember that I love you. You don't know me, but I know you."

"Who am I?" I asked the man.

"You're one of God's saints. He told me to stop by and visit you. He got greater works for you to do. No matter what happened to you, He (God) can restore you," the man answered.

"Who is this He you're talking about?" I asked.

"The one who said, 'I am ALPHA and OMEGA, the beginning and the end, the first and the last: JESUS CHRIST!" the man proclaimed. I didn't know what to say after that. I just sat quietly for a few seconds; then I asked the man,

"Could you tell me your name?"

211

"Yes. My name is James, and your name is Curtis."

"How did you know my name?" I asked.

"From your name tag," the man replied. "Curtis, all is well. Just keep your eyes on the prize. Let me take you back to the party." The man rolled me back to the door of the banquet hall and opened the door for me. I then stopped the man and said, "Can I ask you one more question?"

"Yes."

"Sir, can I have your phone number just in case I need to talk to you later?" He gladly obliged. He then wrote down his phone number and gave it to me. "Thank you so much," I told him. He rolled me back into of the ballroom and then said,

"You have a blessed evening." When I looked back to say something to the mysterious man, he was gone. It was like he just vanished into thin air. I sat there in that ballroom bewildered, puzzled, startled. The sounds of the music and chatter all around me sounded like a faint echo in the distance in my mind. I was physically sitting in the room, but my mind was still outside, stuck at that moment, trying to figure out who that mysterious man was who happened to appear out of nowhere to stop me from committing suicide and then mysteriously disappeared after sending me back into the ballroom.

"Curtis," a voice suddenly called out to me. I was still somewhat in a daze. "Curtis," the voice called out to me again. I started to recognize that voice; it was Melissa calling my name, trying to get my attention, sensing that there was something wrong with me. I just stared at her. My facial expression startled her. "Curtis, are you okay?" she asked. "You look like you just saw a ghost. Baby, talk to me. Are you okay?" At first, I sat speechlessly. But then, I broke my silence and said,

"I'm ready to leave."

"Curtis, the ship isn't scheduled to reach the port for about another hour. So what's wrong?" Melissa asked again. I replied,

"I'm just wrestling with something in my mind." I didn't speak anymore with Melissa about anything, but my mind was still swirling with thoughts and questions. It dawned on me then that the man couldn't have known my name from my name tag because I didn't have one on while I was outside—I took it off and then left it on the table before going outside. Also, the man had on casual clothes as opposed to being dressed like everyone else at the banquet. Also, the man happened to appear out of nowhere at the precise moment that I was getting ready to jump off the edge of the boat. I called for my friend Willie to come over, and I asked him if he would dial the mysterious man's phone number. When Willie dialed the number, all he got was the error message: "I'm sorry. This number is not in service." At that point, it all came together for me. I realized what had just happened. I also thought no one else would believe my story besides my mother. She used to tell me all of the time that angels exist and that they are everywhere.

JUST A LITTLE LOVE & JOY

CHAPTER 23

MIRACLES AND DISASTERS

I T WAS FEBRUARY 16, 1987, AND A PRAYER OF MINE was about to be answered. Earlier that day, I went to all of my therapy classes. Later on that day, the PT/OT techs wanted to see if I'd be able to stand on my own using long-strapped leg bracelets. The techs were trying to get my legs into the bracelets. They managed to get one of my legs in, but not the other. Frustrated, I yelled at the techs and told them to put me back in my wheelchair. I was tired of feeling like a guinea pig. After everyone left, I sat in my wheelchair all alone, thinking about my situation. I decided to look at things differently. Rather than allowing frustration to cause me to shut down, I decided that it would be better for me to cut out my pity-party and try to cooperate with the technicians and physicians who were only trying to help me. "Don't let the disability control you. You control the disability," I reminded myself.

So I decided to give the leg bracelets another try. I managed to get both legs into the bracelets, then I pulled myself up out of my wheelchair while clutching on to a bar; and for the first time in a long time, I started to walk. I took one step and then another one. Tears of joy and happiness began to stream down my face while the other nurses and PT and OT techs were running towards me, astonished over what I'd done. People were clapping and cheering as I managed to take one step after another. Even Dr. Mack ran into the gym to see the "miracle" for himself. When Dr. Mack ran into the gym and saw me walking, he was speechless—it was he who told me that it was highly unlikely that I'd ever walk again. And there I was, walking with the help of those bracelets.

I took one step after another until I finally made it to my room. I was excited about sharing the news with Melissa and my mom. News from other people letting them know that I was walking bombarded them as they arrived at the Shepherd Center. Both Melissa and mom rushed into my room to see me. They were so excited about the news, thanking God for the miracle. Melissa began calling other family members and friends to share the news with them. It didn't take long before the Shepherd Center's switchboard swamped with phone calls from people calling to congratulate me. It was amazing to know that so many people were praying for me. I was so grateful for the miracle; the opportunity just to be able to walk again on my own, even if it was with the help of special leg bracelets.

❦

I was picking up the pieces of my life during this time. I wanted to go back and handle some unfinished business and also move forward with some new ventures, so I decided to go back to college and finish earning my degree. I enrolled again at Morris Brown College.

While I was moving forward with my life in some ways, I was moving backward in other ways, namely in my marriage, which was getting ready to hit an all-time low. I was having trouble performing sexually due to my accident, and this filled Melissa with frustration and put a lot of tension on our relationship. During this time in our marriage, Melissa allowed a relative of hers to come by and stay with us, a cousin of hers from Phoenix City, Alabama. I can't say I particularly liked this arrangement when considering that Melissa and her cousin loved to talk a lot, which caused Melissa to not focus on my needs as much. For example, the house had to undergo certain modifications for me to live comfortably in it, but in the meantime, I had to depend on Melissa for many of the necessities. I needed her to prepare my food for me, help me access certain places in the house, and more. But Melissa and her cousin were more focused on their gossip sessions than they were on me. I felt like a helpless person ringing a bell for help while being ignored by the attendant assigned to help him.

Melissa and I began attending marriage counseling to help our marriage. Our counselor, Dr. Miller, was a very perceptive individual. He easily picked up on the mounting tension between Melissa and me; after all, it was thick enough to cut with a knife. During one session, Dr. Miller asked me, "What do you want from your wife?" With Melissa sitting there, I candidly responded,

"I want her to say 'I'm sorry' to me for what she has done." I felt like Melissa was deliberately neglecting me in many ways and was engaging in passive-aggressive behavior while seeking revenge against me for the things I had done to her earlier in our marriage.

I'll admit that I wasn't the most sensitive husband. I had caused Melissa so much pain due to my affairs; and in spite of all of that, she stuck with me taking care of me. Although I did confess to her all of the wrongs I had done to her and she forgave me for them and continued to put up with me, I expected her to heal too fast, and I also expected her to be more forgiving than I was. I had forgotten that I was also obligated to put up with some things in our marriage and that I had also to forgive some things and let go of some grudges. I liked holding on to things perhaps a little too long, which didn't do me any favors.

Perhaps Melissa was beginning to feel worn out. Maybe I had pushed Melissa over the edge with my stubbornness and selfishness because now she was looking for subtle ways to avoid me. Although Melissa didn't have to work, she chose to work not one job, but two jobs just so that she didn't have to attend marital counseling sessions with me. Melissa had decided that the less of me that she saw, the better. Of course, as a result of Melissa's actions,

I had no other choice but to turn to others for assistance both in and outside of the home. One of the individuals I had to rely on to get me to my therapy sessions and get me to other places I needed to be was one of the nurses named Adrienne. Melissa and Adrienne had a few negative run-ins. Melissa wasn't too fond of her. But I wasn't worried about Melissa's insecurity; I desperately needed help, and Melissa wasn't around to provide it.

As time progressed, Melissa grew even more vocal about her objections to Adrienne being around. She was especially vocal about her desire to not have Adrienne in our house. Things really got heated when, one day, Adrienne came over to the house to pick me up and take me to the Shepherd Center for my therapy sessions. While at the house, I asked Adrienne if she would come in and help me with a couple of things I needed to get done. Suddenly, the phone rang. When I picked up the phone, it was Melissa on the other end hollering and shouting, "Tell that bitch to get out of my house!!!" A few minutes later, Melissa's cousin who had been staying with us pulled up in the driveway. She got out of the car and got straight up in my face and began cursing me out in my own house. She said some of the meanest and most hurtful things to me. *Thank God I was in a wheelchair.* Later on, at about 2:15 am, Melissa arrived home. When Melissa arrived, she immediately began cursing me out. She didn't even take the time to congratulate me on reaching my 30th birthday that day. She was simply on a warpath. She then yelled at me and told me to get out of the house. I responded that I wasn't going anywhere. She ran into the guest bedroom. Being handicapped, I asked Melissa if she would at least fix me something to eat. She just yelled, "Why you didn't let your girlfriend cook dinner for you?" before slamming and locking the door in my face. I was starving. I felt totally helpless because I couldn't position myself in my wheelchair to push the door open. I was also angry because I could tell that Melissa was enjoying the fact that I was completely at her mercy. I began banging on the door using a flashlight. This went on for nearly fifteen minutes until I heard the sound of police sirens outside of my house. I saw red and blue lights flashing through my window. It shocked me that Melissa called the police on me. When I looked out the window, I noticed that five squad cars had surrounded the house. The police began ringing the doorbell. I opened up the door and then one of the officers shouted,

"Where is the knife?!" He had his gun drawn.

"What knife?" I asked.

"Where is your wife?" another officer asked.

"She's in the bedroom with the door locked," I answered. At that point, Melissa opened up the door and ran out of the room and straight towards one of the female officers waiting outside. She was acting like she was totally shaken up—almost traumatized. I felt so embarrassed. Our neighbors were outside watching the whole thing happen. One of the officers kept asking me about a knife, to which I kept explaining I didn't have a knife. I even explained to the officer that due to the deformity of my hands I was incapable of holding a knife. The officer looked down at my hands and realized that I was telling him the truth. He suggested that Melissa and I get some marital counseling. Lord knows, I held my peace. I was terribly upset and disappointed. After the officers left, I simply rolled myself into my room and called my mom. Both of my parents rushed over to the house to check on me. I was angry enough to try to put my hands on Melissa, but I remembered when my dad put his hands on my mom and I swore I would never do that to my wife.

That night, Melissa and I slept in separate rooms in the house. The next morning, we awoke without saying a word to one another. Melissa left the house and went straight to work, and I went to my office to call the marriage hotline the officer had given us. While speaking to one of the counselors, I was in a state of denial the whole time, solely blaming Melissa for the decaying state of our relationship, which wasn't the best idea. I was acting as if I didn't have any problems.

In the upcoming days, Melissa and I gave each other the silent treatment—we didn't say a word to one another. We both pondered much in our hearts, but refused to break the wall of silence between us. I couldn't forget about what she did to me: calling the police on me and claiming that I was threatening her with a knife. I felt betrayed by her. Then I started thinking about other things like all of the money that CFC collected for me, which I had placed in Melissa's care; and the fact that she had power of attorney over my estates. The fact that I had good insurance on me. The money I saved up for a rainy day that Melissa was aware of and the money I had invested in savings and money market accounts and overseas accounts. I had placed so much in the hands of a person I now had my doubts about, and this began to weigh on my mind heavily. All of this weighed on my mind so heavily that I asked Lynda to look into my financials for me to see what Melissa was doing with all of the money I had saved. The report Lynda gave me was discomforting; it was pretty disturbing to me. Lynda revealed to me that Melissa had been burning through the cash in my overseas accounts and was replacing that money with funds from my other accounts to cover herself. I became more and more paranoid around Melissa, believing that she had ulterior motives. I started distrusting her more and more, wondering whether or not she was concealing some secret lifestyle or if she was trying to repay me by burning through cash as payback for all of my extramarital affairs. I didn't know. But one thing is for sure: planted in my heart towards her was a seed of resentment, and it was growing roots and developing into something bigger and more dangerous than I could have imagined.

A deadly mixture of fear and paranoia, desperation, anger, and resentment would transform into madness and produce a toxic atmosphere within me, inviting the ultimate evil into my soul. I had become unrecognizable even to myself.

CHAPTER 24
MURDER SHE WROTE

MY THOUGHTS WERE RACING AT ONE THOUSAND miles per hour. I was obsessed with trying to figure out what Melissa was doing with the money, where she was *really* spending a lot of her time at night and throughout the day, and what she was up to... if she was up to something. She's gone in the morning, and home late at night to avoid me in many respects. She seemed a little too quiet, too secretive; and, at times, a little too happy, but not because of me. I realized that much.

Physical Therapy classes were intense, they were rough, but they were beginning to pay off; they felt like months and months of torture at the hands of sadistic specialists and doctors, but I began to appreciate all of those tough days filled with difficult challenges. I had to rediscover how to do the simplest things like hold a utensil and feed myself. I'd started to regain a sense of independence and embrace the handicap aids in public places. If anything, the hardest thing for me to learn was humility. I now had to ask people to open and hold doors for me, whereas I never had to do such a thing before. But I was starting to get adjusted to my new life.

My body was getting stronger. My muscles were developing. It was getting easier for me to move around in my wheelchair and utilize the many handicap aids like handrails, handicap parking spaces, and more. My house was still undergoing modifications to make it easier for me to get around on my own, so there were construction tools laying around everywhere. I felt like every part of my life at the moment was undergoing construction: my marriage, body, home, etc. In the house, everything was becoming more accessible to me. There was still one problem I was having (of course, besides the inability to walk): due to the deformity of my hands, it was impossible for me to hold small objects. And in light of what I had been planning in my mind, this posed a problem.

Ever since my car accident, I felt vulnerable in so many ways; and since that day, my primary goal became to reclaim much of the control over my life and regain a sense of independence. Melissa posed what I deemed the biggest threat to my independence at this time in my life.

I was living off of her mercy. Melissa had access to all of my financial accounts and the power of attorney over my estate, and she had the power to wipe me out financially. She could easily take everything that I worked so hard to accumulate away from me in a single moment. And due to the volatile nature of our relationship, I lived in fear of saying or doing anything that would anger Melissa. One thing I didn't want to do was incur her wrath and end up in lengthy court battles just trying to maintain a hold on that which took me years to acquire. So, I decided that I would be the sweetest person Melissa knew. I would be there to stroke her hair at night. I would be there to say sweet things to Melissa. I would keep her calm. I would try my best to reassure Melissa of our love and my dedication and commitment to her as a husband. Whenever I got hot under the collar at her, I would think about my bank accounts. Whenever I felt like retaliating against her for something she said or did, I would think about my estate. Basically, she held all of the cards. I just needed to keep my mouth shut and wait. Wait I did. I would wait for a moment to come when I could free myself and regain complete control of my life.

At night, I would dream of horrible things. *Horrible things.* A frightening coldness came over my heart and turned me into someone I couldn't recognize, into someone I had never met. Concealed beneath the contagious smile, heartwarming charm, and bubbly countenance I so often presented was the subtle, gradual transformation. Dark thoughts like hideous roots had grown deep in my soul, and I began to contemplate the unthinkable. I would hear the whispers that so many before had talked about who was in the throes of madness. They were nearly audible voices, like a kind of intuition that comes out of nowhere. Aided I was in my thinking, in my plotting and planning and scheming. Even then, there was the sense that I was ultimately planning my own doom and plotting against my own future. Whatever wanted me dead, it was more content with killing two birds with one stone. It wanted to rob Melissa and me of a future.

As the vision would play out in my head, I would go back again and again to the crime scene to make sure that I didn't overlook or forget anything. Every detail had to be accounted for. Fingerprints were a big thing. My fingerprints couldn't be found on the murder weapon. Timing was critical. Melissa couldn't suspect anything. How to make it look like a robbery or a random occurrence was the big challenge. *What would detectives look for? Missing jewelry? Unlocked windows? A cut phone line or phone line ripped out of the wall? Perhaps these things would add more credence to the claim that it was a robbery. But what about me? What would investigators think about me being present during the supposed robbery? I'll flip my wheelchair over on its side as if I was knocked over by an intruder and then I'll inflict myself with a wound to make it seem like I was also attacked. This would further clear my name and make me look like a victim.* When it was all said and done, this is what I envisioned in my mind the news media reporting:

CHAPTER 24: MURDER SHE WROTE

"Last night, robbers broke into the Lovejoy residence through a side window in the den and entered the Lovejoys' bedroom while the couple was sleeping. One of the robbers hit the female in the head several times with an object while the other robber attacked the husband, slamming his head up against the wall until he was rendered unconscious. Apparently, the robbers were in search of jewelry and cash as items such as wedding rings, gold chains, and watches were the only things discovered missing by investigators. The wife was pronounced dead on the scene when investigators arrived. If anyone has any information in this case, please contact the Atlanta Police Department immediately."

As I thought about the details of my plan and pondered the questions asked by investigators, each question took me deeper and deeper into more madness, into a more demented world. The possibilities seemed endless. I was putting more thought into how to take a life than I was restoring my marriage. And for some reason, this seemed so much easier to do. It seemed easier to kill than to heal. Once I got past the reservation to entertain and contemplate those evil thoughts, entertaining and contemplating them became easy. It was no longer taboo to envision Melissa lying in a pool of her own blood somewhere in the privacy of our house. My biggest concern was figuring out how to get away with the crime.

Curtis, she drove you to this point. She drove you to it! It doesn't matter how much you give her; she is never satisfied. She's spending all of your money. She is devious and vindictive towards you. I think she is on drugs. Large amounts of cash keep disappearing, and no one knows what she's doing with the money. Melissa has been using you. She doesn't love you anymore. I would hear these thoughts in my head constantly during this period. I had to keep repeating them in my head to suppress my guilt. In conjunction with thinking these thoughts, I would keep rehearsing the murder over and over again in my mind to make sure every detail was pinned down.

It's Thursday night, a perfect night to do it. Let me position myself, I thought. I went and got my gloves ready. *Let me practice holding the hammer and swinging it.* Took me over thirty minutes to properly hold the hammer in my deformed hands. Once I got the hang of it, I positioned the hammer under the bed where I could easily access it once the time came.

It was 10:20 pm when Melissa finally came home. I heard her turning the corner and pulling into the driveway. Moments later, I heard her key unlocking the front door. Melissa was home. "Curtis, are you in?!" she asked upon entering the house.

"I'm in the bedroom," I answered.

Melissa entered the bedroom with a pleasant look on her face. I remember her smile. She came and sat next to me on the bed and then planted a big, juicy kiss on the side of my face seemingly for no reason. Then she asked me if I wanted something to eat. I told her I would like a sandwich. She fixed me something to eat first and then jumped in the shower. After her shower, I started to rub her down with some Victoria's Secret Sweet Temptation body lotion. After a few minutes, Melissa began to wind down. She climbed into the bed. I turned some love music on the radio. About ninety minutes later, Melissa was sound asleep. I wanted to make sure she was completely asleep first before carrying out my plan, so I turned on the television just to see if it would startle her or she'd respond to the noise. She didn't respond to the noise. I put on the rubber gloves. I then retrieved the hammer from under the bed and placed it in my lap. At that moment, I slowly rolled my wheelchair closer to the side of the bed where Melissa was sound asleep and then locked it in position. Just like I had practiced, I positioned the hammer in my hands, holding it firmly; I then lifted the hammer above my head, ready to strike the side of Melissa's head when then the hammer slipped out of my hands and fell onto the floor. The heavy thud of the hammer against the floor woke Melissa up out of her sleep. She immediately jumped up on the bed, alarmed. She then looked at me. She then looked down at the floor beside my wheelchair and noticed the hammer laying on the floor. She noticed the plastic gloves on my hands. At that moment, Melissa just stared at me with a look of fear and disbelief while slowly scooting away from me. Her eyes were as wide as an owl's. "Curtis, what in the hell is going on?" she asked while moving away from me. "What are you doing with a hammer in our bedroom?"

"Nothing, baby. I saw it sticking out from under the bed, and I was going to take it back down to the den where the construction workers' other tools are."

"You going to hit me with that hammer?" Melissa asked with tears streaming down her face.

"No, baby!"

"You trying to kill me?!"

"No, baby!"

"Where did that hammer come from?!" she asked, grabbing her housecoat and squeezing it tight.

"I was trying to pick it up and put it back in the den, baby," I said moving towards her and wrapping my arms around her. She was shaking with fear. "I'm sorry, baby, that I woke you up trying to pick the hammer up. It just slipped out of my hand. You know that I don't have any grip due to the accident."

"I don't know, Curtis. It seemed like you were trying to do some harm to me."

"No, baby. I love you too much to do that," I said while holding her in my arms. She had her back pressed against my chest while I pressed my face next to hers. Her heart was beating extremely fast. I was glad that she wasn't looking directly into my eyes because they would have easily betrayed my words. I just kept on saying sweet things to her and rubbing all over her the whole time. I embraced her for the next four hours. While holding her, I kept thinking about the whole thing. "Damn! Why did that hammer fall out my hand?! I blew it!" I thought to myself. I was so angry at myself, I could barely sleep that night...and neither could Melissa.

CHAPTER 25

AS IF THINGS COULDN'T GET ANY WORSE

THE NEXT DAY, MELISSA OPENED HER EYES BRIGHT and early. She appeared as if she hadn't slept any that night. She had heavy bags under her eyes, which were red due to sleep deprivation. I awoke with a purpose. I had a plan. First, I needed to convince Melissa that she was in no danger being with me; that I loved her and would never attempt to harm her. Ever so present was the fear of having my financial world swept out from under my feet by an angry wife. I could sense the fear and nervousness she felt being around me. The tension in the room between us was palpable.

That morning, Melissa chose not to go to work due to exhaustion from not getting any sleep. She didn't want to go into the office looking how she was looking.

I tried to play it cool, but the tension in the house was making it very uncomfortable for me to hang around, so I decided that I needed to get out of there. I then called one of my associates, Willie, to come over and pick me up. I figured that Melissa was going to go to her mother's house and spend some time over there. My only concern was that she might inform her mother of what had happened the night before, which I hoped she wouldn't.

In the upcoming weeks, things around the house seemed to be returning to normal although Melissa and I sensed that things were different. We realized that things would never return to the way they were between us. We would speak to each other, but there was always a hint of suspicion in our eyes; and now, a suspicion of mine was about to be confirmed.

It was the weekend, and Melissa was preparing to go away for the Army Reserves. This was good for me as it would allow me to catch up on some things I needed to do. Melissa was in the shower on this particular morning. I was waiting for Willie to come by to pick me up and take me to my therapy classes. The doorbell rang, and it was Willie. I began making my way down the hallway towards the front door at that moment. While moving towards the door, I hollered back at Melissa who was still in the shower and told her I was gone for the day. I then made my way into the kitchen, heading towards the door; but once I reached the kitchen, I noticed Melissa's handbag lying on the tabletop. For the first time, she left her bag in a position where I could actually reach it. I wanted to retrieve my set of keys from her, so I grabbed her purse and began going through it quickly, looking for my keys. I found the keys, but that wasn't all I found. I also found an envelope with several hundred dollar bills in it, and I found several cards, one being a Father's Day card for my dad; but then, I noticed there was another card there with the name Toney on it. This card had a gold seal on it with the initial "L." I picked up that card and left.

While at the YMCA for therapy classes, my mind couldn't focus on therapy. I couldn't stop thinking about that envelope with the money in it and the card with the name Toney handwritten on it. After I finished my workout, I went to the restroom to change my catheter; and while there, I pulled the mysterious letter from my backpack to begin reading it. When I opened the letter, this is what I read:

To my love, Toney. We've been blessed with each other's love and friendship. Neither one, nor any card I've ever found, nor any words I've ever written, can express the changes you've wrought in my life. I can't wait until we're as one. Everything is going according to plan. Just hang in there with me. Curtis is very analytical and bullheaded. I must do this very quickly. He don't know about the money yet. Thank you for being my lover and my friend. I trust you so completely. I look forward to our tomorrows. I love you with all my heart.

Melissa

After reading this, I felt empty inside. It felt like all of my energy drained out of me. I couldn't believe Melissa had an affair behind my back. *How long had this affair been taking place?* I wondered. I began to feel rage rise up inside of me. I became outraged at the thought of Melissa's betrayal. When I met Willie in the waiting area, he could see it all over my face. "What's wrong?" he asked. I handed him the letter. He read it. While reading it, he kept shaking his head in disbelief. At that time, I picked up a phone and gave Mrs. Battle (Melissa's mom) a call.

"Hello! Mrs. Battle, your daughter, is a DEAD JEZEBEL by five o'clock!!" Then I slammed the phone on the hook and told Willie to drive me to Melissa's job. We arrived at Melissa's job within twenty minutes. When we got there, I asked Willie to go inside of the building and tell Melissa to come to the car; I wanted to confront her about this letter. Willie went inside of the building to get Melissa, but he left out of the building accompanied by a man in a suit who then approached the car window and said,

"Mr. Lovejoy, we don't want any altercations to take place here." Melissa had been informed of my intentions before I arrived by her mother apparently. Not only did the man come out to stop me from confronting Melissa, but I heard police sirens in the background getting louder as officers drew near. Five police cars suddenly arrived on the scene. Officers then got out of their cars and surrounded me. Just then, one of the police officers approached me and said,

"I know that you and your wife are having some marriage issues right now, but we don't want anything to escalate. We're hoping that there is some resolution that can take place today."

"You acting like I'm the one who is going to do something to her!" I responded to the officer. "That isn't the case! You see that damn wheelchair in the back seat?! That's my wheelchair! Look at my hand! Look at it! Why don't you try to shake my hand?! Go ahead! I won't bite you! I was paralyzed from the neck down! All I want is for my wife to come to this car and give me an explanation about this card! Why don't you read the card! Perhaps you'll see the big picture!" I then handed the officer the card, which he read. After reading it, he informed me that he was going to get Melissa and bring her to the car. The officer returned to the car with Melissa. She was crying as if she was in great distress, which I interpreted as an act. Then I questioned her: "Explain this card! Who in the hell is Toney?! You want to be with him?! You love him?!"

"Um. Listen, Curtis. I think that you're receiving this wrong. Toney is just a friend."

"A friend?! That card doesn't say that!"

"I see right now that you're upset with me. This is what my attorney suggests we do . . ."

"What you mean by 'What we should do?!' He doesn't speak for me!"

"He wants me to go by the house and get some of

my belongings and make sure that you're not there when that takes place."

"So you leaving me?"

"Yes, I am. It will be best for both of us. I want to drop by the house around 4 pm. Is that okay with you?"

Before I could say anything, one of the officers intervened and said, "Mr. Lovejoy, as an officer of the law, I would advise you to honor that request. Let her go by the house and get as much as she can. Please don't be there when she arrives. Her attorney gave her some solid advice, and we're witnesses to that fact." After that, Melissa simply walked away crying. "Mr. Willie," the officer continued, "please keep Mr. Lovejoy occupied and away from the house during the hours of 4 pm to 6 pm. I know that he is hurting right now, but separation will do them both good. Okay?"

I'll never forget that officer's name: it was Officer Ricky. After Melissa walked away, he placed his hand on top of mine, looked me straight in the eyes, and gave me these words of encouragement: "I don't know what triggered this problem, but I believe that GOD WILL ORDER YOUR STEPS. The picture doesn't look so good on your behalf because you suffered an accident that paralyzed you, but you can overcome all of what has happened if you just keep your eyes on the prize. Please do that for yourself. Because of your last name, you'll pay it off."

"What do you mean by that?" I asked.

"Brother, just give it time. Time heals everything." Part of me wanted to thank that officer for those words, but I was too angry at that moment. All I wanted to do was unleash my wrath on Melissa for her betrayal.

Willie and I left Melissa's job and drove around through downtown. While sitting in that passenger's seat, I felt numb, bitter, sad, angry; it felt like I was dreaming. I was hoping it was all a dream and that someone would wake me up. I felt like I was trapped in a very long night; as if daylight would never arrive. I then asked Willie to take me to my mother's house; there, I would always find hope, strength, guidance, and comfort when in a tough situation. I just needed to hear my mother's voice.

When I arrived at my mother's house, my mom asked me if I wanted something to eat. Normally, I would jump at the opportunity to receive a home-cooked meal from her. Her fried chicken was to die for. But this time, I didn't have an appetite. Still, she insisted that I eat so that I wouldn't get weak. Mom could sense that I was in dire need of strength. She always seemed to know exactly what I needed even when I didn't communicate with her what was going wrong with me. "Mom, WHY ME?!!" I cried.

"Why not you, Joe?" she responded firmly. "God knows what's best for you. This situation happened for a reason. God wants all of you, not just half of you."

"But she was cheating on me with another guy! I don't deserve this!"

"I know, baby. I know. You're hurting right now. It's going to hurt. You must see yourself through it. It's going to take time. You need time to deal with the hurt, and you need time to put it behind you. It won't happen overnight." She continued, "You'll need to learn from your mistakes. Don't just put it all on her, Joe. You have fallen short as well."

"But mom, she's trying to take away from me everything I achieved," I said, referring to my concern over Melissa's handling of my accounts.

"Son, don't worry about materialistic things. God can bless you just like He did Job. He can give you seven times what you lost. But you both must repent for your sins. God can restore you both. Both of you were young and in-love and made some silly mistakes. Marriage isn't something you can dip in and out of. God ordained marriage. Mrs. Battle called me and asked me if I talked to you yet. She claimed that something was wrong with you and Melissa."

"I hate Melissa!!" I yelled.

"You're just upset right now. But you can't make it into the Kingdom (of Heaven) feeling like that. You need to repent for that as well. Mrs. Battle is probably waiting for Melissa to come home so she can give her the same advice I'm giving you because she loves the Lord with all her heart. Joe, the truth is supposed to hurt, but God's Word must cut like a two-edged sword. YOU BOTH ARE WRONG! It will probably get worse before it gets better. Just don't think or say bad things about her. Just let it go. You should want the best for her since it didn't work out for you all."

"But mom, that's hard to do," I said.

"That's when you ask for forgiveness. It is one of the hardest things for a person to do, but if you're born again, it's easy!" she replied. While mom was talking, everything she was saying was registering with me. She was telling the truth. At the time, I had only focused on Melissa's act of betrayal while forgetting about my betrayal of her trust. I needed reminding of the fact that I wasn't guiltless in the situation. While mom was talking, I then decided that it was time to get something off of my chest that I had been holding on to for far too long. I knew that I couldn't start the process of healing while remaining dishonest with myself and with others. It was time to come clean so that I could clear my conscience and start fresh.

"Mom, I must confess something."

"What is it? I've heard some awful things, so I believe you won't surprise me because once the devil steps in, he wants to drive. So what do you want to tell me?"

"Please brace yourself," I warned. "Three months ago, I tried to kill Melissa by hitting her in the head with a hammer while she was asleep, but the hammer fell out of my hands, and she woke up."

"Boy, what the hell got in you?!" mom hollered while shocked. "Bring me that [anointing] oil over there on the table! I need to anoint my hands and lay them on you because you need Jesus! Shut your mouth!! I don't want to hear no more!" Then mom turned to Willie and asked him, "Willie, did you know that?"

"No, ma'am," he replied, shocked himself. Mom began praying for me. As she prayed, the anger, the rage, and resentment began to melt away. Mom had to strike me hard with the truth of my own wrongdoing, and confront me with the truth behind my actions. I was under an influence, a demonic one, which up until that point that was completely irrational, selfish, and ambitiously in pursuit of destruction. I could see that now. At this point, it was no longer about Melissa; it was about the darkness in my own heart that needed to be expunged by the light of God's truth and glory.

God was protecting me while Satan was trying to kill me in every way. He even protected me from me. He kept me just long enough to see the face of the devil and to surrender my heart, which had departed from God, back to God. Mom's words and prayers washed over my soul like the waters of a shower. It was now time to make my way back to the presence of God. Before then, it had not dawned on me that my departure from Him invited such darkness into my soul. I had to repent, which I did.

After mom finished talking to me and praying for me, I hit her with one last request: "Please fill dad in and the family, but don't tell Rosa Lee what happened. You know that she doesn't get along with Melissa. That will set her off."

"Don't worry about your sisters and brothers. I'll handle them all."

"But mom, I'm worried about Rosa Lee."

"Don't worry, Curtis. Big Momma will take care of everything. Now, you look like you been missing some meals. Get over there in the kitchen and let me fry you up some chicken."

CHAPTER 26
A NEW LOVE

I DECIDED THAT IT WOULD SERVE ME BEST TO GET OUT of town for a few days so that I could clear my head, so I went down to Savannah, Georgia, to spend some time with Lynda. While there, Lynda and her father, Mr. Gore, took a load off of my shoulders. It was good seeing their faces.

Mr. Gore wanted Lynda and me to travel down to Hilton Head, South Carolina with him to check on his father, Papa Gore. Papa Gore suffered a stroke, which left him hospitalized. But Papa Gore was a very independent man. He didn't want to depend on anyone to help him after his stroke. He rehabilitated himself and built his own ramp to his house. He continued to cook, mow his lawn, and take care of himself using only his right arm. And he was 86 years old. Seeing all that Papa Gore was able to accomplish on his own after experiencing a stroke on the left side of his body inspired me to stop complaining about my situation.

When I first saw Papa Gore, I felt concerned for him considering his handicap. I remember asking him, "Where's your girlfriend?" I'd already been made aware of the fact that he was a widow. I also figured that he had someone new in his life as a companion. He responded,

"She doesn't stay here. If you let them move in, they'll want to change the whole house around." His response tickled me, revealing to me just how headstrong he was. He then continued, "I'm at peace. Don't have to deal with mood swings. If I get lonely, I'll make a telephone call and my little sugar momma, she'll make her way over here, and she'll warm up my bed, help me to release my stress, cook me breakfast, and I'll give her a little money for her time. No questions asked. That's the way I like it. No headache."

After meeting Papa Gore for the first time, I could understand why Mr. Gore wanted me to travel with him to meet him. Papa Gore was an interesting person. Set in his ways, he was determined to live and not allow anything to hold him down. He refused to lie down and die and have pity on himself. I needed to see that type of resolve during this time in my life.

I spent several days with Papa Gore, listening to him share wisdom and insights into life. He would talk to me about women especially. "I discovered during my lifetime on this earth," Papa Gore mentioned, "that man will never understand a woman because they don't know why they do what they do at times. Set in their ways and if you try to figure them out, you'll lose your head. That's why the Man above have let me live so long."

Probably most impactful were Papa Gore's words to me about life. He took time to explain to me the things that have helped him to balance his life. Just like a father, Papa Gore took to me. In a sense, he nurtured me back to a state of mental and emotional health. He'd always tell me that I was going to be alright and that I just needed to be patient. Of course, his advice to me regarding Melissa was to forgive her, to let go of the anger and malice in my heart towards her, and realize that if I didn't do so, I would never be able to move forward in my own life.

Papa Gore's advice was rugged, raw, unfiltered in a sense. He didn't hold back the punches; he felt no need to hold back. Some of his advice wouldn't necessarily be good material for a Sunday morning service, but like a farmer who tosses the chaff into the wind and keeps that which is edible, I knew how to do just that. I realized that it would take time for my heart to heal, but my time spent with Papa Gore helped to expedite that process.

I was still attending sex therapy classes. At first, Melissa was attending them with me, but after a few classes, she stopped going; I then started taking a young lady named Saundra with me to the classes. Saundra was a lady from my church. One day, Saundra asked me if I would go down to Sarasota, Florida with she and her friend Tracy, a PT, to visit a friend of hers who invited her there for the weekend. She asked me if I needed permission from Melissa to go. I answered no and stated that I was ready to leave at that moment. I could use a break from the craziness, from Melissa. I hit the road with Saundra and Tracy. While on the road, I began to think about my life again. *All kind of questions began running through my head: What will my life be like years from now? Will I ever be able to go back to work? How long will I have to deal with workman's compensation? Will I ever be able to attract the right woman in my life? Will my family be able to accept my disability and my new way of life? Can I truly pick-up* the broken pieces of my life and move forward? While I was pondering these questions in my head I began to feel the temptation to have a pity party; but then, the thought that came to my head was, *I have to keep moving forward. Even without knowing what the future holds, I have to keep going.*

The next day, Tracy approached me and asked if *I would go* with her to a dolphin show there in Sarasota. Why not? I thought to myself. Between the war raging within me and the chaos surrounding me, it would be a good idea to experience something new, to be a little adventurous; so I went with her to the show. While there, we were seated in the wheelchair section. The place was packed. The master of the ceremony came out and began to introduce the dolphins. There were five dolphins: four dolphins and one main dolphin named Sheba who was the star of the show. Watching those dolphins began to do something inside of me. They were so majestic and amazing to watch. I marveled as they moved with such energy through the water and then leapt into the air with great force, reaching incredible heights. I sat there by that pool like a big kid; my mouth wide open in astonishment; my eyes stretched wide; anxiously anticipating every move the dolphins made, their every leap. I found myself transfixed by the moment, oblivious to everyone and everything that was around me. I was truly mesmerized. The cunningness of the dolphins amazed me. The way they responded immediately to the commands of the master of ceremony fascinated me. After a while, I couldn't resist the urge to interact with the dolphins, so I rolled closer to the side of the tank and tapped on the glass to see if I could get their attention. One of the dolphins actually came over to me. I can tell it was laughing as it wiggled its head from side to side. It was so playful, so jovial. At that point, while the dolphin was moving its head from side to side, I began to imitate its movements. The dolphin just froze in place and began watching me as if it was amazed or shocked. Both of us began to interact with one another. I no longer remembered my disability. I no longer remembered that I was even in a wheelchair. I found myself immersed in an entirely different world.

While watching that spectacle, I was taken aback when the ringmaster jumped into the water and grabbed Sheba's fin and held on to it as she carried him down to the bottom of the tank before bringing him back up after several seconds. The ringmaster then jumped on Sheba's back and held on for the ride as Sheba swam on top of the water. Afterward, the ringmaster fed Sheba some

fish as a treat. It seemed like the two of them had a wonderful, even spiritual, connection. Sheba knew just when
the ringmaster needed air. The two shared an incredible
sense of trust. I began to think about the connection
between the ringmaster and that dolphin had—that was
something I longed for desperately in my life. I was so
zoned out and lost in my thoughts; I didn't even hear
Tracy calling my name trying to get my attention. "Curtis, are you are having fun?" she asked me.

"Uhm, I'm sorry, Tracy. My thoughts were in another place. I can't believe what I see right now. I would
love to experience that and have that close relationship
with those dolphins. Tracy, I wonder if I could touch or
rub the dolphins?"

"Well, there's nothing wrong with asking," Tracy
responded. Tracy and I then decided to wait patiently for
the show to end so that we could talk to the ringmaster
to see if I would be able to interact in the water with the
dolphins. Tracy went over and talked to the ringmaster
and staff after the show, and she began to tell them about
me and my situation. After a few minutes, both Tracy
and the ringmaster started walking towards me with big
smiles on their faces. Then Tracy introduced me to the
ringmaster whose name was Rob.

"Curtis, Tracy tells me that she brought you all
the way down here from Atlanta to see Sheba. She had to
fool you to get you here. So you want to touch Sheba?"
asked Rob.

"Yes, I do. Can I?" I asked him.

"Let me ask you a question," Rob said. "Can you

hold your breath for twenty seconds?"

"I think I can. I can do that."

"I tell you what: Tracy is going to take you to our dressing room to put you on a wet-suit, then you and I are going to get in the tank with Sheba."

"Are you for real?"

"Yes, I am," Rob responded. I started praying secretly for God not to let me drown. I was afraid of water. My heart was beating really fast.

The staff placed me on the side of the tank on a bench. Rob then called Sheba over and introduced her to me. I was a little afraid, hoping and praying to myself that she'd like me. I gently rubbed her face with small strokes. Then all of a sudden, Sheba began laughing and wiggling her head playfully. She then plunged under the water. "Keep your eyes on Sheba," Rod said. While under the water, Sheba began picking up speed; then she began swimming to the top. After reaching the top, Sheba leaped out of the water about 10 feet into the air. When she landed back into the water, she swam over to where I was and rested her nose under my hand. "She likes you," Rob said. I started rubbing her while talking to her. "Are you ready to go for a ride?" asked Rob. I had warmed up to Sheba and the water by now. I answered, "Yes."

The staff gave me a pair of goggles to put on, then two of the team members placed me into the tank. Rob was close by telling me, "Don't be afraid! Just hold on to the fin and don't let go!"

"But Rob, how will Sheba know when to bring

me up for air?!" I asked.

"Curtis, she'll know! She can also feel your heart beating at the same time! Just trust her!"

When I grabbed hold of Sheba's fin, she took off. She pulled me around the tank on the top of the water very slowly. I started looking down into the water to see how deep it was. I was nervous. But then, Sheba took me down under the water. While underwater, I was holding my breath; my heart was beating so fast. Sheba was sensitive enough to realize I was nervous, so she made sure not to go too fast initially; but then, after she brought me back to the surface so that I could catch my breath, she took me back into the water; and this time, she went a little bit deeper and moved a little bit faster. After this, Sheba brought me back to the top where the team members were waiting to retrieve me and help me out of the water. They sat me back on the bench on the side of the tank. Then Sheba came over towards me. Rob gave me some fish to toss into her mouth. After feeding Sheba the fish, I started stroking her again, and this time she began nodding her head at me while laughing and doing the moonwalk.

Before Tracy and I left, Rob had Sheba perform one more trick for us. He held a hula-hoop about 5 feet in the air the water, and he had Sheba to jump through it. This was the most exciting moment, even more, exciting than the moment that I first got up out of my wheelchair and began walking while holding on to the parallel bars in the hospital. That day was life-changing for me because it allowed me to be introduced to a whole new world—an aquatic world, which I would soon refer to as my home away from home.

That night, I could barely sleep. My mind no longer played scenes of torment, and the accident, nor did it ponder questions about my future and my handicap; all I could think about, the only thing that became my obsession, was getting back into the water. All I desired was to get in a pool somewhere, anywhere, just so that I could relive that exhilarating experience Sheba had given me. I could still feel the water on my skin, the euphoric rush as Sheba carried me into the deep, and the tranquility that awaited me at the surface of the water. It was as if I had undergone a religious experience. I had been baptized and emerged a new man. Left at the bottom of that tank was all of the fear, the hurt, the pain, the sorrow, the grief, and the depression I had suffered. Of all of God's creation, a dolphin taught me how to laugh again, how to smile again, how to enjoy life again; it taught me how to leave the past behind me and leap into the great unknown. That dolphin helped me to forget all about my problems; actually, it caused me to discover my new passion and hidden strength of mine. I was now in love with the water. That's all I longed for when I got back to Atlanta. That would become my world now.

CHAPTER 27
WHAT'S WRONG WITH ME?

I WAS IN THE MIDST OF A DIVORCE AND A LEGAL FIGHT with Church's Fried Chicken at the same time. On September 15, 1987, I had received divorce papers from the Atlanta Sheriff's Department; and at the same time, CFC didn't want to deal with me fairly regarding worker's compensation, so I had to hire a lawyer to negotiate with them on my behalf. They offered me around $275,000 as a settlement, but I explained to my lawyer that nothing short of one million dollars would suffice. They had to take into account my medical bills, my living expenses, the fact that behind my accident I lost my marriage, etc. The amount of money they were offering wasn't enough for me to make it on. Still, in the midst of all of this, I found an escape in the swimming pool. My new love afforded me the relief I so desperately needed

251

from the chaos swirling all around me every day.

The Shepherd Center's Therapeutic Recreation Department introduced various sports teams to me, trying to find out which one would fit. The swimming pool was therapeutic, and they thought that swimming would be good for me. I was excited about the swimming team. I inquired about scuba diving despite not knowing how to swim yet. I was eager to learn how to swim ever since I had developed a sudden love of the water following my trip to Florida.

I signed up for scuba diving classes. No one mentioned to me that I needed some swimming ability before I signed up. I thought that scuba diving consisted of putting on an oxygen mask and jumping into the water. During the class, we did classwork. After finishing the classwork, we headed to the pool when the instructor asked me to get in the water. He noticed that I was hesitant to get in so he asked me, "Curtis, can you swim?"

"No," I responded.

"Then why did you sign-up [for this class] knowing you don't know how to swim? I tell you what, I'll work with you, and if you can't float within the next three days, I'll refund your money back. Deal?"

"Yes."

God knows, I drunk a lot of H^2O over those three days, but I learned how to float and hold my breath.

I took my first snorkel in March of 1988 at West Palm Beach and took my first dive in the Florida Keys. I was both optimistic and a little afraid during this time.

Just looking at all of that water made me nervous,

but I knew that if I kept calm and remained relaxed, then everything would work out just fine. My mind was at ease, at peace. I was in good company—other Quads and instructors surrounded me.

While in the swimming program, my body began to shape up. My muscles were beginning to develop, and it was quite noticeable. Everyone could see the definition in my muscles. I also became more health conscious and learned to pay more attention to my body. I was now leg-pressing 185 lbs and bench-pressing 210 lbs. I was also receiving therapy from a woman named Cheryl who had me walking for ten minutes on the treadmill. I was then assigned a swimming coach named Cecilia who gave me one-on-one swimming lessons. The water would loosen up my tight muscles. Cecilia consulted with a professional bodybuilder named Billy regarding developing a specific workout program for me. Cheryl assembled a great team around me.

Not a day would go by when my mind didn't revisit the time I spent in the water with Sheba. I couldn't stop dreaming of swimming after that day. Never had I swam before, nor held my face under water until the day I met Sheba. Some people said I was crazy to ride on the back of Sheba, but I didn't care. That experience changed me. And the more time I spent in the water, the more I could think clearly; the more relaxed I had become; the less stressed and more happy I was, and no one could get me down. While in the water, I would get new revelations in my mind about life. That was my place of meditation.

One day, while at the YMCA, I met a lady named Gene. She was diagnosed as a hemiplegic (a stroke victim)—she could only use one side of her body. Her left arm and elbow were bent and pressing against her chest. She was able to swim using only one side of her body, streaming through the water like a fish. Half of her body remained out of the water the whole time, including her face; and yet, she kept the perfect buoyancy. One day, I introduced myself to her and I asked her a few questions about swimming. She was glad to give me some advice on how to swim better. I asked her how long she swam each day. She said she'd swim for about two miles every day, which would take her about two hours to complete. I decided to pattern my routine after hers and shoot for a similar goal.

I had to fire my attorney representing me on my worker's compensation case and find another. My new attorney was Mr. John Sweetlow. He seemed like a firm, no-nonsense guy. The divorce proceedings were still taking place, so I was dealing with that situation also. But it was official: Melissa and I were done. I began spending a lot of time thinking about things. At times, I'd be happy; other times, depression would hit me. One day, Lynda and I decided to hang out. We went shopping earlier that day; then we ran a few errands before heading off to dinner. Later on, after arriving back at her place, we sat outside on the patio looking up at the moon and enjoying each other's warmth.

CHAPTER 27: WHAT'S WRONG WITH ME?

Right then, it started to get *hot*—and I'm not referring to the weather either. I was definitely in the mood, and so was Lynda. It was off to the bedroom for us. Truthfully, I was ready when I first saw her. We quickly began taking off our clothes, ready to make mad, passionate love. Suddenly, while undressing, something happened: I felt lethargic and was no longer in the mood. I simply lost all of my energy. My entire countenance changed. Lynda sensed the change. At that moment, I started putting my clothes back on. Then she gently took me by the hand and asked, "What's wrong?"

"I got to go," I said.

"Did I cross your religious line?"

"No. It's not you. It's me. I can't explain it," I told Lynda. For whatever reason, I just shut down. I couldn't get in the mood. I didn't know what was happening to me. I had never experienced that before. Something wouldn't let me do it that night. After I left Lynda's place, I thought about that experience the entire drive home.

A week later, I took Demonna out to lunch at the Boston Seafood Restaurant. After lunch, did some shopping. Demonna began inquiring about my mom. So I decided to take her over to my mom's house. My mom and Demonna were having an interesting conversation when I suddenly noticed Lynda's car pulling into my mom's driveway. She decided to stop by unexpectedly. I was stuck and didn't know how I was going to get out of this one. I quickly went over to Demonna and said to her, "Your name is Helen," and then began rolling towards the front door. Both Demonna and my mom were looking at me strangely, trying to figure out what was going on and why I was behaving so weird. Suddenly, the doorbell rang. I answered the door. It was Lynda standing there, asking to come in. She said she just wanted to stop by to check on me since she had not heard from me since the last time we were together. My mom was looking. Demonna was looking. Busted, I couldn't do anything else but introduce the two women I had been secretly seeing to one another. The cat was now out of the bag. "Lynda, meet Helen. Helen, this is Lynda," I said. Both ladies looked at each other, but they didn't get angry or violent with one another; it was more like an awareness that they were both being played and were both victims. They were polite and cordial with one another, but I could sense the deep hurt in their hearts; I could sense the disappointment in my mother's heart as well. I knew I had messed up. There was a brief silence in the room. Lynda then went and sat down in a chair and started talking to my mom. Demonna decided that she needed to leave, so I escorted her to the front door. Once we got to the door, she punched me in the ear and said,

"How dare you disrespect me like that! If your mother wasn't present, I would push you out of that damn wheelchair! I'll never forgive you! Don't ever call me again!"

Lynda and mom continued to talk after Demonna left, and for nearly thirty minutes my ear continued to ring. I couldn't hear out of it. I headed to my bedroom feeling embarrassed. A few minutes later, Lynda came to my bedroom. She had a look of great disappointment on her face. She asked me what was wrong with me, but I couldn't face her. I just sat quiet, retreating into my shell, attempting to tune her and everyone else out. Lynda just stared out of the window at that point, continuing to say hurtful things and express her feelings at the moment. I didn't say a word. She then went over to my dresser and started going through all my mail and papers. She found a card given to me. After reading it without my awareness, she asked, "Who is Sandy B.?"

"What are you talking about?"

"She says that she loves you."

"You have no reason to be reading my cards," I responded. "Sandy was my nurse at the Shepherd's Center."

"So you and she got a thing going on, too?"

"No. There is more than one card saying that they love me. I'm not going to try to explain it to you because you'll never understand. You're taking it out of context," I said. At that, Lynda didn't say anything; instead, she angrily got up and left out of the room, slamming the door behind her. She simply acknowledged my mom before leaving. After Lynda left, I grabbed the phone and attempted to call Demonna so that I could try to explain to her everything that was going on in hopes that she'd forgive me, but she never answered her phone. I left her several messages, but she never returned my calls.

After both Demonna and Lynda left, that's when mom's voice ranged through the house: "Joe! Come here! I need to talk to you!" I knew I was in trouble; still in hot water. "Now, Joe, you can't go around changing a person's name. That is degrading and very low-down for anyone to do. I can imagine what Demonna is feeling right now. Just tell the truth. You're not hiding anything." I just sat and listened, taking it all in. "Did you forget that Lynda was coming over?" she asked.

"No. Lynda came without my knowledge."

"You must be sleeping with both of them?"

"No," I lied.

"Boy, don't start lying to me. I had you. I had those same problems with your father before we married. One night, he came over and fell asleep. I then tied his hands and feet to the bedpost, then I woke him up while sitting on top of him with a butcher's knife to his throat, and I told him he had better get his act together. 'If you ever disrespect me, floating and tipping out on me or having an affair with another woman, I'll cut your penis off!' I told him. Do you read me loud and clear?! And like a baby, he said yes. So far, he still has his penis intact. I've shared that with only you, keep it to yourself!"

"Yes, momma."

"I pray and hope that she (Demonna) forgives you. If she deep down inside loves you, she will. But you'll pay for it. Now, on the other hand, Lynda won't be that calm and nice like Demonna. That girl will take you to your grave quickly. She will kill first and then regret it later...because you made her snap. In the court of law, she will walk away as having committed self-defense. You can't play with a woman's emotions; it will always get the best of you, and a woman always got the power over a man. If anybody tells you something different, they're trying to fool you. The only chance a man has to overcome that power is through the grace of God. THE WAGES OF SIN IS DEATH, Joe, but through God is eternal life!" It all made sense what my mom was saying. I knew she was telling the truth. She added, "Joe, I knew when you were three years old that you would have women problems. You attract women to you. But you'll learn to walk away and avoid smiling at every woman you see. Both of the girls are in love with you and you know it, but you won't choose which one. You can't have your cake and ice cream with the two. You must make a decision and choose one. It's better to learn early in life. But don't mess with fire or you will get burned!"

"Yes, momma."

I couldn't wait to get back into the pool over the next few days—that was my sanctuary; that was also the place where I could think and reflect on my life. Swimming gave me the time to do a little soul-searching. While in the pool one day, I began to reflect back over everything my mom said. I thought about the many times I played with fire and nearly got burned. I thought about the time when I was in college, and I was messing with this one lady—I was over at her house getting ready to have sex with her when her man came home. Thankfully, my legs were working then, so it was easy for me to jump out of the window and escape; but had I been in a wheelchair at the time, someone would have found my body in one location and my wheelchair in another, and I would have been on the six o'clock news that day. I began to think about all of the reckless decisions I made in my life, and I knew I needed to get it together. If I didn't get it together, the *next time* might be fatal.

One Tuesday morning, I was sitting at home getting ready to watch one of my favorite talk shows, *The Oprah Winfrey Show*. Interestingly enough, the topic for the day was divorce and the challenges of moving after having one. At that moment, the thought ran through my mind, "Melissa isn't getting a damn thing from me. She can have her name back." At the exact moment that I thought that the doorbell rang. When I looked out the window, I noticed a police car in my driveway. *This can't be good*, I thought. I opened the door; two male officers were standing there. One of the officers had an angry expression on his face while clutching the gun at his side. "How may I help you?" I asked.

"We're here to serve you your divorce and alimony papers!" the angry officer said.

"What do you mean by alimony?! I don't have any kids!" I responded. The angry officer then hollered,

"You need to take care of your damn children!"

"No! You need to keep your damn nose out of my business! If you're here to serve me papers, then do so and get the hell off of my property!" I hollered back.

"Who do you think you are talking to like that?!" the officer responded.

"If you want respect from me, then you need to show it, not stand there judging me, especially when you don't know what's going on! Got your hand on your piece like I'm going to take-off running. Don't you know I'm in a wheelchair?!" The other officer told him to chill. He then asked me for my ID. *Today isn't my day*, I thought to myself.

After the officers left, all kind of thoughts began to go through my mind. Melissa was filing for mental cruelty, for alimony, and she was running up credit card charges at different stores: Victoria's Secret, Fredericks of Hollywood, Saks Fifth Avenue, etc. I regretted not taking the advice of my lawyer and canceling the credit cards when she told me to. It was starting to eat me alive when thinking about what Melissa was doing to me. Undoubtedly, she was trying to get back at me for the things I had done to her. She was certainly getting the better of me. I picked up the phone and called a friend of mine, Bernard Parham. (Back in 1978, I gave Bernard his first job right out of high school and guided him along the track to becoming a manager himself.) I began to vent to him what was on my mind, telling him I should have finished what I set out to do to Melissa, which was to kill her. Of course, he tried to talk me out of it and get me to calm down, but I kept going, even getting to the point where I asked him if he had a gun that I could use. My way to deal with Melissa, I said, was to take her out. I hated her. The thought of her started to make my skin crawl. He encouraged me to calm down. He told me to talk to my mom about how I was feeling and reminded me that I wouldn't be able to overcome Melissa's attacks through hatred and revenge; but I instead needed to follow Jesus' approach and fight hatred with love and learn to turn the other cheek, and to simply trust God to fight my battle. His words were playing in my mind, but so were those dark thoughts. Eventually, I started to calm down and collect myself, realizing that he was correct. I wouldn't be able to win this battle on my own and with violence and anger. A light switch came on in my mind as Bernard was talking. It dawned on me the whole point about trusting God. This is what I began to think about in my meditation time, the epiphany that hit me:

> What do you do when you don't know what to do and when you're powerless to do anything about your situation? Put it in the hands of The One who can work a miracle in any situation. Put it in God's hands and leave it there. Just keep your heart clean and pure so that you can rest in His peace while He fight your battle. Your way only leads to death and destruction, but God has the ability to cause all things to work together for your good so that not only will the problem be resolved but you will benefit from it in the end. So give it to God rather than listen to Satan who is trying to get you to destroy yourself.

I had only two options: trust God and let him handle what I couldn't, or die from stress and bitterness. Dying from stress and bitterness wasn't going to change anything; therefore, I chose to go with option number one.

CHAPTER 28
COURTROOM SHOWDOWN

APRIL 25TH WAS A DAY I WILL NEVER FORGET. THIS was the day I was supposed to stand before the judge regarding my divorce case. Just a few days before my court appearance, I had to hire a new lawyer to defend me. My original lawyer, Anne Bennett, decided to resign for personal reasons, but she referred another lawyer to me, a man named Freddie Jackson. I was hoping Anne would remain on the case because she is female and she could provide a certain perspective during arguments in the courtroom, but I decided to take a chance on Mr. Jackson—it's not like I had time to shop around anyway.

On court day, I walked into the courtroom on my crutches. I was clean-shaven and well dressed. I was nervous but ready. I looked over at Melissa and noticed that she wasn't looking too good: her hair needed to be fixed, the clothes she had on weren't presentable, and she looked like she desperately needed some sleep. I also noticed that she had one of the best lawyers in the state of Georgia representing her, Mr. Bostic. I figured that I didn't stand a chance with Mr. Jackson. It didn't dawn on me at the time that Melissa was using her appearance to garner sympathy from the court, making it seem as if she was seriously struggling when she wasn't.

Mr. Bostic, in his opening statement, stated that his client, Mrs. Lovejoy, experienced mental abuse from me and put up with multiple extramarital affairs. He said she wanted all of her belongings in the house (a total of 35 items to be exact). She wanted monetary compensation for the next five years, she wanted the house, the BMW, she wanted me to pay for all of her court fees, she wanted the dog (Yes, even the dog!), and he mentioned that I had a total of $325,000 in assets. Mr. Jackson, my lawyer, when it was his turn to speak, mentioned that I was willing to return twenty-five of the thirty-five items requested by Melissa, and he explained that I was willing to give her the BMW and the dog, but not the house since it was especially modified for me due to my handicap. Lastly, my lawyer mentioned that I was unwilling to provide monetary support to Melissa since she was the one who left me. I tugged on Mr. Jackson and reminded him to present the card I found that Melissa wrote to another man revealing her plot to have an affair and manipulate money out of me. Mr. Jackson brought the card out and presented it as evidence of Melissa's intentions, but he didn't do a very good job of arguing on my behalf. It was as if he wasn't mentally invested in the case or at least concern about my interests. He wasn't convincing at all.

One thing that I noticed during the trial was the judge never once looked at me; he never once made eye contact with me. I could sense that things weren't looking too good for me. Suddenly, the judge began to speak. "Mr. Lovejoy," he said in a solemn tone, "this is what I require you to do." "You will pay Mrs. Melissa Lovejoy $400 in alimony per month for the next five years. You will return all thirty-five items back to her; you'll sell the house and give her half of the proceeds and pay her $25,000 from the equity in the house. You'll give her the BMW, she will go back to her maiden name; and by all means, please give her that dog!" My heart sunk into my chest. I then blurted out to the judge,

"You can give her the whole damn kitchen sink as far as I'm concerned!"

"What did you say?" the judge asked, offended.

"You can give her the whole damn kitchen sink as far as I'm concerned!" I shouted again.

"Mr. Lovejoy, you will respect my courtroom! If you cuss in this courtroom again, I'll hold you in contempt!"

"Your Honor, I've never been in jail a day in my life. If that makes you happy, then..."

"Curtis," Mr. Jackson butted in, cutting me off. "You need to calm down and be quiet."

"For what? I haven't done anything at all. I'm the

victim here, not her," I told Mr. Jackson.

"Mr. Freddie Jackson, I think that you need to escort your client out of my courtroom before I give him a night in jail! This order will take effect thirty-one days from today! That's my decision! If there is nothing else to be discussed, this court is adjourned!" I was furious. I was disappointed and confused. When I tried to stand and leave the courtroom, my spasms began to act up, making it impossible for me to move at that moment. My lawyer, in the meantime, was trying to convince me to accept the judge's decision, justifying his decisions using an argument that didn't quite make sense to me. I didn't want to hear him anyway.

"You didn't do a damn thing!" I yelled. "That was probably the worst court display from a lawyer I've seen in twenty years! Have you ever defended a divorce case before?!" I asked him.

"No. You're my first one," he replied.

"And Ms. Bennett recommended you? Wait until I talk to her. Well, you can forget that damn $500 because of a lack of experience."

After leaving out of the courtroom, I proceeded to the elevator; and while heading towards the elevator, I ran into Melissa; she was walking out of the restroom. She had a huge smile on her face. She then said, "I guess you thought that you were going to win. Another one bites the dust." I wanted to take one of my crutches and hit her over the head with it so badly; but instead, I told her,

"If you ever see me again on the street, you should

consider walking on the opposite side because it won't be a pretty sight!" The elevator door opened and she got on. I figured it was best for me to catch the next one to avoid being brought up on a new set of charges, namely assault or murder in a public elevator in the courthouse.

While in that courthouse, I felt like I was in *The Twilight Zone*. My mind was spinning, and I was in a daze. I was feeling nauseated. I finally reached the parking deck where a female sheriff asked me how everything went. "Not so good," I told her. The sheriff then hugged me and said,

"In the long run, she is the biggest loser."

"Why does it hurt so badly?" I asked her.

"You win some, and you lose some," she answered.

Everything was a blur at that moment. I wanted so desperately to end the nightmare. In my vehicle, I decided that I was going to end it all by suicide. I decided to press the gas pedal all the way to the floor, accelerating to a speed of 110 mph on the I-20 expressway westbound. While I was driving, I heard a voice speak to me just as clear as day. It said to me, "Don't do this. It's not worth it. Slow down." I looked in the rearview mirror to see if someone was in the backseat, but no one was there. I realized that it was a voice from heaven trying to spare me from making one of the biggest mistakes of my life. I slowed down and came to my senses and drove home safe and sound.

When I arrived at the house, I cried out to God and asked Him, "God, why weren't you inside the courtroom?!! Why?!!!" God spoke these words in my heart,

"I've always been with you. I was there when you were five years old when you almost fell from a second-floor apartment on Coleman Street. I was there at Park's Junior High School when that gunman chased you through that gymnasium, and I was there when you had your car accident. You think that you lost your legs; you just misplaced them."

A few hours had passed, and I was home all alone. While sitting in my home-office, I could vaguely hear someone calling my name, but I paid it no mind; I was zoned-out. Suddenly, my sister Rosa Lee entered the room and found me just sitting and staring through the window and up at the sky. I was so unresponsive that she had to shake me to snap me out of my daze. After finally getting my attention, she asked me why I was sitting alone in the dark with the phone off of the hook and the front door wide open. "Joe, how long have you been here?" she asked.

"Since I came from the divorce hearing around 4 o'clock. What time is it?"

"It's after 10 pm. I can see that her damn ass won."

"Yes, she did. The court wants me to pay her $500 a month for the next five years, sell the house, and give her half. What kind of BS is that?"

"Don't worry, baby brother. We'll take care of her when we see her."

"No, Rose. Just leave it alone. I want all of this to be over."

"Well, if she thinks that she is going to get away with hurting my brother, she got another damn thing coming. Do you want me to spend the night?"

"No. I'll be alright."

"Have you eaten today?"

"No. I'm not hungry."

"Well, let me see you to bed and I'll lock-up the house for you before I leave."

"Have you told mom?" I asked.

"Not yet," Rosa responded.

"Good. Mom doesn't need to hear that right now."

"I love you, Joe. If you need me or if you need to talk, call me." Rosa kissed me on the forehead and said goodnight. I didn't say anything. I just laid motionless in bed, paralyzed by the debilitating pain of disappointment and what I called a great injustice. I heard Rosa walking down the hallway after she had put me in the bed saying, "I never liked that heifer from day one. She's going to wish she never knew me." The only thought that ran through my mind at that moment was,

"I can't wait to get to the pool in the morning."

CHAPTER 29
A MOTHER'S DREAM

I STARTED ATTENDING MEETINGS OF THE PEER SUPPORT group at the Shepherd Center. During these meetings, peers in the center would discuss their thoughts and emotions with one another. This healing process was so critical to my life. Without someone to talk to, I don't believe I would have made it through this season in my life. At these meetings, one of the things that stood out to me instantly was the fact that I didn't have it as bad as others in the center. One thing you learn in these types of settings is there is always someone else that is in a worse situation than yourself.

Mrs. Oviatts was the group coordinator. I promised her that I would attend one of her meetings and share with the other attendees my experiences. When I went, I began to share with the others about my expe-

271

rience of climbing the corporate ladder while living the good life only to lose everything in one season of my life. But the thing that uplifted the attendees is when I began to express how my faith in God was the only thing that sustained me ... and continues to do so. Look to God: when all hope is gone, and bitterness is attempting to overtake your soul when there seems to be no one available to understand how you are feeling and you feel all alone. When everything that you have worked hard for seems to go up in flames, and left in your hands are only the ashes of your dreams. The only thing you can do is look to God. There are no thoughts, no philosophical sayings, no amount of drugs and other substances that can sustain you; only God can; only falling backward into the arms of Jesus the Christ can help you. And the interesting thing is this: you don't have to be strong; God is your strength.

I explained to everyone that although I was optimistic about being healed and being able to walk on my own without the aid of crutches again one day, I realized that my real strength and peace comes through my daily surrendering to God. I shared these thoughts with everyone in the room; and while sharing them, I saw the hope beginning to burn in their eyes as they began to light up. When I finished talking, everyone started clapping and cheering, and this went on for several minutes. It amazes me how touching the lives of others has the inverse effect of touching my own life. While lifting the spirits of others, my own spirit uplifted. I was essentially reminding myself to totally surrender my hurt, pain, and life to

God so that I could rest peacefully in the assurance of His divine providence and will.

I still needed help and guidance in my own life. I decided to pick up the phone and call Pastor Flemming, Sr. who had been so instrumental in my life, helping me to navigate through tough seasons and situations. It was good to hear his voice again. I told him I needed spiritual counseling. It was interesting that when he picked up the phone, one of the first things he mentioned was that he was expecting a call from me. I found that reassuring. We talked and he reminded me about trusting in God. I remember griping, "How do I cope with the pressures of life along with this disability? My legs don't work like they use to. The insurance company don't want to give me the funds that I need to function—it's always 'red tape' and a bunch of paperwork to slow the process down. My soon-to-be ex-wife telling lies on me just to make me look bad, and I don't like the way I look and how others stare at me. I thought that when the accident happened the pressure would disappear, but it increased. My family members and friends just don't understand me; only my mother does. I feel like my dad treats me like nothing ever happened. I never cry around him because I never saw him shed a tear. And with all of that, I still have to deal with racism and being disabled. When will all of this madness stop?! WHY ME?!" Pastor Flemming's response helped me to regain the proper perspective. He said,

"Why not you? God wants to use you in a great and powerful way. When it's all said and done, you will

touch millions of lives around the world. It's your purpose."

That conversation with Pastor Flemming helped
to put everything back into focus in my life. Rather than
try to bury the stress of a failed marriage and devastating
divorce and lament the loss of my legs and deformity of
my hands, I remembered once more that all of my pain
and suffering was for a reason, one that would catapult
my name to heights that I could only dream of as a child.
It was now time for me to become mission-oriented rather than sorrowful, and let my pain propel me rather than
bury me. I began fasting and praying at least once a week
and reading my Bible. I'd go to the altar at Mt. Carmel
Baptist Church (where Pastor Flemming pastors) during
their 12-noon prayer; sometimes, I would go there three
times a week whenever I would feel like the devil was on
my trail. This way gave me incredible strength.

As the news of my accident continued to spread
throughout the state of Georgia, I began receiving phone
calls and letters from people asking me to speak at their
events about my experience. I recalled my mom telling
me once that when she was pregnant with me, she would
have dreams of me speaking before large crowds. As time
progressed, I started to witness my life shape into something wonderful in light of the tragedies I was facing.

One day, I received a phone call from Cathy Tru-
ett, the owner of Chick-Fil-A. He wanted me to share my
story with his company—there were over two-hundred
employees present. After that, I met a lady named Clark
Cones. She was interested in my story and my divorce

case, and she asked me to stop by her office just to shed some light on the divorce case. I later received the Claimant of the Year Award from the Workman's Compensation Board—that event took place at the Hyatt Regency Hotel in downtown Atlanta, Georgia. Over a thousand people attended the ceremony and listened to me share my testimony. After speaking, I was elated as the people gave me a standing ovation. That day, my mother was overjoyed while watching me grace that stage to receive that award and speak to so many people about faith and hope in the midst of tragedy and adversity. It was just as God had shown her, and this was only the beginning.

At this time, I was attempting to finish up my degree at Morris Brown College. This was particularly memorable for me because I began to get close to another young lady who would fill in the hole in my heart. Her name was Tammy. I met her at the Piedmont Hospital originally where she worked while attending school for nursing at Georgia State University; but later on, she transferred to Morris Brown College to finish up her degree. She had a little boy of her own and had been involved in an abusive relationship—at times, I would be there to be a shoulder for her to cry on. But since that time, we began spending more time with each other, getting to know one another.

I'll never forget the year Tammy took control of my birthday celebration. On May 13th, at 10:30 am, a black limousine pulled up in my driveway to pick me up. Later on, she had a special lunch prepared for me with a pianist playing classical music. Afterward, we went to the mall for some shopping and then took a nice stroll through the park—it was a perfect, sunny day. Later on, we were off to play Ms. Pac Man and Galaxy in the game room. At around 4 pm, we checked-in at the Western Peachtree Plaza Hotel in downtown Atlanta. When we entered our room, I noticed she already had our special dinner attire laid out for us on the bed. But I really loved what she had on already. The shorts she had on revealed the curves of her hips and her toned legs. Our dinner reservation was at the Sun Dial Restaurant on the roof of the hotel. The dinner, along with the white wine, was extraordinary; the restaurant was a unique experience: it spun around allowing diners to see the entire City of Atlanta. After this, we went for a stroll down Peachtree Street. The whole time, Tammy sat on my lap. She didn't care that others were looking at us. Some people thought it was very romantic. Truthfully, who cared. The way she was looking at me was intoxicating; the desire in her eyes was consuming. We went back to the hotel room where she had gifts spread out on the bed for me. Tammy wanted me to open them, but I wasn't focused on unwrapping *those* gifts. Next, she told me to relax while she went into the restroom to get changed, then she told me to close my eyes before stepping out of the restroom, so I closed them. I felt her placing a blindfold over my eyes, and then heard the sound of Luther Vandross. Tammy started teasing me, playing a game where I couldn't touch her but she could touch me using either her tongue, some fruit, or a piece of ice. After that, she told me to remove the blindfold. When I did, I noticed she was dressed like a playboy bunny. The rest, I'll leave to your imagination.

※

While finishing up college I was paying a slew of hefty fines imposed on me by the court during my divorce trial; and I was also battling it out with the AUC (Atlanta University Center), which included a cluster of schools there (Morris Brown College, Morehouse College, Clark University, and Spellman College) over the issue of making their campuses compatible with handicapped individuals. Some of the classes I needed to take I couldn't take because the classrooms were inaccessible to people in wheelchairs. I had that problem to deal with alongside the worker's compensation battle. And now, I had fallen four months behind on my alimony payments and was summoned to court to appear before the judge. My worker's compensation attorney, John Sweetlow, sent me one of his attorneys to represent me in the case. He said he didn't want to represent me himself because he and that particular judge had a bad history together. The lawyer who would be representing me was a man named Daniel. That day, the courtroom was jam-packed. The judge tried to portray me as a rich Black man who was ignoring his wife and kids—as a deadbeat dad. My attorney tried to explain to the judge that I had fallen behind in alimony payments due to the fact that I didn't have the money, and that I was a student in college and I was waiting on the worker's compensation money to come through for me. He reminded the judge that I was a quadriplegic and that I had been under an inordinate amount of stress as of late because of my financial hardships. He asked the judge to simply be lenient and grant me some time to catch up on the payments, but the judge wasn't hearing it. Things didn't get any better after the judge found out that Daniel, the attorney representing me, worked for Mr. Sweetlow, the very man the judge disliked. After that, everything started to snowball. The judge demanded that my attorney and the other caseworker who was also present representing me, Mr. Ramseur, approach the bench. The judge then told them, "From the look of things, I believe that Mr. Lovejoy must have some money because you all walking into my courtroom with your fancy suits on. Mr. Lovejoy looks like he got money. I tell you what, I believe he needs to go to jail. He's just like all of these deadbeat dads who don't take care of their kids. It's my job to teach all of them a lesson." While the judge was talking, I was biting my tongue, thinking to myself this judge was out to get me. Melissa was sitting in the back just looking. The judge suddenly ordered an officer to handcuff me and take me to jail. Determined not to go to jail, I immediately asked my lawyer to grab my car keys out of my backpack, rush out to my car, grab $850 out of the money I had there, and pay the court clerk so that I could get out of that courtroom. After doing so, I was free to leave. Again, before leaving, I reminded the judge that Melissa and I didn't have any kids together, to which he appeared puzzled and embarrassed. Although I was upset about everything and feeling picked on, I was a lot calmer than before, knowing that I had the ultimate advocate fighting on my behalf: God. I was not afraid of anything that Melissa and the court tried to do to me. If no one else understood me, God understood me and He was fighting my battle.

I began to grow in the Christian faith daily. I seized every opportunity available to read the Bible and spend time with God in prayer. I stayed at the altar at my church. I felt a change occurring in my heart and mind. I still had all of the same problems, but I was beginning to have a greater sense of peace in the midst of my problems. My perspective was changing. I was upset over the treatment I was receiving in my divorce case, with the lack of progress in my worker's compensation case, and upset about the lies Melissa was telling among other things, but I was more optimistic, realizing God was up to something big in my life; therefore, the result was going to be good.

February 18, 1990, was an amazing day. That was the day I was ordained as a deacon in my church. The ceremony took place during the 10:30 am worship service. All of my family and friends were there. They were so proud of me. But no one glowed with a brighter joy than my mother who had been praying consistently and relentlessly for me throughout the years. Her heart was now filled with contentment, knowing that not only was her son's soul secure in God but that he had a family of like-minded Believers there to gird him up and keep him rooted. I was now a part of a brotherhood and obtained a role and responsibility that would keep me rooted and grounded in my faith as a Believer.

That morning, as part of the ceremony, the pastor had me to come down to the altar before the entire congregation. He then called all of the deacons down to the altar and told them to lay hands on me. At that time, the pastor began to charge me as a deacon to dedicate myself to a life of prayer and consecration and be a godly leader and example for others to see, living according to God's Word. After that, the pastor began to pray for me. While he was praying for me, he was asking for the "fire of the Holy Ghost" to fall on me. Immediately, I started to feel a warm sensation come all over me. That heat began to shoot through my body. I'd never experienced that before. That day, something broke loose within me. What is difficult to articulate is the unbelievable freedom I felt on that day. The serenity was greater than that which the swimming pool provided. After that day, I was never the same. Never! I could never return to my old ways and be content. Life for me began to take on a completely new meaning.

Written by Tammy from Atlanta, on Sept 1992

Hey Sweetie,

I just got off I-75 N my way here to the hospital. This letter is to give you the real deal. No half stepping; no wanting to say –just plain and simple– the essential truth. First, let me start by saying, I first became "aware" of my true feelings for you before you left for Germany. The day when you came to get my work address and you said I was short and sweet with you. I'm sorry for that but I was not being short, I was pissed because you promise to meet me after work the day before and you were at Lenox Square instead. While you were gone I wondered if I was beginning to care for you in a different way than I did in the past. I could not confirm it at the time; I then received a letter from you when you were in Germany. The letter was very touching and heart-felt. I still could not confirm my feelings for you, when you returned from Germany we began to have weekly lunch dates. We talked and laughed–what a wonderful time. I was still a little confused and w/o my feelings been tested and just thought that it were the same feelings that I already had. Then I met you on a Saturday at the pool for the first time. I felt a little nervous before I got there–then I saw you. You're so relaxed and free when you're

281

swimming; I sensed the joy that the sport brings to your life. After watching you for several hours, I could not focus on my feeling because the life guard kept talking to me. After that day you were on my mind _constantly_. I would wake up, you were on my mind, while driving, working or just sitting, and you are always there. So after about a week of this it hit me and it hit me _hard_ Curtis, I think I'm falling in love with you, yes you read it right the first time I began to realize it. The times we shared talking at your house confirmed what I thought I felt, when I'm around you I get this feeling that I can't explain, when you look me in the eyes, when you touch me, the hugs, the kisses, the calls, lunch at Southern Regional, the wonderful songs on my machine, all of the songs were my favorites, the consideration you always have for me. You name it! I feel like I'm going to melt every time you are around me. Curtis, I have a great fear that I can't explain, I think my fears are originated from the possibility, of something that I feel I would not be able to handle. To love you unconditionally is hard work—both mentally & physically it has nothing to do with your disability because I fell that it made you above all men! Curtis you have me going in circles sometimes, there are many times I don't know if I'm coming or going. I smell you constantly. While I'm walking, working or thinking. I don't know how much longer I'm going deal with this. Please realize (I know you do) the history that we have. When we first met, we immediately clicked. It seem like we had so much in common. The long talks in your car meant so much to me at that point in my life. But I always felt that I was not good enough for you. I felt at time that I could not give you what you deserved or needed due to the turmoil I was experiencing at that time. So the way I am feeling is shocking because I've never had these feelings for you before. I sometimes haves to realize that we have not just met each other. We have been a part of each other lives for about 5 years or so. Even though we lost contact something, we always managed to find each other at some point; I now feel that I missed so many opportunities to have a relationship with you. I guess I'll never know what happened and why. I know that we have talked on several occasions about how and why we didn't become a pair I will take half responsibility or maybe it was not our time at that point. I may never know. Another subject that I need to address with you is intimacy. There are times when we are talking and you begin to talk about making love to me, I <u>always</u> avoid your questions by not answering with my true feelings. I have been doing this to avoid reality. Reality is .... (Pause). I would love to express my "new feelings" for you in an intimate

283

way. The thought of making love to you is a beautiful experience. One _never_ to forget! We have _been_ through a lot together. So much miscommunication in the past, you on one page, me on another. And for us to finally make love would bring our emotions and passions into an explosion of love (damn, that sounds good). But one thing I can't seem to shake is the day after, what will happen to 5 years of friendship. 3 weeks of my feelings going to another level. I cannot imagine losing all of that just stop for a minute and think. I want you to put yourself into my shoes.

************** (The tables are turned now....)
****

What if you were still married to Melissa (your wife) you guys had a nice relationship. And everything was well in your marriage. Then one day you meet me and off and on for 5 years. We establish a great relationship. Then out of nowhere, this relationship starts to go to another level. Lunch dates phone calls all day, love letters, sex messages, you come to my house occasionally, we kiss and hug and hold each other, and then we begin to want to make love with each other. At that point, I want you to be honest and tell me _exactly_ what would you do and how would you handle this situation, (I want your answer).

284

Curtis, I don't to make the wrong decision but I know what I feel as well. So this is the confusion that has been occupying my thoughts daily. How would I feel about myself if I was doing something that I know was not right but feels so right? If I was not married at this times of my life, I would love for you & I to have an understanding, compassionate, intimacy filled relationship with you, By you knowing that I'm getting a divorcé and my two boys mean the world to me, I'm not longing for his financial security but how long will this process take, I feel that I could not give you everything you want even though I want them to, If I never find a solution, I love these feelings I have for you. I love your present, your smile, your touch and your passion. Remember the time you said you are not going anywhere, I hope that you never stop feeling that way.

Well let me close by saying, I did confirm, those feelings I talked about earlier in my letter. And I can <u>finally</u> say, Curtis I love you !

   (Boy, it took me 5years-I am always late (smile [happy face sign]

                    Love Always
                    Tammy

JUST A LITTLE LOVE & JOY

CHAPTER 30
A DARK FAMILY SECRET

M Y BROTHER WiLEWIS WENT TO THE HOSPITAL
for a routine check-up only to discover that
he needed surgery on his kidney and his small
intestine due to his many years of alcohol abuse. All of
that Seagram's 7 and Crown Royal had finally caught up
with him. He loved to drink. He would get so drunk he
would forget who he was. One time, he got so drunk he
thought he was Superman and he believed that he could
fly, which wasn't good since we were on the 3rd floor of
our apartment building on Coleman Street at the time.
Another time while drunk, he thought he was Bruce
Lee, and he tried to kick down a wall. The next morning,
when he awoke, he discovered that his foot was nearly
the size of a grapefruit—it was swollen that bad.

One thing that WiLewis was known for in our

household and by those who were close to him was his
hatred of White people. He didn't have any problems
with letting his contempt for Caucasians show either. At
the hospital, you could sense the uneasiness in him while
being treated by the White nurses and doctors. Whenever I would ride in the car with him or go anywhere with
him, whenever we'd encounter a White person, WiLewis's facial expression would change, his demeanor would
change, he'd become defensive, tense, and would openly
express hostility and contempt towards them. If he were
at a gas station or someplace where he had to engage in
a financial transaction with a White person, he'd insist
that the person place the change on the counter as opposed to placing it in his hand. He didn't want his skin
to make contact with a White person's. In one incident,
WiLewis was at a store making a purchase and the man
behind the counter, who was White, was trying to hand
him his change from the transaction. WiLewis told the
man to simply place the change on the counter, insisting that he not place it in his hand. Even though the
man was very polite and gentleman-like, WiLewis' contempt was fuming. WiLewis was secretly clutching his
switchblade, which he concealed under his shirt. After
we left, WiLewis stated, "I can't stand them bastards who
burn-up my granddaddy! I hate them pecker-woods! If
he had touched my hand, I would slit his throat!" And
he meant it. I was scared to be around WiLewis after
that, especially when he was in the company of someone
White.

For a long time, I wondered why my brother hated White people so much. I can understand the general contempt that many within the Black community had for Whites due to some of the things I had seen growing up and the things my parents saw and experienced growing up. But deep down inside there was always an understanding that racism was a matter of the heart and not skin, and that not everyone possessed the same views. In other words, many within the Black community endeavored to avoid generalizing all White people as being the same. And furthermore, we teach that we are to fight hatred with love and avoid becoming like the very individuals who carried out hatred and violence due to the ignorance and bigotry in their hearts. Mom would always stress to us the importance of love and forgiveness and keep our hearts pure before God, knowing that it is impossible for a person to enter into heaven with that stuff in their hearts according to the Christian faith. But WiLewis held a deeper contempt. His was more personal, more intense. It was like cancer slowly eating away at his core throughout his many years on earth. *But why?* I would often wonder. One day, I asked him, "Why do you hate White people so much? God said to love everyone."

"Joe," WiLewis said calmly, "just keep on living."

"But God said to love everybody regardless of their skin color."

"Joe, they low-down! They don't love Black folks! They have always discriminated against us! In their eyes, we are just niggers to them." WiLewis then mentioned a dark secret in our family's past. "They killed your granddaddy! They boarded his windows and doors of his house in the country and set the house on fire!!" I couldn't say anything after that. I was in a state of shock. I could feel the hatred spewing out of my brother's heart as he said those words. The more we dived into the subject, the angrier and more worked up he got, so I decided not to push the issue further with him. But I was still curious about what happened to our great-grandfather. I waited until I saw mom and then I asked her about what happened. She explained to me,

"Yes, Joe, it's true. Your daddy never talked about it."

"How do you and daddy feel about it?" I asked.

"It has been very hard on your father. I wish he never told your brother (WiLewis) until he reached the age of accountability. You father told him at an early age. During that time, your father expressed his feelings only because if he didn't release that pressure, it would eat him up. That sad injustice had an effect on WiLewis, which caused him to be bitter, and hatred set in his mind."

"But mom, what about you?"

"All I know is God is the only one who can heal the heart of people. It takes a lot of praying. We tried to raise all nine of ya'll to honor the true and living God and know that we must love one another in spite of and that no one can make it to heaven hating one another. God loves us so much that He gave us His own begotten Son so that whosoever believes in Him will have everlasting life. That's the Word. When everything else fails you, you must stand on God's Word and hide it in your bosom."

�֍

WiLewis was going through chemotherapy treatment. During this time, I would visit him frequently. During one visit, I asked him how he was feeling. He responded that he was tired. But then, he went on to share with me an interesting dream he had. "Man, Joe, I was asleep for an hour or two, and then I began to dream."

"Dream about what?"

"Heaven," he answered. I was shocked. "Everybody was so happy and singing a lot. Everybody was well he continued to say. No sickness. Then I drifted off back to sleep. But I dreamed about you, Joe."

"What was it?"

"Well, it didn't make any sense to me, but I saw you in some strange country. Don't know why you were there, but you were so happy, and lots of people were surrounding you; they were giving you a standing ovation—different kind of White folks who were not from the United States. But the kids had a fit over you, my baby brother. Then I went back to sleep. I'm getting a little tired now. If I close my eyes, you know why."

I was startled by WiLewis' dreams. I figured God spoke to him and began showing him things because of me and momma's prayers and because his time was coming to an end. But to hear what he saw me doing in the future was interesting because it was similar to a dream that I had of myself being in a foreign country and winning gold medals in swimming in a stadium that was packed with thousands of people that were giving me a standing ovation. It was a little strange, but also a confirmation to me that I was supposed to be in the swimming pool. All of this sent chills up and down my spine. After leaving that day, I went straight to the swimming pool and swam for four and a half hours straight without stopping. WiLewis' dream birthed in me a greater hunger for the water, a drive I hadn't possessed before then. It brought light to my purpose which, up until that moment, was still veiled by obscurity. Now everything was clear; it all made sense. The accident, the loss of my legs, and the changes I underwent in life were all leading me to this place, which was my place of destiny. I could see it now.

It was the morning of June 6, 1990. I was on my way to the gym to swim when I decided to stop by the hospital to pay WiLewis a visit. That morning, while the two of us were talking, WiLewis really opened up to me about some things that were in his heart. He told me that he opened up his heart to receive Christ as his Lord and Savior; he did this just prior to receiving a visit from Pastor Flemming who he described as a humorous individual that was a lot of fun to talk to. He began to release all of the hatred in his heart of White people. "I need to let my baby brother know that I asked God to remove the hatred from my heart," he said. "I don't want to go to hell hating anybody. Yes, I do love White people!!" he shouted. He continued talking, telling me about how he repented for disrespecting mom and dad. I was completely overjoyed. My heart was at ease. I realized at that moment that whatever happened to my big brother, everything was going to be alright. After our discussion, I left the hospital and went about my way. That was the last time I saw WiLewis alive. He passed away right after my visit. His time of death was 10:41 am.

After WiLewis's passing, mom decided to go into detail with me about what happened to my grandfather. She shared with me the gruesome details that WiLewis knew, which caused him to burn with anger and hatred towards Whites. As was revealed to her by Aunt Bessie Mae, this is what occurred:

My grandfather's name was Eddie Lovejoy. He was born in 1889 and grew up in Greenville, Georgia. He spent all of his life picking cotton. He was married to Bessie Harris who worked on a farm and took care of all ten of their kids: five boys and five girls. But Eddie's troubles started when he began having an affair with a White woman. As you may well know, this was not viewed favorably by the town's population, especially the White community. The White lady's name was Lucy.

One day, Eddie and his brother, Frank, were making moonshine. Present with them were a few of the White neighbors called the Vogue brothers and Lucy. As they were all getting drunk, Lucy started coming on to Eddie. She even put her arm around Eddie. That's when

Uncle Frank knew it was time to leave. The Vogue family certainly weren't too pleased with such a display of affection, and they felt it necessary to take matters into their own hands to let Eddie know that interracial relationships would not be tolerated in their community or anywhere else.

Granddaddy began to have a full-fledged affair with Lucy. He began seeing her quite frequently. Word of their affair began to circulate around town, thereby placing a lot of negative attention on his family. Many Whites, when spotting Eddie's family in passing, would shout things like "Stick with your own kind!" angrily at them along with other racial slurs and threats. Many of the town's Whites would even display nooses at Eddie's family with smiles on their faces before shooting birds at them. The tension was getting thick, but none of this seemed to deter Eddie from seeing Lucy. When his wife confronted him about the situation, granddaddy (Eddie) would just tell her that it was just hearsay and that nothing was happening between him and Lucy.

One night, at about 11 pm, granddaddy was making his way home; he was walking alongside the roadside when several trucks pulled up and surrounded him. He knew he was in trouble. All granddaddy could see were the headlights. He couldn't see the faces of the men, but he could make out the voices of some of them—some of them were the Vogue brothers. "Hey, Nigger, what is your problem? Why can't you stay away from our women?" one of them asked. Granddaddy didn't say anything. "Nigger, the cat got your tongue?!" another one shouted out. Finally, granddaddy said,

"I'm done with that girl! It's over! I promise you I'm done!" After he shouted I'm done, it got silent completely. Suddenly, one of the guys let off a shotgun blast into the air. Then one of the men shouted,

"Don't you come near Lucy! Understand, nigger?!" Afterward, another guy let off another shotgun blast. Frightened and startled, granddaddy responded,

"Um, um... Yes, sir!!" After that, the men jumped into their trucks and sped off.

After that night, Eddie started going home early rather than spending time with Lucy. In fact, he began avoiding her like the plague. But one day, while he was walking through the downtown district pass the courthouse, he heard a woman shouting his name out in the open: "Eddie! Eddie! Eddie!" When he looked back, it was Lucy. Despite his best effort to avoid making contact with her, the appearance of a White woman associating with a Black man in broad daylight in full view of the public sent shockwaves throughout the town. And it was this act that spelled doom for Eddie.

The day was hot. It was ninety-eight degrees Fahrenheit outside. Mrs. Bessie was out in the field picking cotton that day while singing to the Lord. Strangely, she felt a startling, unshakable conviction in her heart like a nagging feeling or itch that just would not go away. She began to sing louder until finally crying out to God. She sat down in her rocking chair and began to pray to God: "Father! Jesus! What you trying to tell me?! Where is Eddie?! Is he alright, Lord?! Lord, don't leave me! I need you to lead me!" Just then, she heard a voice calling out her name,

"Bessie!!! Bessie!!! Bessie!!!" It was a woman named Helen—a neighbor. When Mrs. Bessie ran to the door, there was Helen standing there almost out of breath with tears streaming down her face. "Eddie's house was set on fire and we believe he was inside of it!!!" she hollered. "Is Eddie here?!!!"

"No!!!" grandma Bessie answered. Grandma and Helen immediately rushed to the house where they discovered that it burned to the ground. Instinctively, grandma knew granddaddy was in that house; she knew that he was gone. Windows and doors nailed shut prevented granddaddy from escaping. But that was more of a formality at this point considering that, as it was later discovered and revealed by investigators, before being killed, granddaddy was tortured and dismembered. His hands and feet, shoulders, arms, legs, and his penis had all been cut off, and he was burned alive. Upon discovering the gruesome scene, grandma fainted.

The family took granddaddy's death hard. Grandma's church family did their best to console her and her kids. There was much talk about revenge by the Lovejoy family. Most of them wanted to strike back at the Vogue family, especially my father, James. The hatred that developed in his heart not just for the Vogue family but Whites, in general, raged out of control like a wildfire in his heart, but grandma wouldn't hear any talk of revenge. As she explained, we must not seek vengeance; but rather, put the situation in the hands of the Lord; for

He declared in His Word, "Vengeance is mine." Grandma stressed that if they would have sought revenge on the Vogue family and burned their house down killing them all, then the bloodshed wouldn't end there, jail and death would await them all, and they would be no different than the killers themselves. Daddy didn't agree.

One of the most difficult parts of it all was the funeral. En route to the church where the funeral was being held, our family had to drive past the Vogues' house. While the funeral procession was passing by their house, the Vogue brothers dared to hang out on their porch and drink and laugh at the procession as it passed. Grandma immediately grabbed daddy and held him close to her bosom and started singing *Amazing Grace*.

Everyone in town knew that the Vogue brothers were responsible for granddaddy's death, but the sheriffs couldn't seem to find any witnesses to come forward. Basically, the entire town was responsible; every person knew what happened but refused to speak up for justice. In the wake of a formal investigation, the killers took their time beating up granddaddy. They would take turns beating on him and burning him. Beer cans were found all over the crime scene. As each killer took turns cutting off a piece of Eddie's body, I can imagine him screaming for dear life. They didn't just kill him; they killed him slowly and painfully. To this day, I can't imagine what kind of evil can possess a person and cause them to do the things they did to granddaddy.

When I think about it all, I'm reminded of why a place called hell exists; I'm reminded of how strong

Black women are and had to be, and I'm amazed at how deep God can penetrate our hearts and bring about forgiveness within us. I didn't understand it until I heard the whole story behind granddaddy's murder—which, by the way, has yet to be solved—how much God had to work to heal my brother's heart. I didn't realize until then just how powerful God's love is: that it can not only match the intensity of the evil surrounding us, but it can even supersede it. For, where evil abounds, God's grace abounds even more (Romans 5:20).

That day, I discovered the true meaning and power of the words "love" and "forgiveness" and realized that they only come from God. Only He can give us the grace to love and forgive so that we can not only counteract the effects of hatred but also avoid being both consumed and destroyed by it.

CHAPTER 31

THE DEPARTURE

THE YMCA (YOUNG MEN'S CHRISTIAN Associa-
tion) is where I would spend the majority of my
time. I would go there and swim for hours in
order to relieve my mind; but now, swimming had taken
on a new meaning in my life; it was about to transition
from a hobby to a career. It started when I joined the
Shepherd Center's Swim Team. There was a total of six
athletes on the team and they practiced every week on
Mondays. The oldest swimmer on the team was a woman named Gene; she was the one I met earlier who gave
me swimming tips when I first developed an interest
in competitive swimming; she was the hemiplegic who
would swim gracefully on one side of her body; she was
54 years old.

☙

I had forgotten how dangerous the water is. Just because you can swim like a fish doesn't mean you are one. One day, while I was at swimming practice, I had a lot on my mind. I was thinking about other things that were going on in my life that were bothering me, but I was still very eager to get into the water so that I could forget about it all. I had just finished warming up and I wanted to get an unofficial time on my 25-yard breaststroke. Everything was going smoothly at first. I had just passed the 13-yard line when I suddenly missed my timing and ended up swallowing water. I began to panic, then choke, and then sink. The more I struggled, the more I sank. All I could do was cry out to God under the water while my lungs were filling up with water. "Oh, Lord!!!!!" I cried.

When I was a child, I would hear grandma talk to us about outer-body experiences. She would share with us the experiences of others who claimed to have died only to come back to life. Many of these people, would describe in vivid detail ending up in a place that was strange to them, one that was foreign, but one that was indescribably beautiful after being revived. We refer to this place as Heaven. But not all near-death experiences (or NDEs) saw Heaven. Some NDEs ended up seeing the opposite place, which we know as Hell. The sheer terror in their eyes when describing Hell is enough to convince anyone that this is not a place you'd want to end up.

I never thought I would join the ranks of individuals who talked about having a near death experience and briefly seeing the joys or terrors that await every soul in the afterlife, but I did. Sitting at the bottom of that pool with my lungs full of water, I drowned. I couldn't tell how long I was at the bottom of the pool before someone noticed me and pulled me out of the water, but my transition was instant, it was seamless. In a split second, I was out of my body. I was no longer in the water, no longer drowning, no longer in a panicky state, no longer conscious of the plight of my physical body. All I could see all around me was the purest white I've ever seen. As my vision seemed to adjust, the scenery became more clear. Wherever I was, I was not alone. I saw people gathered around. There was a sense of peacefulness and a serenity I had never known before. The place was like earth, but it wasn't earth—it was too glorious to be earth.

Suddenly, everything was over. I was no longer in that strange place. I opened my eyes to the sight of the team's coach, Jennie, and the other teammates huddled around me. They all had concerned looks on their faces and were asking me if I was okay. Now responsive, I was able to reply, "I'm okay."

Right before I rolled into the pool to begin my 25-yard swim, I set my timer so that I could time myself. Shortly after regaining consciousness after being rescued from the water, I looked at my stopwatch and noticed it was at around twenty-eight minutes. How long was I in the water? I can't say. Might have been five minutes, ten minutes, twenty minutes. All I do know is after a certain period, the brain, when deprived of oxygen, will experience significant, irreversible brain damage; I also know beyond a shadow of a doubt I was not supposed to live through that. My being here today is simply a miracle, but it's also a statement: For a child of God, death is not in control. It wasn't my time to go. God said, "No. I am not through with Curtis Lovejoy." So I lived. But I'd also seen something while in that water that I can never forget.

My first swimming competition was at the Dixie Games in May of 1988. I had to compete in six events: 50-meter breast, 100-meter breast, 50-meter freestyle, 100-meter freestyle, 50-meter backstroke, and the 100-meter backstroke. I placed first in each of these events, winning gold medals. It was an exhilarating experience. Of course, there are the obvious butterflies that flutter around in one's belly before a big competition like that; but once that horn goes off, all of those butterflies disappear and the only thing that kicks in is the intense training you took your body through to prepare for that specific moment.

After the competition, my coaches congratulated the other athletes and me. Many of them were amazed that I had done so well for my first time in a swimming competition, let alone swimming as a Quadriplegic. Not everyone was happy to see me shine during the competition. I could see a few negative looks on certain people's faces, but I dared not allow that to eclipse my glorious moment. I knew I had found my place, my niche, and I

CHAPTER 31: THE DEPARTURE

was excited about my future.

✷

Not too long after the Dixie Games, mom had to admit dad into Georgia Baptist Hospital. He was experiencing shortness of breath and pain every time he would urinate. The doctors began running tests on him to try to figure out what was going on in his body. Throughout this process, mom was daily by his side. My siblings would take turns going to the hospital to be by dad's side daily. Dad wouldn't eat anything—he no longer had an appetite. There was nothing anyone could do. He would barely speak to anyone. His condition went on for several days.

One day, while at swimming practice, all I could think about was my daddy. Whenever I was worried or deeply concerned about someone or something, I would swim as a way to relieve my anxieties and fears. That day, while thinking about dad, I swam for four hours straight, not even realizing I had been in the pool that long. After my swimming session, I went down to the hospital to visit dad. When I entered his hospital room, I noticed he was asleep. One thing I'll never forget about that day was his eyes: they were a soft yellow color. My dad would sometimes sleep with his eyes opened. It stunned me to see his eyes so discolored. To me, it appeared as if he was suffering deeply due to intense pain. That was a sight I could barely stand to see: discolored eyes; a tube running from his nose; his irregular breathing. I wanted his suffering to come to an end. I began to pray for God to end his suffering and take him home rather than leave him in the state that he was.

After about forty minutes, dad finally opened his eyes. "How you feel?" I asked him.

"Not so good, Joe. But it's all in the Master's hands."

"Yes, I know, dad. Is there anything that I can do?" I asked. In a small, child-like voice, dad responded,

"Yes, you can, Joe. Take care of my wife," he said looking me straight in the eyes. "Promise me that you will take care of your mother," he said while squeezing my hand tighter and tighter. I paused for several seconds, and then asked,

"Why me, dad?"

"Because I know what's inside of you. When you make-up your mind, nothing can stop you. I've seen it all during your childhood and adult life. Even in a wheelchair, nothing can stop you. I know that I may not be around when you get-up out of that wheelchair and walk without any crutches, but it's in your heart. You have a lot of me inside of you. But you also have much more to offer your family and the world. One day, you'll make the name 'Lovejoy' proud and respectable. So promise me that last request."

"Yes, dad. I'll do that. I love you, dad," I said. A few seconds later I said to him, "But sometimes I get a little scared along the way."

"That's okay, Joe. You are just human. God will shape and make you. You just walk through every door that is about to open for you, son."

CHAPTER 31: THE DEPARTURE

Because tears were running down my face, I wanted to let my dad's hand go just so I could wipe them away, but something wouldn't allow me to let his hand go. I began to feel heat running from my dad's body into mine; it was like fire running through me. During this time, it appeared as if dad was trying to muster up a smile on his face. Wanting to let go of his hand so that I could wipe the tears away from my eyes, I said to him, "I'm trying to pull away from you, dad, but something has a hold on me." After I said those words, dad lets go of my hand. He then spoke these words to me, which would be his final words to me:

"Joe, let me rest now. I'm very tired. Tell your mother to come to see me tomorrow."

"Yes, sir. Love you, dad."

"I know. I know," dad uttered while his eyes slowly shut and dozing back off to sleep.

After dad fell sound asleep, I just sat quietly and soaked up the moment with tears streaming down my face. Strangely, I experienced a sense of peace in my soul, which prompted me to smile. I then left out of the hospital and headed back to my van. The moment I got into my van, an overwhelming sense of despair came over me, and I found myself sobbing uncontrollably. I began to cry out, "Daddy, don't leave us now!!!!" I was wailing and weeping inconsolably. Just then, a Bible verse popped up in my mind—I thought about the words of Jesus in the Gospel of John where He said, "If you ask me anything in my name, I will do it." At that moment, I began to cry out to God again,

"God, don't let my dad suffer! Take him in his sleep!" I continued to pray for this with tears streaming down my face all the way home.

It was Sunday, June 26, 1994. Mom got up and got herself ready to go to church. We went to service that morning; and afterward, at her request, I dropped her off at the hospital so that she could spend some time with dad. After dropping her off at the hospital, I informed her that I was going to run and get me something to eat, and then I'd be right back—I felt starved after service. I rushed home to get something to eat, and while warming up the food I felt this uneasy feeling in the pit of my stomach. Suddenly, the phone rang. It was mom. "Joe, your daddy is gone home." I just paused there with the phone in my hand. Suddenly, peace fell over me. I felt relieved because dad's suffering was over. It was just as I had prayed. I wanted dad to slip away quietly, peacefully, painlessly. I wanted him to make the most important transition of his and everyone else's life while content and in a state of peace.

"Mom, are you alright?" I asked her.

"I just lost my best friend," she uttered.

"I know, mom. You can't have a peanut butter sandwich with no jelly. You two were that close. I know you're going to miss him a lot, but we're going to get through this together because those were his last words to me."

Dad was seriously ill. He was dealing with prostate cancer, emphysema, heart trouble, and shortness of breath. The doctor told me that my father's lungs were the same color as black coal. Dad never liked going to hospitals. At times, I witnessed him slumped over and out of breath, but he still refused to get checked out by a doctor. Dad would often grab his chest due to pain and mom would tell him, "James, let's go and see the doctor." She would beg him to go with her and get checked out, but he never would. Dad preferred the old country remedies instead.

I believe that had he seen a doctor much sooner; he would have stayed around a little bit longer; at least, he wouldn't have endured so much pain and suffering; he would have caught those health issues a lot sooner. I realized right then and there the importance of seeing a doctor before things get out of hand and it becomes too late. That's a lesson I will never forget.

JUST A LITTLE LOVE & JOY

CHAPTER 32
AWAKENING A MONSTER

"**M**OM! MOM! THE AJC (ATLANTA Journal-Constitution) is featuring Joe!" my sister hollered. "It says, 'He's Broken but Not Defeated!' It goes on to say, 'He didn't know how to swim then but was told by the SSC staff that the activity was good rehabilitation.'" The story was exciting news to my family. To be highlighted in the AJC was truly a big deal, and still is. The article featured a sit-down interview with me, detailing the events that led up to me taking to swimming; it also covered my condition as a person with quadriplegia and my workout routine among other things. The writers even referred to me as a daredevil, detailing how I participate in para-sailing, water skiing, and scuba diving. One thing the article stated is,

"People who have spinal cord injuries are high

risk-takers." This statement is certainly true because, as I stated in the interview,

"Nothing scares me anymore."

When you've faced death and had something important taken away from you (like a limb or limbs), then you're not worried about dying or losing limbs anymore.

After that article, I began receiving calls from more people wanting to interview me and write about me. The AJC did another article about me entitled "Dove Into His Destiny To Be A Winner" by Karen Thurstan. She wrote, "At age 37, the fear of water didn't stop Curtis Lovejoy from becoming a medal-winning swimmer." She went on to describe the many community volunteer and outreach activities I was involved in, from speaking to students at schools to conducting wheelchair basketball games to working with the Cub Scouts and more. I was then contacted by Hal Lamar of WAOK radio station in Atlanta to appear on their TalkBack Atlanta show. He, along with Mike Roberts and Carol Blackman of WVEE-103, held a fund-raiser for me at the Chick-Fil-A Greenbriar Mall along with Cynthia Inman, the store's manager, to help raise money for me to compete in the 1996 Paralympic Games in Atlanta, Georgia.

Now it appears that everyone wants me on their show or to speak at their school or event. Joe Washington of WXIA-TV 11-Alive wanted to interview me and showcase footage of me swimming, fencing, in peer-support groups, working out in the gym, and interacting with my mom. Ron Sailor of WIGO Radio 1340 wanted me to appear on his show for the Paralympics in the public school system. I did an interview on TalkBack Atlanta with Mike Roberts, Carol Blackmon, and Good Morning America's Robin Roberts. Morris Brown College, Georgia State University, and the University of Georgia wanted me to speak to their student bodies. Seeking me to make guest appearances were Georgia Tech and also Ansley Mall to address fifty of its elderly citizens. I spoke at Workshops in Carrollton, Douglasville, Augusta, and Rome, Georgia; at Quad-Rugby competitions in West Palm Beach, Florida and Tennessee; at a local fencing competition, the World Congress Center where I had to do a fencing demonstration for CNN and the 1996 Paralympic Swim Trials at Georgia Tech. WXIA-TV 11-Alive honored me at their 20th Annual Community Service Awards celebration aired on live television and shown via satellite throughout the United States and the Caribbean. These are just a few of the public appearances I was being requested to make, and they were all coming back to back. It felt as if my head was spinning at times; I was so busy.

During the 11 Alive awards ceremony, in what was a heartfelt speech before a captive audience, I shared how after my accident I couldn't see the light at the end of the tunnel and how I felt like giving up on life. I shared with them how I fell into the grip of truly dark days; but now, it seemed surreal that I was preparing to do something I couldn't have imagined myself doing as a child and it all happened so suddenly. One minute I was in the grip of darkness, contemplating suicide, and the next minute I was sitting on the world's stage, immersed in lights while preparing to compete at the 1995 Paralympic Swim Trials to win a spot on Team USA for the 1996 Paralympic Games. God did more than I could have ever imagined with my life. It was a humbling thought, one that reminds me that our lives are not our own and that even our tragedies in life serve a greater purpose when we turn to God and trust Him. I had heard others say this, but now I was experiencing it—I became the evidence of it. It weighed heavy on my heart the debt I owed to my parents. I could only think of the fact that anyone who had ever accomplished something extraordinary in life—Arthur Ash, Muhammad Ali, Dr. Martin Luther King, Jr., Lance Armstrong, Michael Jordan, etc.—had to experience dark days too before becoming successful. They didn't have it so good, but they were surrounded by and protected by excellent parents or people who saw something inside of them that set them apart from the crowd. With a heavy heart, I shared those words, remembering all of the days my parents would remind me that I was predestined to do something great. They believed in me when I didn't believe in myself, which is what made such a huge impact on my life.

Team USA stayed across from the Atlanta Stadium. It was nearly unbearable to sleep in the same room with one of my roommates because he snored louder than anyone I'd ever heard before. His snoring was so bad that I recorded him one night, knowing that others wouldn't believe it unless they heard it for themselves. It was now day one of the competition, and I was not well-rested. I looked at the competition and felt a sudden chill. I had never seen some of these S2 swimmers before. Although I didn't know any of them, they were aware of who I was. In the dressing room, they practically watched my every move. I could feel the pressure on me. After suiting up in my swimming suit, I waited for my name call so that I could enter the pool area and take my position. I had to remind myself that I belonged there although I was nervous and trembling.

They called my name, and I went out and got into position. I was in lane number three. I could feel the eyes of onlookers gazing at me while the other athletes and I were getting into position for the race. To help me deal with all of the stares from strangers in the stands, I tried to locate my family and friends. I needed to see a few familiar faces to set my heart and mind at ease. Thank God, I spotted their faces. I was ready now.

In the pool, I placed both feet on the wall and waited for the signal to take off. "Swimmers, take your mark!" the timekeeper shouted. Then the horn went off and off I was rotating both arms backward. My heart was beating so fast. I ended up swallowing a little water, but I kept concentrating on swimming. *Curtis, swim your race*, I thought to myself trying to keep it together, but panic began to set in, and my legs began to sink; it felt as if they had five-pound weights on them; also, my body began to drag in the water. It became difficult to swim straight. "What should I do right now?" asked myself. "I hope that when I get to the end of the pool and look at the clock, I'll have a good time." I finally I made it to the end of the pool and looked back at the scoreboard to see where my name appeared in the rankings. I was crushed to realize that I had finished fifth. I finished at 1:55.03, which was way too slow.

I heard my sister Diane shouting, "Way to go, Joe!! We love you!!" Still, I knew that my performance wasn't going to earn me a medal. I was so disappointed with myself that I didn't even want to go into the stands and greet my family, but I did anyway. Mom just hugged me and told me she loved me and that I did well, but I couldn't shake the feeling that I could've done a lot better. I wasn't satisfied. I looked at my mom and said,

"Mom, that wasn't good enough," referring to my performance in the water.

"I know, Joe. But you must learn to lose first before winning. It takes time, Joe. It takes time. That's something you cannot buy, just like grace."

After the trials were over for the day, I began to think hard about what happened and what I needed to do differently the next time. I felt a strong urge to go to the altar at my church and pray and seek God for His wisdom and guidance; I also felt the need to talk to my head coach about sleeping in another location away from Ken, my roommate who snored like an animal. I knew that I could never give my best performance if I could not rest. My coach obliged and granted me permission to sleep at home granted that I am present by 6:30 am to ride on the bus with the other athletes to the competition.

Later on, I went to the church to really clear my mind and receive some guidance and direction. When I arrived, I was glad to see Rev. Flemming, Sr.'s car. I went in and spoke with him about my disappointment with my performance. "My first day of competition didn't go well," I confessed. "I swam my worst race, and I got the 50-meter breaststroke race coming up Sunday."

"Brother Lovejoy, God has His own timing. He never left you. He is always there because He said that He would never leave nor forsake you. Just put that swim behind you and go forward. God will show up tomorrow and show out. You must believe that and keep the faith, okay?"

"Yes, sir."

"You'll be telling me how good God is next week." After that, Pastor Flemming began to pray with me.

"Good morning, everyone. Let me welcome you to day two of the competition of the 1995 Paralympic Swim Trials here at the Georgia Tech Aquatic Center. This morning, let's welcome the S2 Swimmers for the 50-meter breaststroke!"

My heart was beating fast. I was nervous but ready. I was well rested and determined to outdo my last performance. I came prepared to do damage. This time, I wasn't concerned about the people, the competitors, the faces in the crowd, nor the chattering and mind-games played in the waiting area; all I cared about was the race.

This time, I was in lane five. "Swimmers, take

your mark!" Silence fell over the arena as we awaited the sound of the horn. The horn finally sounded. Off I went. This time, I was off to a good start. *I can't let my legs sink and drag this time*, I thought. I got to make this arm go faster. *I can see across to the other end of the pool. Come on, Curtis! Let's keep our eyes on the prize! Just two more strokes, Curtis! Come on!* I kept saying to myself. Finally, I touched the pad at the other end of the pool and looked back at the scoreboard to see where I ranked. It was so noisy in the facility that I couldn't hear the announcer. I took my goggles off to get a better look at the scoreboard. My mouth fell open. I was sorely disappointed. From what I saw, it appeared that I had placed fifth again. I couldn't believe it.

While getting out of the pool, I noticed Diane and Sallie making their way over to the pool with excited looks on their faces. They were hollering my name. All I wanted to do was get out of there and go back to the dressing room. I didn't want to be bothered with anyone. I felt like hiding from everyone, so I hurried up and went to the back to change before anyone could get to me. After I finished dressing, I left out of the dressing room; and it was at that moment I heard someone yell, "Curtis, good job!! Good swim!! Way to go, Lovejoy!!!" I was thinking that everyone was just attempting to encourage me, but I wasn't in the mood for that. So I left and got on the elevator. When I got off of the elevator, a group of friends was standing there, and Sallie, Diane Ann, Rose, and Carl began to embrace me in a celebratory fashion while chanting "Lovejoy! Lovejoy! Lovejoy!"

Still, I didn't want to be bothered. All I really wanted was to see my mother. When I spotted my mom, I rolled toward her. She just embraced me with a big hug. Sensing that I was feeling distressed, she asked,

"Are you okay?"

"No, mom. I don't feel good. I didn't swim well at all. I'm sorry that . . ."

"Joe," mom cut in, "what are you talking about? You got the World Record in the 50-meter breast!"

"Mom, what are you talking about?! You got it wrong! I came in fifth place."

"No, Joe! You were in lane five, but you won the race!!"

I couldn't believe it. I was floored. Speechless. Tears began to flow from my eyes. I then discovered that I read the scoreboard wrong. Around that time, a large crowd of people came around to congratulate me on my victory. Suddenly, I was hearing my name being announced over the PA system telling me to report to the awards room. When I got to the dressing room, the head coach, Gail, said, "Where were you? We were looking everywhere for you. You know that once you earn a medal, you must go out to the award ceremony." I felt like I was in a daze. "Well," Gail continued, "this is the time that everybody will know that you're a gold medalist and I'm proud of you!"

When I rolled out for the award ceremony, the announcer stated: "And with the World and Pan-American record performance in the 50-meter breaststroke in 1:38.21, the winner of the gold medal for the United

States of America: Curtis Lovejoy!" After the announcement, the American national anthem started blasting.
While the national anthem played, they placed the gold
medal around my neck. I envisioned my dad saying to
me, "Don't let the disability control you; you control the
disability." I could feel him right there beside me along
with both of my grandmothers, wearing huge smiles on
their faces.

That gold medal was one of the most beautiful
pieces of art I'd ever seen; it glistened and shined almost
as bright as my spirit. Hearing my peers and others calling my name was one of the most enjoyable feelings I
had ever experienced. After the ceremony, everyone
wanted to take pictures with me. All I wanted to do was
get to my mother so that I could put that gold medal in
her hands. But when I saw Diane, she wanted it more
than I did. So I took it from around my neck and placed
it around hers and rolled over to my mom who gave me
one of the biggest and warmest hugs.

✸

After the trials were over, I sat patiently by the phone,
waiting to receive a call from Team USA's swim coach,
Joan, telling me that I had made the Paralympic Swim
Team and that I would compete on Team USA in the
1996 Paralympics in Atlanta, Georgia. Unfortunately, I
received no such phone call. Finally, after several days of
waiting, I received a message on my answering machine:

"(Beep) Hi, Curtis. This is Joan. I want to let you

know that you DID NOT make the 1996 USA Swim Team. I'm very sorry. You're considered as an alternate. Please hang in there and keep training. (Click)"

After hearing that message, I was floored. I felt devastated. My devastation then turned to anger. I was not going to sit by and do or say nothing about this. Being that I set a new World Record in the 50-meter breaststroke, I needed an answer as to why I didn't make the cut for Team USA, so I called Coach Joan and left her several messages, but I never received a response from her. I began to ask around to find out who I could speak with regarding the decision, and I was informed by a reliable source that there was someone who could reverse the decision regarding my situation, but I would have to try to set up a meeting with this individual. Whatever it took, that's what I was going to do. I met with this individual and presented my case, but she never gave me any indication that she would look into it. I left her office feeling like I had just wasted my time.

My next option was to hire a sports attorney and try to fight what I perceived as highway robbery being committed against me. I headed down to 500 Baker Street in downtown Atlanta. I didn't have an appointment nor knew the names of any of the lawyers in the firm there, but I knew that Dave Justice's and Deion Sanders' attorney was stationed there. I entered the building and the security officer approached me: "Can I help you? Who are you here to see?" I could not give him a name. "You must have approval before seeing an attorney," the guard stated. Right there, I poured my heart out to that guard, explaining to him why I was there. Afterward, he said to me that he was going to walk back to his seat and that he didn't see me. He let me get on the elevator. I took the elevator all the way to the 51st floor. When the elevator door opened, it looked like a scene out of a Hollywood movie—it was that luxurious. The receptionist on that floor greeted me. I briefly explained to her my situation. She then escorted me to a meeting room that had a beautiful marble glass table. A moment later, I was approached by a well-dressed, impressive looking attorney. I began to explain to him my situation. At first, his body language conveyed one thing, but once I mentioned to him that I also had Attorney Sweetlow representing me in another case, his body language changed. I could see the dollar signs in his eyes. He knew of Attorney Sweetlow and that he wasn't cheap. He then said to me,

"Curtis, I'll need a $5,000 upfront retaining fee and two other attorneys to assist me, which will be $250 an hour." At that point, I looked that attorney straight in his eyes and said,

"Do you know attorney John Sweetlow who represents my workman comp case?"

"Oh, yes. He's one of the best in Georgia."

"Well, that's who's representing little ole' me. You increased the cost when I told you the name of the person I went to for help after thinking at first that I couldn't afford you. But yes, I can. You see, money isn't the issue here. I passed the criteria to make the 1996

Paralympic USA Swim Team, but they cheated me out of my spot on that team, and now you want to 'BS.' I'm just an athlete who loves to compete. I don't play games. Listen: When I get a sour taste in my mouth about a person, and my gut feeling says to me that something in the coffee isn't clean, then I don't fool with them. So I don't need a person like you because you'll sell me out. Just show me the elevator, please." I left that office still feeling upset that I hadn't gotten any further in my quest to change and overturn things.

I went to my mom's house to talk to her about the situation. She shared these comforting words: "Don't worry. God will fix it all." But my heart was still filled with anger. I really didn't feel like hearing that particular message, but I humbled myself and received it. I then went to my room and fell down by my bed and began to cry out to God. Suddenly, one word popped up in my mind: "Fast!" I realized that complaining and grumbling weren't going to solve anything and that I needed to do what I sensed the Holy Spirit leading me to do. Therefore I went on a six-day fast with no food, only liquids, and doing nothing but praying and exercising. I spent plenty of time praying at the altar at my church for guidance. At times, I would speak with Pastor Flemming who always encouraged me to be optimistic because God was going to set things straight. I needed that encouragement.

When the 1996 Paralympic Games came around, I had to grit my teeth and bear the humiliation of being asked by people who witnessed me in the stands but knew that I should've been in the pool, "Why aren't you down there? Why are you up here?" I didn't want anyone questioning or bothering me. I felt embarrassed. At one point, I wanted to leave and avoid being present at the games altogether. Of course, I called my mom and shared with her the pain and humiliation I was feeling, to which she simply responded,

"I know it's hard, Joe, but see yourself through it all. Just use your mind and put yourself on that field because the day is going to come when you are there. Use it to your advantage, Joe. Smile through it all!" Her words struck a chord with me; they set me on a path and sparked something inside of me.

Just as mom had instructed, I began to visualize myself in that arena awarded with the gold medal. My focus shifted from being wronged to getting even. I even became angry. At that moment, I vowed to myself I was going to break every record in the book and make sure that everyone knew that Curtis Lovejoy was the best in the world. Bitterness kept me chained to my hurt and trapped in a useless ritual of blaming and self-pitying, so I ditched the bitterness and focused on becoming better. They were getting ready to have no choice but to chant the name "Lovejoy" and bring me center-stage. It was on. They done did it now! They've awakened a monster!

CHAPTER 33
BEAST MODE

P ISA, ITALY, THE WORLD INTERNATIONAL Wheelchair Fencing Competition, April 9 – 16, 1997.
A total of 18 countries represented, and during
that competition, I placed first in Foil and Épée fencing,
winning two beautiful gold medals and silver plates. I
quickly ascended to the number one rank in the fencing
category and becomes the first American to win an international medal in the sport. Shortly after this, I competed
at the Disabled Sports USA Competition in Springfield,
Connecticut, July 16-20, 1997. There, I set my second
World Record in the 50-meter breaststroke swimming
competition. I broke my first record by a whole ten
seconds and went on to win three gold medals in the
50-meter backstroke and the 50-meter freestyle swimming competitions. Six days later, I was on my way to

the World Wheelchair Games in Stoke Mandeville London, England where a total of 40 countries were competing. The three USA swimmers, Jacques, Fred, and I, brought home a combined eleven medals in swimming. Afterward, we spent the rest of the day in Paris, France, which was a beautiful city, especially at night with the Eiffel Tower lit up. After that, I was in Budapest, Hungary from November 12-20, 1997 where I had never seen so much pretty white snow in my life. It was cold there, but not freezing. In fencing, I competed in "B" classification, was ranked 38 coming in, but moved up to #29 in the world. I was able to compete with some of the top fencers in the world, and I held my ground.

On July 20, 1998, the USA Fencing Team journeyed to Frankfurt, Germany for the International World Paralympic Fencing Championship where 67 countries represented. There were three classes of competition: A, B, and C (also known as 'Tera"). When I was preparing and training back in the US, Coach Stawicki wanted me to fence in the class "B" competition. But once we got to Germany, he found out that I was really a class "C" fencer and told me he wants me to fence in the class "C" event to bring home the gold. My reply was okay, but I asked him to explain to my teammates why he made this sudden change since they were counting on me fencing in the class "B" event.

While preparing for my match, I began to reflect back to something Coach Stawicki shared with me before the entire team one day. He looked me in the eyes with a serious expression and said to me, "You will be our first World Champion for the USA very soon. There's nobody that can beat you or touch you! It will happen! I've traveled around the world coaching, and I haven't seen any other Tera fencer come close to beating you. So train hard because that day is coming for you!" That thought stirred me up so before my match that I felt like I was on fire; it felt like something went through me. Of course, I went on to win the gold medal in the Foil fencing competition and gold in the Épée fencing competition. At the end of the competition, I brought home a total of twelve victories and no defeats. I can remember during the last bout of competition, hearing the entire USA Team shouting "USA!!! USA!!! USA!!! USA!!!" For the USA once again, I brought home the World Champion. Coach Stawicki and my teammates were crying tears of joy. All I could say was,

"We did it!!! We did it!!!"

My teammates responded, "No, you did it!!! You brought home the gold!!!"

After winning that second gold medal, the feeling was so sweet. I just wanted to relive that moment over and over again; it's a feeling I can't put into words. Just know that there was a profound sense of appreciation for all of the hard work put into preparing for that moment. Athletes from other countries were telling me, "Curtis, you're the best. I've never seen a Tera with your disabilities that demonstrated a will to win like that."

I was humbled, and could only thank those athletes for the kind words. But I was not done yet. I was just getting started. I had more than just the 2000

Paralympic Games in my sight; I had a legacy to establish, one that would leave no doubts when it came to who is the best.

The Paralympic World Swimming Championship was being held October 10-18, 1998, in New Zealand with a total of 125 countries represented there. They were competing for three medals: gold, silver, and bronze. I felt honored to compete for this was an opportunity for me to take my performance to another level. I didn't take that opportunity lightly.

New Zealand was breathtakingly beautiful. It was amazing to see the clear water and the amazing marine life, especially the whales. New Zealand also had excellent food, and they're known for their perfect stones.

At this competition, there were plenty of competitors, but only one stood out to me: a young man who looked like a little person with feet turned backward. I was amazed to see him walking down the stairway. I wondered how he did it and concerned that he might fall forward. He was Pakistani.

Our tour guide took the entire USA Swim Team on a boat ride to see the whales. I remember the Captain yelling, "Everyone, look to your left!" Looking in that direction, we saw a gang of baby whales about 60 yards out; they were playing with one another. Around 200-300 yards away, we saw three grown whales leap five to eight feet into the air. I wanted to get in the water with those whales. That was one of the highlights of that trip, but it wouldn't be the main highlight. The real highlight would come later on during the competition.

Two weeks before the competition, I heard the Holy Spirit whisper in my heart these words: "All of the records will fall into your hands." There was a warmness on the inside of me, a supernatural peace that filled me. I was confident that I was about to do great.

Team USA was awesome! We cut thirty-one seconds off of the 50-meter freestyle, twenty-one seconds off of the 50-meter backstroke, ten seconds off of the 50-meter breaststroke, eleven seconds off of the 150-meter IM, and six seconds off of the 100-meter freestyle. Before the event, I visualized myself on the podiums receiving medals, and I received them. In fact, I ended up breaking two records in two more events that I had never competed in before.

God kept His promise. I broke several World Records, received several medals, and was even voted by my teammates to be the team captain. Everyone was calling me Captain Lovejoy.

March 26-27, 1999, in Montreal Quebec, Canada, The American Fencing Cup was held. I won the gold medal in Saber fencing while competing against class "A" and class "B" fencers even though I was only a class "C" fencer. Nothing could stop me. I was on a roll. Before I would score a single point, I would visualize myself first scoring that point.

It was June 10, 1999, in Minneapolis, Minnesota, the USA Swimming Championship Competition. I had told my swimming coach that my goal was to bring home the gold for Team USA at the 2000 Paralympic Games in Sydney, Australia. I was determined to get there. At the swimming competition, I set two new World Records in the 50-meter backstroke and the 50-meter breaststroke. I missed two more World Records by only .100 tenth of a second. But I still went on to set five new American records and bring home seven gold medals.

I was working my behind off to get the opportunity to represent Team USA at the 2000 Paralympic Games. On the way to the Paralympic Games, I needed to prove myself in several of the events prior to the games. I sought to compete in both the swimming and fencing competitions. This was considered historic because it had never been done before and I wanted to be the first. A big part of my successes was due to my focus and determination. I never got the big head. Regardless of how many medals I won, I realized that I needed to stay focused. I can't say all of my teammates carried this same drive. Some of my teammates wrestled with remaining humble, especially after securing big wins in competitions. For example, in one of the fencing tournaments held in France, some of our teammates racked up on gold. After the tournament, we all went out to celebrate. I could never stand being in certain environments, especially around cigarette smoke. I decided to retire for the night a little early. But it wasn't just the smoke that disturbed me; I saw what was coming. I had a brother who drank all of his life. I knew what would become of a night of wild drinking and partying.

Mixing alcohol and beer isn't the best thing to do. One of the fencers drank so much that her appendix burst. Whenever someone would tell her to slow down or stop, she'd shoo them away and continue on. At one point, a Polish fencer was pouring alcohol down her throat while she was leaning back in a chair. The next day, while the rest of us were preparing to board a plane and leave out, that young lady was in surgery at the local hospital. That was her first international trip...and it would also be her last. She never fenced again.

I made sure to keep myself healthy. I needed to remain sharp both mentally and physically. The mental part was the most difficult. Like any organization or competition, there tend to be a degree of behind-the-scenes politics that come to play. A teammate may grow envious and attempt to sabotage the success of another. It's happened to me on more than one occasion. You try to overlook it and stay positive, but it can get to you and tamper with your peace. For example, in the fencing department, from the beginning fencers tend to get a bad reputation. Nearly 97% of fencers smoke. During the 1996 Paralympic Games, the International Paralympic Committee (IPC) regularly observed fencers smoking outside before and after competitions; this behavior causes fencers to not be regarded as elite athletes—to some, fencers aren't seen as athletes at all. It's bad to see both males and females smoking like chimneys right before they have to compete in a serious physical event... one that involves a lot of movement. How can you compete in any physical activity if you destroy your lungs and your health? I am so thankful for the smoking laws here in the USA. But even more disturbing than the smoking habits of many US fencers was a practice often carried out by many who wanted to give each other a boost during competitions. It was commonplace for certain fencers to deliberately lose to their friends just to put them over while working to hold back the teammates they didn't like. I found myself on the butting end of such an attack. But the thing that kept me in a state of peace and gave me confidence was remembering the encouraging words from my pastor and the promises of God concerning my life. I realized I didn't need to try to fight against the internal politics raging behind the scenes; instead, all I needed to do was keep my eyes straight ahead and realize that my being there was ordained by God. *If God is for you, then who can be against you?* That is the ultimate confidence booster.

The 2000 USA Paralympic Fencing Trials held in Austin, Texas, was fast approaching. Before that was the Swimming Trials to determine who would make Team USA. I was excited about competing in them both and representing the USA in both sports. But not everyone was happy about me representing the USA in both sports as I discovered after receiving a message on my answering machine from Vickie, the fencing team leader:

(Beep) "Hi, Curtis. I just want you to know that before you head to the fencing trials in Texas, you need to choose which sport you're going to do: swimming or fencing. You cannot do both. If you have any questions, we can address them when you get to Texas. Please call USOC at [...] and let them know which sport. Thank you, Curtis." (Click)

When I received that message, I started to get upset, but my mind suddenly went back to the Sunday before I got on the road to head to the competition. That Sunday, the pastor laid hands on me and prayed for me. At that moment, the entire right side of my body got hot; a heat ran through it. The pastor then looked at me and said, "God is strengthening your right side for the journey." When I heard that message, I realized that what God was doing in my life ran counter to what some people wanted for me. Some didn't want me to compete and make history by competing in two sports, but God had other plans. The thought then entered my head: *God was preparing me for the fencing trials.* And guess what, I went on to compete in the fencing trials and defeat three of the top guys in the division to earn my spot on the 2000 US Paralympic Fencing Team. Regarding Vickie, the USOC attorney met with her, me, and head coach, Stawicki. He informed them that they could not make me select one sport over the other because I had the right to compete in multiple sports if I qualified. I learned that day to be quiet and let God fight my battles.

JUST A LITTLE LOVE & JOY

CHAPTER 34
THE ROAD TO SYDNEY

THE ROAD TO THE 2000 PARALYMPIC GAMES IN Sydney, Australia, was a long one. There was a total of fourteen events I had to compete in while en route to the Paralympic Games, including the trials for both swimming and fencing. The first event I had to compete in was the European Championship, which took place in Oviedo, Spain. By this time, I moved from being ranked 13th in the world as a class "B" fencer to the rank of eighth in the world. In fencing, Team USA also moved to fourth place in the world; I had also been selected at this time to carry the American flag during the opening ceremony for the 2000 Paralympic Games, which was a great honor.

I had to travel to Cleveland, Ohio, where it was cold, to compete in the fencing Nationals. I ended up with fifth place in Foil fencing, fourth in Sabre fencing, and third in Épée fencing. Based on the national rankings, the fourth, fifth, and sixth place spots for the USA Paralympic Fencing Team were wide open. It was getting down to crunch-time. During moments like these, that's when you find out who can handle the pressure.

❧

I had just reached my 43rd birthday, and I felt like I was in the best shape of my life. I was still on a roll. I had just broken several more World Records for swimming in the Pan-American Games. I set new records in the 50-meter freestyle (time: 1:33.0) and 50-meter backstroke (time: 1:35.23). Currently, I held seven World Records, four Pan-America records, and seven American World Records in swimming. According to the World Ranking Records, no other American—let alone African American beside the great Mark Spit—has made such an accomplishment in my sport. But I couldn't get comfortable and settled. I had to keep pushing myself to higher heights and higher levels of greatness. I understood that God wasn't through with me yet and that I was not through by a long shot.

The swim trials had arrived. This was the event that determined who made it onto Team USA for the Paralympic Games in Sydney, Australia. It was game-time! On day one of the trials, the first event during the preliminaries was the 50-meter freestyle. The World Record holder at the time was Jim Anderson from Great Britain. As I entered into the pool and got into lane three, I said a short prayer: "Jesus, let's do this." At that time, the official hollered,

"Swimmers, take your mark!" A brief silence fell over the place, and then the horn sounded. We took off. I swam the first twenty meters with my head under the water without coming up to take a breath. I could hear the Holy Spirit saying to my spirit, "Now is the time." When I reached the end of the pool and touched the wall, I emerged from the water and looked at the scoreboard. The scoreboard read "1:05.57 for Curtis Lovejoy." It happened! I did it! I set a new World Record! The crowd was jumping and going crazy! Music was blasting throughout the arena! The announcer lost himself. I think that he was just proud that a quad from the USA finally arrived. As I got out of the pool, I glanced around at the people in the stands. Many were happy for me; others were in a state of shock and disbelief. My heart was beating super fast as if I were going into cardiac arrest. I could barely catch my breath. The reality of what had just happened was still settling in in my mind. The moment that I rolled off of the pool deck and hit the media stand, the media bombarded me with questions. All I could see were light bulbs flashing. All I could think was "To God be the glory."

After the preliminaries that morning, I went and got something to eat and some rest. I wasn't done. I still had records to break and goals to accomplish. The finals were later on that evening. When the time came, I was well-rested and mentally prepared. Earlier that day was gone; only the present existed in my mind. When

I arrived at the venue for competition, I changed into my swim clothes and began to visualize myself winning the race. I saw myself with my hands raised, the winner. When it was time for the race, all of us competitors got into the pool; I got into the fourth lane. We were ready for the 50-meter freestyle finals. Just before the race started, the announcer called out my name: "Can Curtis Lovejoy swim beyond his World Record from this morning?! Let's cheer him on, fans!!!" he shouted. And the fans began to cheer loudly. Then a hush fell over the building. "Swimmers, take your mark! . . . . Go!!!" The horn sounded, and off we went. This time I felt completely at ease while racing; I felt like a fish; like one of those dolphins back in Florida that I saw. It was as if I was one with the water. I swam effortlessly. Upon reaching the end of the race and touching the wall of the pool, I raised my head and looked at the scoreboard. It happened again! I set another World Record, surpassing the record I set earlier that day! My score was 1:02.01. I beat my previous score by three seconds. Again, the place went crazy. People were cheering and clapping. Some people were speechless and amazed at what I just did. Afterward, I didn't want to talk to the media or anyone else at the venue; all I wanted was to get back to my room to call my mom and Tammy and give them the good news: I had just broken two World Records, four Pan-America records, and four American records in a single day. Still, the media was waiting for me; they had the side door I was planning to escape through blocked, so there was no way around them.

"Curtis! Curtis! How does it feel to be the World Record holder?!!"

"It feels like a heavy burden just lifted off of my shoulders. Can't take any more questions because I have to get ready for the prelims in the morning—I got the 50-meter backstroke."

"Wait! Wait! Hey, Curtis, can we expect another World Record?"

"I cannot answer that question right now because God says in His Word to never let your right hand know what your left-hand knows. So . . ."

Day two of the trials had arrived, and I was ready for what the day had to bring. Today, it was the 50-meter backstroke. I finished the race with a time of 1:25.0 setting a new Pan-America and American record during the preliminaries; but not a new World Record. In the finals that evening, I swam a 1:26.11. That wasn't my best performance, but it was still a good one.

Day three came, and it was time for the 100-meter freestyle. I entered the swimming pool with confidence. I knew I had this race in the bag. "On your mark! Go!!!" Once the horn blew, we were off. For the first 50 meters, I was doing great; but then, after touching the wall to do the last 50 meters, it felt as if my legs had cinder-blocks strapped to them. I felt a dragging sensation in the water as if someone was holding my legs underwater and my energy was pouring out of me those last 50 meters. I struggled just to get to the end of the pool.

I went back to my room feeling defeated after that race. I had no idea what happened to me in that pool. I expected to do much better than that. As I had made it a habit of doing, I turned my attention towards God and began crying out to Him in prayer. Before the race, I felt like the power of heaven was coursing through my veins; but after the race, I was left wondering if God was even with me in that pool. I cried out to God and asked Him what happened, but there was only complete silence. Later on that night, this thought emerged in my spirit: *Curtis, you have nothing else to prove. Just wait until you get to Sydney, Australia. There, men will see the power of God and know that His grace is sufficient for you.* Curtis, be patient. After that, I began to smile, cry tears of joy, and feel an indescribable sense of peace in my soul. I was now at ease, at rest, no longer bothered by what had occurred earlier that day. I remembered the long journey getting to where I was at the moment, recalling all of the miracles along the way that pointed to the fact that this moment was ordained by God for my life—that none of this was an accident or coincidence. I reminded myself of the unseen hand of the sovereign God and how that hand brought me to where I was, and I reminded myself that He wouldn't abandon me. Afterward, my blood started to boil. I felt the heat rising within. That same heat is what I'd feel every time the anointing of God would fall on me; it was what I'd feel every time Pastor Flemming would pray over me. I knew at that moment that my journey hadn't come to an end; it was just beginning.

Later that evening, all of the athletes were to return to the pool to receive their medals. I was ready to be handed my three first place gold medals. At that moment, I was informed by someone that a reporter wanted to interview me after the ceremony, so stick around. After the last medal was given out to the winning athlete, the announcer came over the PA system and announced, "We have now come to the most exciting part of the swimming championship meet where we present to all IPC officials, coaching staffs, athletes, and spectators the female and male Phillips 66 Athlete of the Meet!" I figured that the female athlete of the meet would probably be Erin Popovich and the male would be Jason Wennings. I was half right...because the announcer called out my name: "Curtis Lovejoy, the Male Athlete of the Meet!!!" I was totally stunned. That took me by surprise. Every athlete wants this award on their resume because it's one of the most prestigious awards one can acquire; it separates you from all of the other athletes.

After receiving that honor and recognition, the lady who first informed me that I had an interview and told me to stick around, Gail Drummond, presented me with the Athlete of the Meet Award. When she handed it to me, I grabbed her and simply held her tight. While I was embracing her, she whispered into my ear and said, "I have another award to present you." All I could do was give praise to God; His blessings were so abundant in my life. *What more could God give me at this point? I could only think of one thing.*

It was June 26, and all of the athletes had gathered together in the Grand Ballroom of the Hilton Inn for the announcement of the athletes who made the cut for the USA Swim Team at the 2000 Paralympic Games in Sydney, Australia. All of the training and hard work had led up to this point. I doubt any of the athletes got any sleep the night before. The anticipation, anxiety, and excitement wouldn't let us sleep. Finally, the day had come, and we were about to find out who made it onto Team USA. There were only 29 slots available to be filled: 19 slots for females and ten slots for males. At the moment, the name of the fourth male athlete was being announced: "From the city of Atlanta, Georgia, Curtis Lovejoy!!" After announcing my name as the fourth member of Team USA, the place erupted in applause. Rolling to the place of honor at the front of the room, I began reflecting back on the last seven years of my life that it took for me to arrive at this point. The number seven means "completion" in the Bible. It was as if God was saying to me that He was paying me back for all of the pain and disappointment I had endured. Everything had finally come full circle. The journey was worth it, every bit of it.

✕

I made the USA Paralympic Swim Team, but I still had the battle to face getting onto the fencing team. The fencing trials were coming up, and I was still catching flak from some of the powers that be about me being able to compete in both swimming and fencing. Again, Vickie, Coach Stawicki, and I, along with USOC Attorney Mr. Ambrose, had a second meeting to discuss my situation.

Attorney Ambrose again reiterated to Vickie and Coach Stawicki that they didn't have the authority to make me choose between sports and that I had the right to compete in both sports, especially if my competing in both sports would increase the USA's chances of securing gold medals in both events. Finally, the issue settled, I was allowed to attend the fencing trials for Team USA in Texas.

Day one of the Épée Fencing Trials, I had to face a man named Joel Royal who was one of the best counter-attackers in the sport. I knew this was going to be a tough challenge, but I was determined to win. Throughout the entire match, we tied in points—14 to 14. Joel had a cheering section filled with family and friends rooting him on, and I had mine. The place was going wild. Whoever scored the next point would be declared the winner. As we prepared for the final round, I thought to myself, "This is it, the moment where I have to go for it. I have to go for it all." I had my sight set on the spot where I wanted to strike Joel: his upper right chest. I figured that Joel wasn't going to expect me to make such a move. "Ready!!" the official yelled. My heart was beating extremely fast. Pressure was mounting inside of me. I waited until the final light that signaled the beginning of the round went off and then I went for it: I struck Joel right where I planned to strike. I hit my mark and won the match 15 to 14.

After a morning full of competition, I began preparing for the next day's competition. It was important that I be sharp and alert.

Day two of the competition had arrived. That morning, while I was at breakfast, Vickie came by my table and continued to hassle me about choosing a sport as if she didn't hear Attorney Ambrose who warned her to get off of my back and leave me alone about the issue. But I refused to let that get to me. I remained focused on the task at hand: winning my spot on the USA Paralympic Fencing Team. I just went back to my room and prepared for my match. I had to compete against Joel Royal again in what was my final qualifying match.

Early in the match, Joel was in the lead. He had a seven-point lead on me. The score was 8 to 1. The official then allowed us to take a one minute break before resuming the match. After the break, I returned with a determination in my heart. Before the second half of the match, I tapped Joel on his shoulder with my weapon to get his attention and then I said to him, "You will not beat me" while smiling confidently. Once the match resumed, I scored 13 points straight, closing the gap in the points. I could see the frustration on his face as he sensed the match slipping from his hands; as he sensed victory and a shot at being on Team USA quickly slipping away. I could see his wrists getting tired and heavy. I was determined to win at all cost. And I did. I won the match 13 to 9, earning both a bronze medal and a spot on the US Paralympic Fencing Team.

Sydney, here I come!

When it was time to announce the Fencing Team

members who would represent the United States of America in Sydney, Australia, I could sense that many of the athletes and coaches weren't pleased with me to be one of them. Some of them felt that I had already made the swim team and that I should've backed out of the fencing competition allowing the other athletes to shine. The outspoken person that I am expressed to those who didn't want to see me on the team that I wished I had four more *Curtis Love-joys* on the team because the work ethic of some of the athletes wasn't where it needed to be—it wasn't on an elite level. I felt like many of the athletes didn't work as hard during the off-season as they did the on-season. I let them know that if respect for the USA was going to be among the world community of athletes, then we had to promote the hardest workers and the best athletes rather than showing favoritism to certain individuals. I worked my butt off to get where I was, and I wasn't going to lie down and surrender to backstage politics in the industry because this was my time to shine. Why? I gave my all to get there and to be the best.

CHAPTER 35
SHOWTIME!

AN ONSLAUGHT OF MEDIA PERSONALITIES AND media coverage descended upon me after the announcement of my placement on the swimming and fencing teams representing the USA at the Paralympic Games in Australia. Brenda Woods of WXIA-11-Alive contacted me for an interview. She wanted to do a story to air on prime-time during the opening ceremony of the 2000 Paralympic Games. CNC and Imani magazines also contacted me. I had a second interview with Hale Shepherd of WXIA-11-Alive and featured again in the Atlanta Journal-Constitution. Jet and Good Life Magazines featured me; WeMedia, WSB Channel 2's Monica Kauffman, and FOX 5's Amanda Davis interviewed me. It was like a whirlwind of media coverage. Everyone wanted to have a story about the man who

suffered a devastating car accident that left him a Quadriplegic and didn't learn how to swim until handicapped
and in his thirties. My story was like a "raised from the
dead" testimony. No, I didn't die physically, but I might
as well had died since I had become dead mentally, emo-
tionally, spiritually, and in almost every other way. I was
a hollow shell of a man who had all but pulled the trigger on himself. The truth is, I attempted suicide several
times only to have every attempt blocked by some act of
God. And now, there I was, sitting on top of the world,
inspiring millions and living the dream. Had I not lost
my legs, my life would not have turned out so spectacular; my name would not have become so great. Simply
put, I became a living example of what God can and
will do with a man when he chooses to get better rather
than get bitter and surrender his heart, mind, and bro-
kenness to Him. God puts men back together in strange
and miraculous ways when they yield to Him. Never before would I have thanked God for a handicap. If asked
which would I choose? To have my legs back and continue living the mediocre life I was living or to continue in
my wheelchair and live the extraordinary life I'm living
today. There is no doubt in my mind what my choice
would be: I'd prefer to roll into my greatness rather than
walk in mediocrity.

>~~

September 15, 2000, was the big day; it was the ceremony for the opening night of the 2000 Paralympic Games
in Sydney, Australia. I had prime-time. Brenda Woods of

the WXIA 11-Alive was running their story on me called "Miracle Quad" before the ceremony. During this time, Brenda also made a big announcement concerning me: I had been voted by the IOC (International Olympics Committee), IPC (International Paralympic Committee), and the WSUSA (Wheelchair Sports USA) as the "Elite Athlete Of The Year" out of a pool of 40,000 athletes all over America. I was humbled and shocked. My mom and I were watching the special on television at the time; and when that announcement was made, we were both speechless and in tears. I had no idea I was about to receive such an award.

October 12th would be my last night sleeping in my bed over the next month. Early that morning, I was so glad to see Tammy, who came by to spend a little time with me before I got on the plane to fly out to Sydney. She came by around five in the morning. When she slid into the bed beside me, it felt like heaven. She never took off her clothes, and we didn't have sex; we just laid there and talked for a while.

The hours just seemed to fly by. Suddenly, it was time to head to the airport, and Tammy drove me. Once we got to my gate and checked my wheelchair, I looked back and noticed Tammy had tears rolling down her face. She looked me in the eyes and expressed sincere regret over not being able to stay and watch me board the plane because she had been missing too much time at work. It was hard for her to part. It was more difficult than she thought it would be. "I asked your mother how does she handle this part; seeing you head out once again to far away countries. She said that you're doing something that you love; but mostly, you're touching lives around the world and you're doing what Jesus commanded each and everyone of us to do. I'm trying to handle that side of you." After this, Tammy handed me a package. She instructed me not to open it until I got on the second plane heading to Sydney, and to call her as soon as I touched down in Dulles. She then told me she loved me and gave me a kiss before turning to walk away. I rolled up to the ticket counter to check in; while there, I so desired for Tammy to turn and look back at me one more time. I didn't want to part with her without a sense of closure. I watched at her walking away while whispering under my breath "Turn, baby, turn." And she did! But not only did she turn back, but she ran back and landed in my arms. I was lost in that moment. No one and nothing else existed in that time and space beside Tammy and the love we shared. Our desperate longing to feel one another's arms again, to hear each other's voices once more, to immerse ourselves in the deepest depths of passion we shared for one another was one of the most powerful things I'd ever experienced. I needed that. It was the closure my heart needed before leaving. Afterward, I knew in my heart that she was going to be fine. We held each other and kissed until I was finally escorted onto the plane.

I arrived in Sydney, Australia at around 7:30 am. It took me nearly two and a half hours to get through customs.

CHAPTER 35: SHOWTIME!

Afterward, I arrived at the Olympic Village and to my room, which was in the fencing team's suite. Being there, took a while to completely sink in that I was actually at *the big dance*: the Paralympic Games. I remember visiting the aquatic center and the feeling of chills going up and down my spine. It began to dawn on me that I was going to compete in that very pool against other athletes. I just closed my eyes and soaked the moment in, taking it all in.

While preparing for the Games, I would visualize myself winning; this became a ritual of mine. I would see myself in my mind winning gold medals in each of my events. Visualization was a big part of my success. I am convinced that victory begins with the mind, not the body. If you picture yourself winning, you will ultimately set yourself up to win. If you see yourself losing, you will set yourself up to lose. There is power in the imagination. Some people may refer to this as the Law of Attraction, but I believe this is a basic tenet of faith. As a Christian, I believe what the Bible says when it tells us, "As a man thinketh in his heart, so is he" (Proverbs 23:7).

There are two ways to enjoy the opening parade ceremony of the Olympics: watching it from the stands or the field of the Olympic Stadium. I was preparing to march onto the field with my fellow peers in front of over 90,000 screaming fans while music blasted loudly and fireworks exploded overhead. Marching ahead of us was the USA delegation dressed in white hats, white mocks, red vests, blue slacks, and blue and white tennis shoes laced with red shoe strings; each item had the USA logo on it; each delegate wore a million dollar smile.

While we (Team USA) were in the tunnel getting ready to march onto the field to take our place, we were chanting, "Who let the dogs out?!! Whoop! Whoop! Whoop! Whoop!" While we marched through the tunnel, the Aussies joined in with us in chanting "USA! USA! USA! USA!" After the Aussies marched into the stadium, the place went wild. Then the cauldron was lit, and the Paralympic Games were officially declared open. It was showtime!

October 22nd was the big day for me; that was the day of my first competition at the games. In Sydney, I was greeted by so many generous people in the days prior. People would often approach me and ask to take pictures with me. I'd meet people who were Christians who were rooting for me because they wanted to see a Christian on the winner's block. I received so much love. Of course, I still felt the cold shoulder from certain of my teammates, but I didn't want to focus on that. It was time for me to do what I was there to do. And my first competition was the Sabre fencing competition.

I told myself that I had nothing to lose and that the only thing I was obligated to do was perform to the best of my ability while having fun doing it. I just needed to relax. My first opponent was Ty Hoon from Korea. We went toe-to-toe. At first, I was beating him 14 to 13. I just needed one more point to win. But Ty was able to score a point and tie-up the match. It was now 14 to 14. Ty then scored the final point and won the match.

Afterward, he congratulated me on a good match and commended me on my skills, and so did Coach Stawicki who expressed how proud he was of me for doing such a great job against a top-tier fencer. Coach then explained to me that I had moved up in the World Record ranking to at least the eighth or tenth place in the world. She told me that I represented Team USA very well.

My Sabre fencing teammates were Mario, an amputee, and Gerard, who has paraplegia. I was able to do well, but Gerard was the star here. He did the impossible, and he refused to lose. He scored twelve unanswered points to seal the victory over Kuwait. I could see the fear in the Kuwaiti fencer's eyes; he was crying because he knew he was about to lose. Gerard won 45 to 42 for Team USA. Everyone was shouting "USA! USA! USA! USA!" in celebration of Gerard's victory. We advanced to the next round where it is my task to face David from Great Britain. I went on to defeat David five to one; Gerard also defeated Great Britain's Peter five to one. The USA had ten wins, and Great Britain had two. Mario lost to Great Britain's Jack, one of the top fencers in the league. Jack scored 13 unanswered points, and Mario didn't score a single point during his match. But still we could make a comeback because we were sure that Mario, our #1 class "A" fencer, would have no problem defeating David who was Great Britain's weakest class "B" fencer. But that didn't happen. David defeated Mario.

When I faced Jack in the final round, the score

was Great Britain (40 points) and the USA (35 points). We ended up losing to Great Britain 45 to 38. I was able to score three points on Jack, their best fencer, who only had a slight limp when he walked as opposed to me, who has quadriplegia using specially made quad-gloves and more. Coach Stawicki was extremely pissed with Mario but pleased with me and Gerard, both of whom he said fenced wonderfully. Sadly, Mario let the team down. After thirteen hours of fencing I was exhausted. All I wanted to do was get something to eat and lie down.

The next day, was more fencing. Unfortunately, Team USA didn't fence well at all. Apparently, everyone on the team except me came down with a bug. I was able to secure two victories out of my five matches. Several of my other teammates caught the flu. I decided to let one of our alternate fencers named Roy finish the Épée competition in my place so that I could direct my attention to the swimming competition.

On October 24th, it was time for my swimming competition. At the last minute, my teammate Jason informed me that I was suddenly added to the 4 x 50-meter relay race. We finished 5th in that race.

CHAPTER 36

GOING ALL THE WAY
TO THE END

I T WAS OCTOBER 25, 2000, AND I WAS PREPARING FOR another day of competitive swimming. Over 20,000 screaming fans anxious to watch the preliminaries packed the aquatic center. This day's challenge was the 50-meter backstroke, which wasn't my favorite event—I had been focusing mainly on my freestyle. Jim Anderson of Great Britain was the World Record holder in this event with a swim time of 1:10. That morning, he finished second place with a time of 1:08.54. Penn of Poland finished third with a time of 1:11.21. Hector of Spain finished first and set a new Paralympic World Record with a time of 1:05.02. After being observed by IPC, I figured classifiers might move him up to Class S3. I was blessed to finish with a time of 1:19.21, thereby setting a new American record while coming in 4th place. But there was no time for me to celebrate. Coach Maxwell approached me about an urgent matter. He appeared stressed and asked to speak with me in private. What could this be about? I wondered. We went downstairs to talk. "Curtis, some country is protesting against your classification," Coach Maxwell shared.

"Me? Why me?" I couldn't believe it. "This was my first time competing in the Paralympic Games, and I already have protesters from another country attacking me," I murmured. Immediately, I began to pray. I sensed that this was an attack against me by Satan; it had to be a demonic attack. I began to declare, "No weapon formed against me shall prosper." I had come too far to suddenly let all of my hopes and dreams get snatched away from me over something like this. While I was praying about the situation, I sensed the Holy Spirit whispering in my heart to stand still and watch the power of God move on my behalf. A calmness came over me at that moment. I knew that God was fighting on my behalf.

Coach Maxwell and I went into a room where two classifiers met us. They stated that the country protesting against my swimming abilities wanted them to conduct a muscle and swim test to determine whether I was a true S2 category athlete or whether I should place in a higher classification. They didn't want to tell me which country was protesting me, but I later found out that it was Great Britain.

I cooperated with the officials during this process. They began by asking me a couple of questions.

"How many times do you practice a week?"

"I practice six days a week—a total of four hours swimming; two hours in the morning and two hours in the evening. And that's just swimming. Not counting the time I spend in the weight room."

"Curtis, the average Quad swims twice a week, anywhere from a total of 60 to 90 minutes on any given day," one of the officials responded.

"But I'm not your average Quad. Please accept what I'm about to say. First of all, I am a Quad. I don't look like a Quad because I refuse to accept how people say a typical Quad should look. Don't just look at my muscular upper body and compare me with another person with paraplegia. These muscles come from working out in the gym. All I want you all to do is to be fair with me and take into consideration my hands and leg-control. I have bad spasms. Can you all be fair with me?"

"Um... Um... Okay. We can do that. We want to start in the pool. We want you to swim one lap of each: freestyle, backstroke, and breaststroke."

I complied with the demands of the officials. As I swam the backstroke, one of the classifiers shouted, "I know you can do better than that with all of those muscles!" I grabbed the wall, took off my goggles, and hollered back,

"Don't push my buttons! You asked me to backstroke, and this is what you're going to get! Okay!"

Finishing all the strokes the classifiers requested of me, they led me to a private dressing room for the muscle tests. It was 95 degrees outside, but extremely cold in the dressing room because the thermostat for the AC was set very low. To make matters worse, I was wet from the cold water from the swimming pool. So I was sitting wet and cold due to these officials. That didn't sit well with me. The cold would cause me to have spasms where my body would jerk uncontrollably. My upper body was fully exposed because I was wearing a pair of swimming jammers only. I kept telling the classifiers that I was cold, but they weren't paying me any attention. One classifier asked me to transfer to the massage table, which I managed to do on my own by pushing and scooting with my upper body until finally in position. Once I was on the table, the officials straightened both of my legs out until fully extended. I was lying there wearing nothing but my swimwear. I was freezing and shivering while the classifiers stood over me discussing whether or not they should start with my legs or arms. Suddenly, my body involuntarily jumped off of the massage table and hit the floor with a loud thud. Now, the classifiers wanted to take me seriously. They started behaving apologetically and asking me if I needed to see a doctor and insisting that I see a team physician. They asked me to get dressed and return to the pool stating that they would share with me their findings later. While getting dressed, my nose started to run. The classifiers were now afraid. They were nervous and edgy because they didn't want my medical report to read: "Swimmer got hurt while in the classifiers' care."

I returned to the pool deck where the classifiers and Coach Maxwell were waiting for me. One of the classifiers revealed to me the results of the test: "Curtis, you are a true S2 Quad. Everything is okay. You're allowed to swim in the S2 class." I shook both classifiers' hands and thanked them for being fair.

"That was a close one," Coach Maxwell said, "because we're expecting you to win the gold medal. Stop by and see the team doctor. Get some food and some quick rest for the finals tonight. Come back to the finals and set my second new American record in the 50-meter backstroke with a new and better time of 1:16.23."

Hector had finished 1st place in the 50-meter backstroke event, but due to being misclassified, he was not allowed to compete in my classification any longer for the rest of the games. He still got the gold medal, but he was bumped up to a higher classification, which was good news for me.

❦

I had cold chills running throughout my body. My head was aching. I prayed that I wasn't coming down with the bug that was spreading throughout the Olympic Village. I called Coach Maxwell and told him how I was feeling, and he immediately sent the team doctor to my room to see what was going on with me. After examining me, the doctor determined that I had come down with the flu. Undoubtedly, going from cold water to a cold dressing room took its toll on me. The doctor told me to eat something, drink plenty of fluids and get plenty of rest; then he said he'd check on me early in the morning to see if I was fit to swim the next day.

I didn't sleep at all that night. Even with a space heater in the room, I couldn't get warm. With my roommate's heater pointed towards me; I still felt cold and chilly. I dozed off to sleep at around four o'clock. Being that I had to get up at six to eat breakfast and board the bus to the aquatic center, this didn't fare well. The doctor returned to my room at around 6:45 am. When he got there, my nose was completely stopped-up; I couldn't breathe except out of my mouth, which was quite uncomfortable. The doctor said, "Curtis, you look horrible. I personally think that you need more bed rest and, perhaps you need to be excused from competition today, but it is solely up to you if you want to go forward and compete." About that time, Coach Maxwell entered the room and overheard the doctor's remarks.

"Well, Curtis, what do you want to do? It rests in your hands," Coach Maxwell stated. While coughing, I paused long enough to respond,

"Coach, I'm going to compete. I didn't come this far to be pampered. I'm going to lay it all in the pool this morning. Doc, can you give me something for my head? My head is killing me."

"Only some aspirins. No medications at all because you're subject to be drug-tested."

"Okay. If I can make it to the finals, I will recover by then. Let's do this!" I didn't want to miss that morning's competition because it was the 100-meter freestyle event, for which I was slated to win the gold medal. For this event, I had trained my butt off. Now, I had flu-like symptoms attempting to prevent me from competing. I decided I was going to fight through this. No one said victory was going to be simple. Along your journey in life, unexpected twists and turns will arise and try to throw you off course. I already knew this. I should have anticipated this. The devil won't simply let you walk right into your destiny without putting up some fight. Life won't make things easy for you although you may have things planned out a certain way in your mind. Fight through it, nonetheless! That's what my parents taught me.

The 100-meter freestyle competition was scheduled for 10:15 am, so I had a little time to lay in bed and rest. Thank God! "I'll have one of the coaches bring you some breakfast," Coach Maxwell told me. "Doc, will you bring Curtis over to the pool at around 9:15 am?"

"Curtis, will that be enough time for you to warm up and report to the ready-room?" the doctor asked me.

"Yes. I'm planning on doing a couple of laps. I want to save as much energy as I can."

"Also, doctor," Coach Maxwell jumped in, "make sure that someone is pushing him. He needs to save his arms for the race. Curtis, no matter how this may turn out, I want you to know that you're making a gutsy decision and I admire you for making that call. That's the American spirit."

It was morning around eight o'clock, and all kind of thoughts were running through my mind. I was wondering if I should continue with the race or just count my losses. I was trying to hang on to the belief that God sent me there to the Paralympic Games for His glory. I was trying to trust in God's power to see me through. I didn't feel well at all. My body was telling me to stay in bed. I was beginning to second guess myself and my purpose in life. I began to search for something to motivate me—anything desperately! I was trying to remember words spoken to me by my mom and dad. I needed to light a fire within. At that time, I grabbed my backpack and noticed a light purple envelope with my childhood name on it: "Joe the Cocomo." It was my mother's handwriting. I immediately opened the card. It read:

To My Son From Your Loving Mother

I have watched you go through life as only a child can – laughing, crying, so sure of yourself and at the same time so often full of doubts. My heart broke for you when life was unfair. I would have shielded you from pain and heartache if you had let me. I wanted to protect you but you needed to grow-into your own person. So I had to let go of you a little at a time. That was one of the hardest things I've ever had to do. Your childhood is gone now, and I still miss those wonderful times, the tough decisions you'll make at the right times, but I am so proud of the adult you have become. I Love you, and whatever path in life you may choose to embrace, my love will be with you. And I will cherish you always.

Love Mom,
GOD Bless you!

By 9:30 am, the only thing I could think of was the words from my mom. I dashed into the bathroom before heading towards the ready-room so that I could steal a moment to pray. I prayed, "Father, I never thought that I would say this to you, but it's from my heart: I can't do this, so please move me out of the way, and you swim the race. I don't want your energy or strength; just swim the race for me. Amen." Once I got to the ready-room, I observed the playing of all kinds of mind games. I simply pulled my hood over my head and tuned everyone and everything out until escorted to the block where I entered lane two. As the announcer called my name, I quickly glanced at the stands and shifted my eyes to the bright yellow swat pad. Beside me was Jim of Great Britain in lane four—he was a World Record holder with a previous time of 2:31.00; also, France was in lane three. The second that the horn sounded, I took-off. I pushed off the wall with my legs and glided into my streamline. I was still feeling weak though. After the first 15 meters, I looked to my left and noticed that Jim was ahead of me. I started praying in my head, "Lord, we need to speed up." Suddenly, it was as if Jesus Himself took me out of the race and placed me at the end of the pool. Strength came out of nowhere. When I touched the wall for the final 50 meters of the race, I looked up at the scoreboard and noticed that it was displaying my time, which was 2:12.89—that was a new Paralympic and World Record in the 100-meter freestyle event! I shattered the old record by 30 seconds.

"Curtis Lovejoy just broke and set two Paralympic and World Records in the 50-meter freestyle and 100-meter freestyle!!!" the announcer shouted over the PA system. I grabbed my head and hollered,

"Thank you, Jesus!!!!" Everyone in the aquatic center went crazy. People were screaming and chanting,

"USA! USA! USA!"

The Aussies can appreciate great swimming. Still, this was only the preliminaries. I still had the finals later on that night.

As I struggled to lift myself out of the pool, I felt weaker than ever, but my spirit was high. The entire USA Swim Team was chanting, "Lovejoy!! Lovejoy!! Lovejoy!! Who let the dogs out!!! Whoop!! Whoop!! Whoop!! Whoop!!" As I rolled towards the Wall Street press box, all of the media groups swarmed me like sharks having a feeding frenzy; they were trying to interview me, but I rolled right past them. I simply gave them a big smile. I didn't feel like being interviewed at the moment. I wanted and desperately needed to get back to my room so I could rest up for the finals later on that evening.

Word quickly spread throughout the Village that I set new Paralympic and World Records. I was just glad to reach my bed and lie down. While in bed, I was soaking it all in. I started thinking about the word the Lord placed in my heart while I was at the trials in Indianapolis: *You have nothing to prove in the USA. Just wait until you get to Sydney.* "Thank you for your faithfulness, God," I began to pray. My body was still too excited to go to sleep, so I simply closed my eyes and laid still as if meditating on that morning's victory...and miracle. I knew *that* wasn't my strength that kicked in; *that* was something extra, something I didn't have. In my weakest state, not only did I win the race, but I shattered my old records, the ones I set when I was at my strongest. That was supernatural. But I wasn't done yet.

When evening time came, I had rested a little more and prepared for the finals. I arrived at the ready-room and prepared for my match. Everyone in the room was quiet and staring. Perhaps amazed by my performance from earlier in the day. Or maybe they were concerned about whether or not I'd be able to repeat my performance from earlier. Maybe some of them thought I was a superhero. I don't know. All I do know is my mind was in the zone and focused on getting in the water. Again, with a prayer in my heart and God's sovereign favor upon my life resting on the front of my mind, I was ready to make history again. I knew that's why I was there.

I got into my lane, which was lane four, and looked around again like before. I was ready and waiting for the horn to blow. My concentration was razor-sharp. I had forgotten at that moment about my sore, hurting throat, the temperature I had (feeling feverish), the aches in my body, and my stuffy nose; I was just ready and anxious to hear the sound of the horn signaling the start of the race.

Once the horn blew, I was off. I streamlined like before in the water, going from one end of the pool to the other. I'd sensed during the match that I was in the lead, but when I stuck my head out of the water and glanced at the huge scoreboard, I saw the lights flashing another message: "New Paralympic and World Record: CURTIS LOVEJOY of the USA. Time: 2:10.48." I didn't match my record from earlier that day; I surpassed it, beating it by two seconds. It was now official: I became the first athlete in the history of the Paralympics to set three Paralympic and World Records in one day. It was unbelievable. The crowd was on their feet, clapping. They didn't stop clapping until I left the pool deck.

The world had come to know the name "Curtis Lovejoy" as I was being handed the gold medal in that swimming competition. I was in tears as the IPC official placed the medal around my neck and read off my credentials. Tears fell from my eyes as I watched the American flag being raised and heard the American national anthem played in my honor. All I could think about was my family. I was envisioning my dad looking down on me from heaven along with my brother, WiLewis, and my grandmother. I could see the smiles on their faces. There was nothing more I wanted at that moment than to get to a phone and call my mom and girlfriend, Tammy. I wanted to hear their voices and celebrate with them over the phone. Even though I had one more competition to face, the pressure was now gone. I called my mom and informed her that I won the gold medal and excitement completely overtook her. She always believed I could do it, and that I would. She then shared with me that Pastor Flemming instructed the entire church family to pray for me and that God had revealed to him that Satan was going to attack me in different ways; therefore, I would need supernatural strength during the competition. How right he was. After speaking with my mom, I did not doubt where nor how my strength comes. Divine favor makes this case. Sure, I was a hard worker, but there was something extra that allowed me to do what I did.

After talking to my mom, I contacted the Shepherd Center to break the news to everyone there. I talked with Amanda Davis and shared with her my accomplishments in Sydney; she burst into tears and began rejoicing over the news.

October 27th was my last day of competition. As I said earlier, I didn't feel any pressure to perform. I had already solidified my name and legacy and made history, but I was ready to perform nonetheless. When the time to compete came, I got into lane four like before, did my normal routine, and waited for the horn to sound. When the horn sounded, I was off just like before. When I touched the wall at the end of the race, I looked up and noticed that the scoreboard was flashing: "New Word Record: Curtis Lovejoy! Time of 1:00.67." Unbelievable! I just broke my own World Record again!

The media was trying hard to get my attention, but all I wanted to do was relax and absorb the wonderful feeling I was experiencing. I just wanted to soak it all in, to once more close my eyes and shut the world out for few minutes. It took me almost forty-five minutes to make it to the stand where my teammates were because everyone was pulling on me. My teammates were shouting, "Curtis, you're the man!! You're the man!!" But it wasn't over yet. That was just the morning's competition; I still had one more to do that evening. That night, I did it again: I broke my own record and went on to be the only athlete in history to break a total of five World Records in three days. This time, my time was 1:00.01. The other swimmers just stared at me in shock and disbelief; one of them approached me and asked me if I was a ghost. Another one claimed I was from another world. Back in the dressing room, one athlete hollered out at an official,

"You need to drug-test him!!!" I didn't allow any of that to get to me. My smile was plastered on my face as if sculpted on. The joy and happiness in my heart were unshakable. I felt on top of the world.

I set a total of four new World Records over two days: the first World Record was set in the 100-meter freestyle during the preliminaries, shattering the old World Record by .32 seconds; then at the finals later that night, broke that World Record by setting a newer World Record in the 100-meter freestyle. The following day, I set a World Record in the 50-meter freestyle during the preliminaries, returned that night and broke that World Record by setting another one for a total of two World Records on that day. In total, I had set five World Records along my journey leading up to the final day of the 2000 Paralympic Games.

❦

October 30th was the day of the closing ceremony for the 2000 Paralympic Games. Athletes from all over the world converged on Sydney, Australia, to compete; their eyes set on winning gold, silver, and bronze medals and having their names recorded in the annals of time. I was blessed to win two gold medals. Some athletes were going home without any medals; still, nothing can replace the experiences shared over those few weeks while there. The Olympics and Paralympic Games is a collective, unifying force that helps to bring the global community together for the sake of peace, love and harmony, and to celebrate a common goal, which was evident during the 2000 Paralympic and Olympic Games. With or without a medal, I was just elated and excited to be a part of such an event. Those experiences, I will cherish for a lifetime.

The closing ceremony was as grand as the opening ceremony, being filled with amazing fireworks and a party-like atmosphere with over 4,000 performers, a sea of Paralympic athletes blanketing the field; a roaring, screaming crowd of 75,000 people looking on; and pyrotechnics dancers, singers, and more. People were coming up to me all night congratulating me and complimenting me on my successes. One Chinese female swimmer said, "Curtis, you're an amazing swimmer! You, by far, are one of my greatest mentors!!!" Regardless of having a

few differences with some of my colleagues on this journey, we were able to put all of that drama behind us and
enjoy our fellowship together. There were no big I's and
little *you's*. We had developed a real sense of unity.

In the Olympic Village, if you are an athlete that
earned a medal, you get special attention from the ladies. Of course, that's always a plus. When you get a
medal, you will be broadcast all over television and all
throughout the Village. Yes, you become a celebrity to
the public and even to the other athletes. But one thing
I learned early on was always to conduct myself with dignity and respect even after all of the events, lights, and
the celebrations have ended. Some people don't understand the importance and significance of being famous;
they don't understand the responsibility it carries. Many
of the athletes were getting wasted after the games; they
were drinking beer and wine and cutting loose. But just
because the games were over, that didn't mean we could
all forget about our ethics, and that didn't mean we were
no longer beholden to the rules of the Village. All of
the Team USA swimmers were under the USA code of
conduct, which meant no drinking was allowed. Violat-
ing the rules carried a heavy punishment. For example,
a swimmer named John got so drunk during the closing
ceremony that he started talking out of his head, sway-
ing from side-to-side in his wheelchair until he fell out
of it. Two of the USA coaches escorted him to his room,
placed him under house arrest, and then put him on
a plane the very next day heading back to the United
States. We (USA Swim Team) later found out that they

stripped him of his World/Pan-American and American record. John mentioned that he was going to go out with a bang and get completely drunk, but he never imagined that doing so would have such dire consequence.

When it comes to the USA swim team, the coaches believes in following the US code of conduct to the letter. I probably could have gotten away with one drink, especially since I stayed in the suite with the fencers and their coaches who were laxer when it came to the rules, but I couldn't afford to throw everything away that I had just worked to establish. What a shame it would have been to be stripped of my achievements after the games because of misconduct. I didn't just break records and win medals; I inspired people, raised hopes, brought attention to my Christian faith, and created a legacy. I didn't want to give the devil an opportunity to destroy all that God worked hard to establish in and through me. But I did take the luxury of enjoying a few things I had deprived myself of during the competition. So I went down to the McDonalds in the Olympic Village and got two Big Macs with French fries, two apple pies, six chicken nuggets, and one large Coca-Cola. It was on! My appetite had returned, and I wasn't concerned about my weight or anything else.

Over the next few days, I stayed in Sydney, Australia, and enjoyed the sights. It felt good not having to get up in the morning at a certain time, and not having to go to a facility to train. I enjoyed being able to sleep in as late as I wanted to. It was relaxing to get up and look out of my window at the surfers trying to beat the incoming waves of the ocean. I transferred my luggage to the Courtyard Hotel in Murrayville in Parramatta City with two of my teammates, Mr. Bruder and Aimie. We enjoyed eating dinner at Dudley Restaurant where there was a great view of the harbor. The seafood was excellent, especially with the 1975 dry red wine. Once the cork popped, you could smell the grapes permeating the air in the dining room. We relaxed while listening to the live jazz band play music that soothed our souls. It was time to unwind. Afterward, we strolled down to the harbor to capture some fresh air. The weather was perfect. As the cool breezes washed over me, it was like they were blowing over my heart and soul. The solitude brought back thoughts of my childhood to my mind. I thought about my beginnings as a child: coming into this world looking like a girl; being picked on by other kids who would call me a girl, among other things. I thought about my days in grade school, graduating from high school and moving into my own apartment while hoping that college basketball would become my career, only that I was too short to make it I was told. I thought about Melissa. I thought about the day of my car accident, recalling all of the nights that I wanted to end my life, thinking that I would never amount to anything since I no longer had the use of my legs. I thought about all of the ups and downs I encountered over the years leading up to this point. As the winds whistled overhead, my mind went deeper into my vault of memories. It all culminated in that one moment with me sitting in my wheelchair on the harbor, feeling the indescribable peace and tasting sweet redemption. Divine favor had manifested in the form of fame, victory, unparalleled success, and happiness like no other. The one thought that resonated with me at that moment was, "It was all worth it, every bit of it. Every tear I cried was worth this moment."

I was basking at the moment, but I needed to get back home to see my loved ones. I wanted to see mom, my siblings, and Tammy. The experience wouldn't be complete without the ones I loved by my side. And to be honest, no amount of gold could fill the hole that was in my heart. I was especially excited about seeing Tammy. I wanted and needed someone to share my life. Over the upcoming months, Tammy and I shared some incredible moments; but as fate would have it, that, too, would come to an end. We eventually broke up. She left for certain reasons of her own. But we remained friends. Even still, God sensed the loneliness in my heart, and He would bless me one more time beyond my wildest imagination with a woman who would become my wife.

Mamie and I met on a sunny day in 1997 at the Shepherd Center. That day, I was rolling down the hall, pass the Apothecary station, when I happened to glance through the window and notice the most beautiful short lady with the most incredible smile. I stopped and stared at her, unable to move. I sat and watched as she moved about with such grace, elegance, and with a demeanor emanating pleasantness. I was nervous about approaching her, being that I didn't know what to expect; but when I finally did, I wasn't disappointed. She was every bit as lovely, pleasant, and clean as I had hoped.

Mamie and I began dating from that moment—we dated over the next eight years. Her family was a lot of fun to be around. Her parents loved me. It was during this time that I began to discover that she was the woman for me. She was a godly woman, full of wisdom and discernment. Of course, I aggressively sought after sex, but she would turn me down because of her personal convictions. Eventually, she did give in.

While dating, Mamie would come to church with me. At that time, several ladies would come around who were interested in me. Mamie saw everything: the stares, flirting, etc. She saw the other women and how they would look at me and act around me. But I'll never forget the words Mamie shared with me one day: "Curtis, I'm going to give you six months to get your act together. Call off all of the lady dogs and get them out of your system." She made it clear from day one that she wasn't going to play those games. I knew I couldn't mess this up. This woman was God-sent, and I had grown up and matured enough to realize when I had a good thing.

It was December 25, 2008, and I was preparing to propose to Mamie. Originally, I planned to propose to her during the halftime at the Lakers vs. the Spurs basketball game that was airing on the Turner Broadcasting Station (TBS). I set everything up with the network over a week in advance, but the producer got the date mixed up. That's when I came up with plan B. I took Mamie to my mom's house where I had waiting twenty-five gifts for her to open; I had more gifts waiting for her at her parents' house. Once we got to her parents' house, I had

six more gifts waiting for Mamie there. She started opening the gifts. The excitement was palpable. Everyone was
on the edge of their seats to see what was in those boxes.
In one of the boxes was a $2,500 mink fur coat. Mamie
was blown away by that gift. But I urged her on to open
the rest. In the other boxes were a charm bracelet, a pair
of expensive shoes, a set of expensive earrings, an elegant
dinner dress, and another dark brown fur jacket; but the
final box I wanted Mamie to open held the real surprise.
As she prepared to open up the box I had intended for
her to open the most, I began to move closer towards
her. She sensed that this box had something special inside of it. I could see her shaking and trembling as she
picked up the small box to see what was inside. Finally, she opened the box. At that moment, tears began to
stream down her face as she pulled out of it the engage-
ment ring I purchased her. At that moment, I took Mamie by the hand and asked her, "Will you marry me?"
The family was screaming with excitement. Mamie was
stunned, speechless as tears are flowing from her eyes. At
that moment, her father said, "Girl, the man is waiting
on an answer! If you don't marry him, I will!" Everyone
bust out with laughter. Mamie, bubbling over with excitement, shouted,

"Yes!! Yes!! Yes, Curtis!!!" We kissed. Everyone was
so happy for us. A peace and sense of assurance resided
within me: a sign that I had made the right decision, one
that was divinely ordained.

On October 11, 2009, I beheld the greatest gift
given to me by God as she walked down the aisle of the

sanctuary of our church. It was a dream come true. Everything was coming full circle. I felt like Job from the Bible—like all of my pain was being transformed into beauty, all of my suffering transformed into joy, and all of the days of darkness turned into sunshine.

When I look back at my journey, all I can think about is my last name. Is it a coincidence that God decided to showcase His love and joy on the world's stage? No. I noticed that love, according to the Bible, is not an emotion; it's who God is. Joy isn't an emotion either; it's the supernatural Kingdom and power of God dwelling within us. As long as God's presence and power are reigning in our lives, challenges simply become stepping stones, obstacles become character developers, and every situation we encounter actually serves the purpose of ushering us into the greatness God has predestined for us to experience.

As the old saying goes: *There's a light at the end of every dark tunnel.* That light is the hope we find in God. If you want that light to flood your soul, all you have to do is open up your heart and allow just a little love and joy to come in.

**Written by: Jeff Currier (newspaper writer)
on December/ 2004**

ABC's Wide World of Sports used to open with Jim
McKay's voice talking over pictures that showed
victorious athletic performances, while lamenting, "And
the Agony of Defeat." Those words and images basically
summed up athletic competition in the heat of battle,
essentially giving the audience a quick glimpse into the
word of the elite athlete, the top-notch physical specimen.
   The term champion describes someone who is a top
competitor, doing something better than someone
else does it. The American way of life thrives on
competition; Atlanta, as well as the state of Georgia, has
its fair shares of champions. Play hard, win, and you
can be one of those people who attain destiny. Being
products of the American way of life, most people have
expectations of their champions. The majority of this
nation and the world does not and would not view
someone with a disability as a champion. Think about
it! Today's society has the idea, perpetuated by television-
cable, satellite-direct or otherwise-and even that old
fossil network standard, which was defined by words
Broadcast, Broadcasting Company, or System, combined
with the words American, Central, and National, that
the sculpted. Muscular specimen is the picture of athletic
completeness, both amateur and professional. Fortunately
that idea does not always define every elite competitor.

   Being a champion is one thing, however, being a
champion who overcomes a disability is quite another.

Curtis Lovejoy, S-2, embodies the latter. After having a November 11, 1986, auto accident that left him as a quad (10 days after the author's own ABI-causing, fiancée-killing wreck), Curtis, before Shepherd had its own pool, used to go to the Jewish Community Center pool across Peachtree Street for his therapeutic recreation. Augusta Chronicle Online reports in an interview with Curtis that he"... never swam a day in my life until (he) got introduced to water by doing therapy." Later he tells the author, he started swimming at the YMCA in a lifejacket. After a month of depression, Curtis Lovejoy decided to take control of his life, meaning that he had to learn at Shepherd how to do the standard things. Combine having to re-learn how to function in your life, your new life, with having to leave your old life behind, and you have an idea of what this Paralympics champion faced in the time before he became a victor.

The Augusta Chronicle Online, in an article about the swimmer, reports the start of his swimming odyssey: "They gave me a life jacket. After a year-and-a-half, I told the coaches I wanted to learn how to swim.

"So I took off the jacket," and he turned into a Paralympics champion, the torchbearer for the 2004 Paralympics in Atlanta, in addition to being a world record holder. In addition to those championship aspects of his sports career, he is also a quad fencer.

Just competing at any level is tough; that just how

world works. Add that idea to the fact that the competitors are unable to use their legs-body parts crucial to being a swimmer-and you can get an idea of what kinds of challenges these Paralympics swimmer face.

When asked about what happened to him as a result of his paralysis, he did not hesitate to reveal the emotional toll that took place, in addition to loss of motion below the waist:

Remembering, he says, "You were walking before. Now that's all taken from you: you go through a period of depression." Imagine weighting 175 pounds, and dropping to 95 in five days, while losing bladder and bowel control, lack of sensation, and blow-to-the-head. O by the way fracture left wrist, two things everybody takes for granted whether he or she is a victim of paralysis or not. In any case, that situation is not very favorable. These kinds of things happen to you, often the result of your particular affliction, when you are on your way to becoming a Paralympics champion, causing Curtis to shed light on what it's like, being a first-time quad.

"At that time-you were walking before. Now it's all taken away from you; you go through a period of depression. So I had about 30 days of that."

Taking Back Control

Tired of what his injury had brought him, he made a crucial decision," After that month of depression," I said, I'm going to take control of my life."

And take control of his life is what he set about doing. His initial efforts involved trying to reclaim critical elements his accident had cost him-things he had relearn, including bladder & bowel control, lack of sensation, and blow to the head, thing about which most people never have to worry. (Author's note, as an Acquired Brain Injury: Believe me, you do have relearn. Bodily functions do not just control themselves). Shepherd offered classes to help him regain command-things such as learning to manage his time, which involves scheduling proper time to get essential things done; making sure he shifts his weight; and learning how to communicate because a lot of people don't know how to communicate-in Curtis's words,"… don't know how to empower themselves."

Recalling his experiences, he further observe, "Adults will just sit back and look at you while they try to figure out what they're goanna say to you,"

Further explaining, he say that people's reaction often reveal confusion. "A lot of times, when you go various places, people look at you differently, especially able-body people."

Conversely, "Now kids' walk up to you and say whatever's on their mind. So kids-they're the ultimate."

Single, Lovejoy is winner of various awards, which include, among others, the WXIA Community Award, the Super 17 Award, the Martin Luther King Award, and numerous others, including"…the Community Service Award through peer support at the Shepherd Spinal Center."

I addition to being named as a winner of the previous

"Humanitarian" awards by the groups that give them, and being Paralympics swimming champion, Lovejoy is a world-ranked wheelchair fencer. Although he had been ranked number one in the quadriplegic class, which he had dominated for five years, he "...got so good at it now I've decided to move up. "I dominated the class for so many years; I got so good at it now, I've decided to move up in the rankings from quad to paraplegic."

At the time of this interview Curtis Lovejoy had done something few people can claim having done. Not only does he swim competitively, but he also owns world records. While most people might not be accustomed to thinking of a disabled person as an athlete, Curtis Lovejoy, with this next recollection even might change a mind or two. "So far from '96 to 2000. I said; if I've got to break every world record to the 2000 Paralympics Games. That's what I'm going to do. And that's what happened. I couldn't lose; I refused to lose."

In 2000 Curtis's five world records at Paralympics resulted when he broke the record he had set earlier in the world record in 100-meter freestyle, combined with the fact that his 50-meter in the 100 was also a record time.

He's even a greater competitor than people might think, since he came down with the flu the day before his event in the 2000 Paralympics. Because he was the ultimate international competitor, he could take no medication. His coach asked him what he wanted to do.

"Curtis responded as any true champion would: "Get

in and give it all I've got!" The story continues: "Once I got to the pool and said my prayers, after that I shattered the world record by 32 seconds, not three-tenths of a seconds, but 32 seconds.

"For the last four years I've been getting letters from Australia, appreciating what I've done. It's been amazing. My life hasn't been the same." Based on his successes, Curtis makes this observation: "When I'm swimming, I'm in a "ZONE". And when I'm in a zone, I'm unbeatable. I see no competitors. I'm in place I consider to be "Paradise". There's no pressure on me."

Every year he tries to add something new to his workout routine. Inspired by Lance Armstrong's Tour de France, he began doing the spin bike-essentially a bicycle for the arms. Like all champions, this champion has a competitive philosophy, which he calls the Four F's, which are Faith, Focus, Follow-through, and Finish-the-stroke-strong. So, he has been able to apply that to his swimming. That ideology must work, based on Lovejoy's successes.

Because Lovejoy says 2008, when he'll be 51, will be his last Paralympics Games, the world of adapted sports will miss one of its GREATEST competitors.

Written by: Chaquita Williams from Atlanta, Ga. on April/1998.

My name is Chaquita Williams. I'm nine years old. You see, I write you to tell you about a blessing that GOD has put in my life. I'm included in the statistics of a single parent household. My real father left me and my mother when I was four years old. But my GOD sent me another father. He is special and like no other. He is my hero. His name is Mr. Curtis Lovejoy. This man has shown me generosity, bravery, persistence, service, courage, and compassion. Mr. Lovejoy was in a car accident in 1986 that left him paralyzed from his neck down. He was told that he would never walk again. He did not listen to what people had to say. He started swimming for his rehab. Now, he is a World Class Paralympics Swimmer and Fencer. He travels around the world swimming and fencing against others. Whenever he goes on his trips, he always brings me something. He brings me things like candy from Spain and Australia, a T-shirt from Poland. He teaches me about the different countries. I now know that the capital of Poland is Warsaw. He tells me stories about different people and their cultures. He shows me pictures of all of the pretty places. He has even seen the strongest man in the world. But to me, he is the strongest man in the world.

He is so loving and caring. He is always concern with how I'm doing, how my day is, and what was am I thinking about. He cracks jokes with me. He lets me play around in his wheelchair. He plays with me as if he has no disability. He makes sure I eat healthy, and all my meal. He never forgets my birthday. He knows exactly what I want. He does not forget holidays either. You know sometimes when school is out and my mom has to work, he lets me spend the day with him. He came to my cheerleading competition. I was so upset because I placed second, but he talked to me, took my picture, gave me a hug, and I felt better. He helped me pick out my mom a birthday present. He helps me with school projects. He lets me come to his competitions. He let me help pass out pictures at one of his fund-raisers. He lets me have his comics out of his newspaper before he reads it.

Mr. Lovejoy not only shows me love, but he gives his service to others as well. He coached a wheelchair soccer team; volunteered for Big Brothers, Big Sisters; and is a Boy Scout Leader. He loves children. He does not have any children of his own, but he acts like a dad to me! He goes to different schools talking to children about his accident. He helps them see that they can make it if they keep trying and take one day at a time. Mr. Lovejoy is one of kind. There is no other as compassionate as him. He gives me hugs every time I see him. He wears a smile all the time. He has made a different in my life. I know that as long as you keep trying, you can reach your goals. You can be what you want to be. Do not give up. I thank GOD for sparing his life because he knew a little girl would come along longing for a father, a girl that does not care if he have legs or not because he has a Big Heart!

Love you Dad,
Chaquita Williams

Dear Curtis,

Thank you very much for responding to my request. I been wanting to write you for long, long time.....now! At The Germany World fencing cup we will finally succeed hopefully! Yes I am doing ok. I really enjoy fencing, but practice very little because of my job. Only little money is coming into the family, that is why I must work. At the end of 1998, I missed several international events; too much work and the coach did not like me missing too many practices. That is why you didn't see me during that time. I started new joy working with young kids with drugs problem....It's very intense, but I'm absolutely excited what GOD will do when you ASK HIM! When I saw you at World Championship, you had this "shine Glow" about you which make me think about you so much. I knew in my heart that you were saved and love JESUS CHRIST! That is what attracted me to you, because when I compete it's hard to find Christians to fellowship with. When I heard you witness to another athlete, it touched my heart and that is why I asked Roy, your roommate to introduce me to you. Roy will have a rush on me, but I don't know. Hope to tell him that I'm content right now, but he never give-up. I was praying that the right time will come so we can fellowship, but when it happened, you was very proud, talking about JESUS CHRIST, and you were never ashamed to talk about HIM OPENLY. But that is really BOLD.

When you talk about how "JC" plays vital role in sports, I never knew that until you talk about "Samson" who was the strongest man in the world, who lost his strength by laying and sleeping in the wrong woman lap! It was an amazing story telling, but very true, because you told me were to go & find the story in the bible. You said victory come by prayer and supplication. GOD gives us the abilities to perform, but we must pray for the victory. By some chance that you don't win, that don't mean that GOD is not with you, it only mean that it may not be your season at that time or GOD is preparing you for something BIG down the road, but it only come with a sacrifice and GOD sometimes Laugh at us while we're competing. HE get pleasure out of us when we don't leave it in HIS hand, then panic set in. It's a sin to worry. Just continue keep doing what you're doing, let GOD HANDLE HIS BUSINESS, stay out of HIS way. And the next day during team competition in "Epee", our girl team (Germany) was in the finals fencing France. We were leading by 40 to 20. I (Silke) only need 5 more points to win it for our team and France start mounting a comeback on me, scoring 19 unanswered points. My coach called time out. He asked me what the hell is wrong with me. All you need to do is score 5 points. This France girl is not in the same class as you, so you need to put her way "fast" ok, now! I was glancing in the crowd to see if you were present but things were moving so fast, there wasn't enough time, so I began to think about what you said the night before. I then scored 2 points, only 3 more to go, but France tied it up 42 to 42. I began to tell GOD, "I need you right now. Please give me the victory. Control my point. Control" (HE DID) I went up 44 to 42 only 1 more point to go, but that France girl was getting louder as she then scored the next point. Now we were tied 44 to 44. The atmosphere was loud and intense, a lot of pressure was on my shoulder right. I must go to my famous move, a straight direct attack with all my power, make sure that I block her out; the director said "fencers-read-Al-lay"! On his command I went with all that I had in me and scored the last needed point for us to win. When it was over, in my mind I was saying, "Thank you JESUS CHRIST"! GOD made me work for that. When I was able to see you, you had this big smile on your face saying, 'I told you GOD plays a very important role in sports! The next day when you went for the GOLD in foil, I watched your bout and you were up 9 to 0 with only 2 more points to finish the bout, then the Sweden fencer scored the next 2 points and you shared with me the prayer you told GOD: "Listen GOD, I'm not Silke, so don't do me like her, let's finish this Right Now In The Name Of JESUS"! And you scored the next and final point to win the GOLD for USA! I now know why you got the next point; you spoke it "IN THE NAME OF JESUS"! There is so much power in the tongue, Curtis!

So this is what I need of you, when you return in November, I want you to conduct bible meeting with the athletes at World Fencing Cup. I will post flyers letting everybody know that there will be bible story telling and praying before competition start. I know you don't speak German that good, so I'll have Andrea to translate for you. In the meantime, I'm putting things together on this end, but I'll call you around September. I'm so excited about the Move of GOD and How HE IS GOING TO USE you! I already know that you will do it for the "Love of GOD"!

Please think about this project and be prayerful about everything. I look forward to our next fellowship. Congratulations on your World record in swimming!!!! You're incredible-you always breaking records. JESUS Life and More bountifully!

GOD Bless you!

Written by: L.B. from Atlanta, Ga. On March 28, 2008.

To: Carol Olsen at Shepherd Center.
Attn: Carol Olsen and CC Parties.
RE: "OVERSIGHT"

Dear: Carol, (To whom it may concerns)
Let me share just little about me, I prefer to use my initials want to remain anonymous. I'm sales rep who had the pleasure to do business with Shepherd Center for the past 6 years.

Let me take this opportunity to say that without the Shepherd Center, where would people be who have disabilities. The largest freestanding hospital devoted to research, medical care and rehabilitation of people with spinal cord injury and disease, acquired brain injury, multiple sclerosis, chronic pain and other neuromuscular problems. The Best Catastrophic Care Hospital in the World! I've had the utmost respect for individual who bouncing back from injury.

Please accept this letter as a way to continue to improve on making the Shepherd Center go down in history. I think that you'll have over look one individual who "Everybody and I know that he the most recognize person around the World who has disability and make United States proud to be an American from Atlanta, Georgia.

I'm talking about Mr. Curtis Lovejoy! Last month I was walking through the hallway on the main floor and notice

389

all the history of Shepherd Center posted in glass frame about the 1996 Paralympics Games that were held in Atlanta Georgia. The 1st time I met Mr. Lovejoy were 1996, not knowing that this is the same guy who just won the 11Alive Community Service Award in 1995. When I saw the event on TV. I said to myself what a humble wonderful person and when I meet him face-to-face and even once again in 2000 when he return home from 2000 Paralympics Games in Sydney, which he won 2/Gold medal, set (5) World, Pan/ American in swimming, also the 1st athlete to compete in (2) non-related sports which were swimming and fencing, he presented him as "still being that humble young man who I saw on TV that day!

So I felt that since he were not post in one of your glass frame, I took it as being "Oversight" on somebody part at the top, so I took time out of my schedule and tour all the floor at SC, not one beauty smiling photo of him post in the center, unless I miss it alone the way. Perhaps I'm ahead of myself; the SC must be planning on doing something special in the next several months on Mr. Lovejoy! I wanted to make sure that I've the right facts down about this "Overachiever"/ "Athlete" and "Humanitarians" individual. A special thanks to Mrs. Mary Kay who is the librarian, who shows me all the information that you'll had on Mr. Lovejoy and I call USOC who provide information that really blow my mind about this man accomplishment There is too much to write about but I'll only mention some of his accomplishments, which is not posted at SC.

* 1st Athlete to compete in (2) non-related sports, Swimming and Fencing in

Sydney and Athens. Maintain Elite status in both sports since 1996.

· Winner of Gold medals in Paralympics Games in 2004 and 2000.
· 1st Athlete to win Gold at World Championship in both sports 2006,
2005, 2002 and 1999.

 * Currently and only Athlete who hold 98% of the World Record in swimming
 and #1 Quad fencer in the world since 1995. (10) World, (13)

Pan/American and (13) American record in swimming.
· 2000 Olympics Games ceremony he was won the 2000 Athlete Man of the Year, out of a pool of 40,000 athletes by USOC, IPC and Wheelchair Sports USA.
· 2001 selected as the "Icons" of the Paralympics Swimming.
· The 1st African American to win GOLD in Fencing for USA.
· Winner of 431 Gold, 35 Silver and 10 Bronze in swimming, 75 Gold, 29 Silver and 20 Bronze medals in fencing.
· 2004, 2002, and 1996 Olympics and Paralympics Games Torchbearer.
· 1st African American to do so many things.
· Winner of the TBS/17 Super Station Community Award, alone with a boatload of Humanitarians in USA and (4) outside the USA.
· 1987 to present: a Shepherd Spinal Center Peer Supporter (which his name is post on plague) and Volunteer.
 (I see that Mr. Lovejoy sit on the Advisory Board)

I'm not the only one who make this statement:

Mr. Lovejoy is not the one who will talk about his accomplishments; he learns to let others do that for him. That is why he "Great", what every he does, because he shows so much humanity toward other, willing to put other before him.

It's an "oversight", I hope that you'll review this matter and do the right thing, because he is an pioneer, one who has change this world to be better place, show other what you can do with your life after a car accident I read in one of the article that he never knew how to swim until the accident and one of the therapists introduce H2O to him for therapy.

The most amazing thing about Mr. Lovejoy, that were said about him during the 2000 Paralympics Games from David Rosner of WeMedia "Curtis Lovejoy. An individual left paralyzed from the neck down and told by doctors he would never be able to use his body again. Now, after 14 years defying medical science, he has defined sports science in different kinds of test....Proving that a quadriplegic can be an elite athlete as driven as Olympian". His USA Paralympics Coach told me that they don't sometime believe that they're seeing, because as he get older, he continue to get BETTER! He in his 50's, she believe that Mr. Lovejoy have at less 2 more Paralympics Games left in him, beside China/2008, quad just don't do these thing"!
Finally, I hope that when other people visit SC and take a tour of your facility, that they see photo of him and read about him and actually, physically see man in action in the pool or the weight room working out Anytime when you can see thing for yourself it has a lasting long effect on

the individuals. Don't let this man pass away before you'll give him rightful place in Shepherd Center history, now is time! Everybody knows Mr. Lovejoy, he have given and done so much in all our lives, He's a living example that you can record your name in the HISTORY BOOK!

Sincerely yours,

L. D.
Pharmaceutical/Rep

CC. Gary R. Ulicny President, Ph. D. /CEO at Shepherd Center
289

Donald Peck Leslie, M.D./Medical Director at Shepherd Center
Matt Edens, Sport Team Coordinator at Shepherd Center
Curtis Lovejoy, Motivational Speaker and Athlete/ Shepherd Center

Written by: Eric Craig G. on December 9, 1998

Curtis,

I appreciate you sending me your address - I've wanted to write you some time now. To ask for your continued prayers; I feel fortunate to be in your thoughts. I call your name personally in the spirit of my prayers (for your well-being and continued friendship to me and my family)..... You're the epitome for dealing with Life's up's and downs the way you've dealt with challenges, proves that "Self" can change and adjust successfully.

I have made some bad decisions and mistakes in my life - but I have never hurt anyone (but myself)! And of course my family; but I've "never" did anything violent in my life.... I take full responsibility for my disobediences of the law; but the current unstable and "confused" system has me caught-up in the middle of political strategies. The Board of Pardon and Parole has departed for too far, from what the original guidelines were to be!!! As though I committed a violent crime. I am in for a sale of control substance. (In which was so small, they didn't have any remaining from LAB testing). I must also stress that I was a "user"... addicted to a drug in which turned (30) yrs. Old. So I'm not a career criminal. I truly believe I needed more help than punishment! I've never sold the drug for money or to support a Lifestyle. Only in support of the Habit. I'm praying Gov. Barnes inputs his campaign promises for non-violent offenders?!! I'm an extreme likeness to his vision to relieve the overcrowded situation. Of course I give all Praise, Glory and Trust in the LORD. (And not man) - but I'm praying for reconsideration of the Board members to reduce the time to be physically served. I also realize the importance of outside civilian help. My brother, I'm going to keep holding-on Curtis, and continue to do my best with unscarred institution conduct!!!! Well, my friend, it's been

394

nice to be able to talk to you, but I'll let you go before boring you any further. Please send me some spiritual literature from your church.

Take care of yourself, and may GOD Continue to BLESS you.

Eric Craig G...

Dear Curtis, I hope that you & USA/team
made it home. From the day you left Durban, the Hilton
staff really missed you. Not only did you have an
impact on them, but you touched my life & "Miria"
echoed the same. You opened-up your heart and let us
in. I personally want to come to America, but after
hearing you shed light on your life there, it's only fitting
that myself & others can really make a better life for
us there. We pulled your name up on the internet and
all I can say is "WOW!" You're an Amazing Athlete. If
you resided here you would be "King" here. Millions of
people would cherish & love you because you're a hero.
So many would love to be you, yet alone overcome
your disability. When you said that you were "Quad"
I could not believe that because the Quad I know &
seen cannot do the thing that you're able to do. So I
really count you as a "Miracle" made by GOD! During
the time that you were here, I never seen you upset,
mad or dismayed. The smile that you carry is a smile
of hope, love & joy! Yes, your last name was

predestined; it fit everything you do. Remember the movie star/model who was in the lobby taking photos? I noticed that all the guys were staring at her, but you rolled over to her while photographers were taking pictures and you said something to her, but she immediately & gave you a kiss & hug! She was staying in the hotel here, so I asked her what did the guy say to you who was in the wheelchair. She said, "Oh, you talking about Curtis Lovejoy?" "Yes." "He told me that if I relax & be true to my heart then my smile will reflect my heart. and he was so right. Not only was he a gentleman, but he acted like a Happy Angel! Believe me, he is a true sent Angle. I wanted to invite him for lunch, but I haven't seen him." I told her that you left and was going back to the United State the next after kissing him. She walked away saying, it's my lost!

Curtis, people can easily love you because you're a class act person, you speak from the heart, you don't waste words, you seen to know what to say at the right time, to do this w/o been nervous, the way you keep eye contact to the person you talking to, you make people react to what you say but they can't really believe that this is happening to them, so they Kindler hold back, because you're too good to be true!

Everybody (the ladies) in the restaurant said "hello" and was wondering when you were coming back to Durban, especially "Gugu". Did you tell her that you're going to get her to the State? She not only admires you but she's even more focused & determined to finish school and go on to college because of you! Thank you for planting that seed in her spirit. "Xolile" said that by you grabbing her hand, you felt her heart beating so fast, then you began to rub her hand, saying, "It's ok to be nervous but don't fear anybody, ONLY FEAR GOD." She said that she will never forget that. "Busi" said that she thought that she was the happiest person on the earth until she met you! When "Nomali" asked you if she can give you a hug, you said ok. she did, then you said it's something else she wanted to do, but she did not ask, so you pointed to your right dimple, (I been wanting to do that when you smiled at me the 1st time I seen you) after Kissing your dimple, she went to into Kitchen lean-up against the wall & started sliding down the wall as if she was just melting. You made her not be afraid but just ask 1st!

398

"Zanele" said thank you for telling her that you loved her hair. When you asked can you touch her hair you ran your hand around her head. She said that triggered currents down her spine! "Lindiwe" is the quiet one of the bunch. She thinks that you're the sexiest man she ever met. She saw you with your spandex on one morning when she entered your room to bring you breakfast, but she had the wrong room. She felt so bad at the time, but you were so nice about the mistake, saying "It's ok. Everything is fine. No problem." That's all she talks about: your muscles in your arms, chest & butt! And finally "Miriam" said you reminded her of her father who was strong-minded and a go-getter, and never stopped until he got what he wanted, and he loves his wife. He always put himself last & others before himself, and spread love to all. I pray one day that I meet someone just like Curtis Lovejoy. She wished that you were available, but you told them all that you have someone special back home that you're planning on marrying one day. She had problems sleeping when you're away from her, but once she laid her head on your chest she'd fall right to sleep just like a baby!

Curtis, it took me several days to put this letter together because I had to wait on everybody to write their part down. I know that your life is a open-book. I hope that one day it will turn into a book and a movie for the world to see because no matter what came your way, you've been able to overcome it all. You travel around the world meeting lots of people and showing them how to be happy & content with life. It's ok to be optimistic about your future, but you must make it happen and act like you only get 1 chance at life and complete it without any excuses! I personally want to thank you for not just coming to South Africa, but for wondering into my shop, telling me what you wanted and asking me to be real with you about the "Mother Land"!

Now you have my email so stay in touch with me as you travel the world. I know that once you see water, you're in "Heaven"! Take care. May the wind blow you to every inch of the world!

My brother! Peace & Love

Career Highlights

2012 PARALYMPIC GAMES
August 2012 in London, England
Sport: Swimming

2008 PARALYMPIC GAMES
September 2008 in Beijing, China
Sports: Fencing and Swimming

2004 PARALYMPIC GAMES
September 2004 in Athens, Greece
Sports: Fencing and Swimming
Medals Won:
- 1 Silver Medals in swimming
- 1 Bronze Medal in fencing
- 2 Gold Medal in swimming
New Records:
- 1 World Record set in swimming
- 1 Pan-American Record set in swimming
- 1 American Record set in swimming

2000 PARALYMPIC GAMES
October 2000 in Sydney, Australia
Sports: Fencing and Swimming
Medals Won:

- 1 Silver Medals
- 1 Bronze Medal
- 2 Gold Medal

New Records:
- 5 World Records in swimming

1996 PARALYMPIC GAMES
August 1996 in Atlanta, Georgia
Sport: Swimming

SWIMMING HIGHLIGHTS

- A total of 700 medals won
- A total of 13 World Records
- A total of 12 Paralympic Records broken
- A total of 39 Americans Records broken
- A total of 13 World Championship Games competed in

FENCING HIGHLIGHTS

- A total of 200 medals won
- A total of 12 medals won - 6 of them gold medals
- A total of 10 World Fencing Championships competed in

CURTIS LOVEJOY IS...

- The 1ˢᵗ American/African American to win gold for Team USA in the Paralympic Games
- The most decorated male athlete for the USA in swimming and fencing

For a complete record of Curtis Lovejoy's accomplishments, go to www.TheCurtisLovejoy.com.

Curtis Lovejoy at 7 years old

James and Sallie Lovejoy, Cur[
Lovejoy's parents

Sallie L. Lovejoy (mom),
Curtis Lovejoy (center),
and Carl Lovejoy
(brother)

Great grandfather, Eddie Lovejoy

Curtis Lovejoy and fellow athletes being honored at the White House by President Barack Obama, Vice-President Joe Biden, and First Lady Michelle Obama

Curtis Lovejoy being honored at the Governor's mansion by Georgia State Governor, Roy Barnes (on the left)

© ATR / Panasonic Lumix

1-6 Add and Subtract Whole Numbers and Decimals

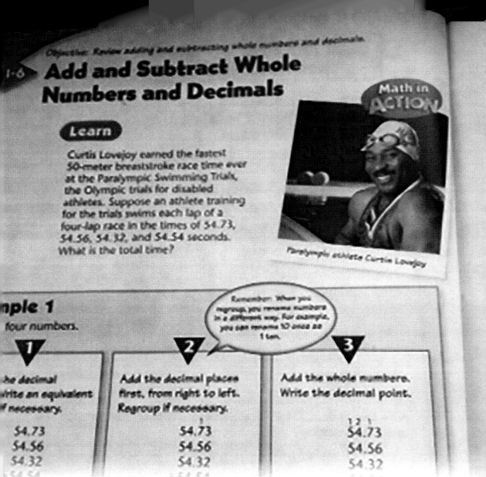

Math in ACTION

Learn

Curtis Lovejoy earned the fastest 50-meter breaststroke race time ever at the Paralympic Swimming Trials, the Olympic trials for disabled athletes. Suppose an athlete training for the trials swims each lap of a four-lap race in the times of 54.73, 54.56, 54.32, and 54.54 seconds. What is the total time?

Paralympic athlete Curtis Lovejoy

Example 1

four numbers.

Remember: When you regroup, you rename numbers in a different way. For example, you can rename 10 ones as 1 ten.

1	**2**	**3**
the decimal. Write an equivalent if necessary.	Add the decimal places first, from right to left. Regroup if necessary.	Add the whole numbers. Write the decimal point.
54.73	$\overset{1}{54.73}$	$\overset{12\ 1}{54.73}$
54.56	54.56	54.56
54.32	54.32	54.32
54.54	+ 54.54	54.54

You know you've made it when your picture is featured in a public school Math textbook as seen in the above photo. Curtis Lovejoy is a recognized hero and inspiration to many, including the youth

45c
Australia
SYDNEY 2000
PARALYMPIC GAMES

Yes, Curtis Lovejoy has his own stamp. Being such an inspiration to people around the world, a stamp was created in honor of this world renown, world-class athlete

Wedding Day! Curtis Lovejoy getting married to the love of his life, Mamie Lovejoy

Curtis Lovejoy and his wife, Mamie, at a church function together

oto of Curtis Love-
display at
oints Art Gallery in
ta, GA. The portrait
old for $4000.00

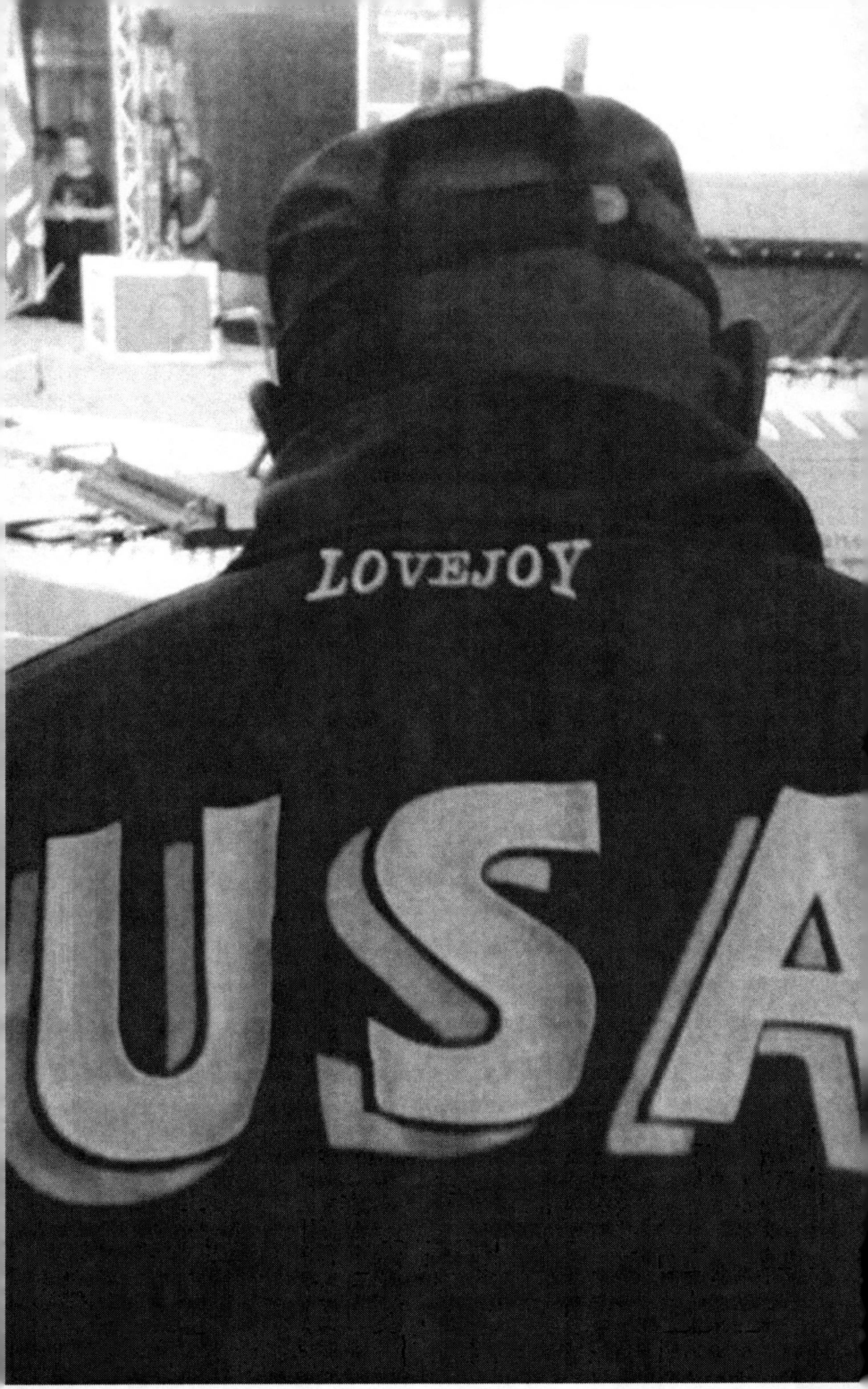
LOVEJOY
USA

ABOUT THE AUTHOR

Curtis Lovejoy, affectionately known as "Living Legend" to his fellow athletes, is a five-time Paralympian. He is an accomplished competitive swimmer, having represented his country at Paralympic events around the globe. He has become the most accomplished and decorated male athletes in Paralympic history for the U.S.A. Curtis Lovejoy was first introduced to the water as a form of physical therapy following a life altering car accident in 1986 that left him as an incomplete quadriplegic, which in Lovejoy's case means he is in a wheelchair and has limited use of his arms. In 2000, Lovejoy beat the odds and became the first athlete to win gold medals in two non-related sports, swimming and fencing. Currently, he has won over 500 gold medals in swimming, 200 in fencing, has set 12 world records, and is ranked the number one fencer in the world.

Curtis Lovejoy's mission is to inspire people from all walks of life to face down their fears as well as build awareness and education, rehab, fitness, and career opportunities for those who are faced with Spinal Injury challenges. He serves as a peer supporter for the Shepherd Center's patients, and he speaks to corporate, school and community groups about overcoming adversity. Lovejoy, who earned a bachelor of science degree in therapeutic recreation from Morris Brown College now mentors others, including the Shepherd Sharks swim team.

Officially sponsored by the US Paralympics, Curtis Lovejoy remains the most decorated Olympian of all time.

TO CONTACT THE AUTHOR, GO TO:

www.TheCurtisLovejoy.com
love1982002@yahoo.com
Facebook: Curtis Lovejoy
Twitter: @curtis_lovejoy9
Youtube: CLovejoy988